D1557553

MegaTraits

12 Traits of Successful People

Doris Lee McCoy

Wordware Publishing, Inc.

Library of Congress Cataloging-in-Publication Data

McCoy, Doris Lee.
Megatraits / Doris Lee McCoy.
p. cm.
Includes index.
ISBN 1-556-22056-1
1. United States—Biography. 2. Celebrities—United States—Biography. 3. Success. I. Title.
CT220.M43 1988
920'.073—dc19 88-9626
CIP

1506 Capital Ave.
Plano, Texas 75074

Printed in the United States of America

ISBN 1-556-22056-1

10 9 8 7 6 5 4 3 2
8808

All inquiries for volume purchases of this book should be addressed to Wordware Publishing, Inc., at the above address. Telephone inquiries may be made by calling:

(214) 423-0090

ACKNOWLEDGMENTS

I would like to express my gratitude to the following people:

Dianne Pietila for reading and editing, as well as Suzanne Henig and Rhonda Lee McCoy; to Irene Schaffer, Alan Garner, Jeffrey and Suzanne McCoy, Doreen and Mark McCoy and Margaret Hickey for their counsel and support; to Fay Adell Wells and Grace Capilitan for typing; to Peter S. Wahren and Anne Ring, and the American Intercultural Student Exchange for enabling some of the interviews to take place; to Nightingale/Conant Corporation for allowing me to include three of the interviews that I did for their "This I Believe" series; to Russ Stultz, Jana Gardner-Koch, and the Wordware Publishing staff that worked as a team to get this book out; and to the many people whose prayers encouraged me during the long, exciting journey it took to write this book.

— Doris Lee McCoy, Ph.D.

Photographs on cover: Lady Bird Johnson, by Frank Wolfe; Maria Martinez, by Jerry Jacka; Mary Cunningham, © 1982 by Thomas Victor; Peter Coors, by Olivia DeCroce; Norman Lear, by Linda Solomon; Forrest Shumway, by Charles Schneider

DEDICATION

This book is dedicated to my mother and father Alvena and Bernard L. Raymond, who taught me that you can learn something from each person you meet, and that success comes in many different forms.

SPECIAL THANKS . . . .

A special thanks to the many people who took time from their extremely busy schedules to share their process, way of life . . . the good parts as well as the struggles and hardships . . . so that you the reader might be able to learn from their journeys through life and grow. I will always be grateful to them for wanting to return something to the world from which they gained their success.

Very gratefully,
Doris Lee McCoy, Ph.D.

CONTENTS

FOREWORD

Why are successful people successful? While such a question is not easy to answer, it *is* fun to ask. Doris Lee McCoy asks that question again and again of successful people in all walks of life in her new book *MEGATRAITS—12 Traits of Successful People*. From politicians to athletes, from business leaders to actors, Doris Lee has gotten in touch with some of the most successful and fascinating people of our day to probe the secrets of their success.

The answers she received led her to identify a dozen traits she felt most enabled the group of people she interviewed to be successful. The traits she categorized have the face validity of common sense—yet they ring true at a deeper level as well. For example, Trait 1 is "They enjoy their work." While certainly it makes sense that anyone successful enjoys what he is doing, how many people continue to work in jobs and careers that they do *not* enjoy? More people than those who do enjoy what they do, I'm afraid.

It becomes an easy jump to assert that enjoying one's work is an important factor in becoming successful at that work. A related corollary could easily be that if you hate what you do for a living, you should do whatever you can to change to a field of work that you find more satisfying, because you will otherwise quite likely undermine your own success.

Or consider Trait 2: "They have high self-esteem and a positive attitude." Who could argue that such a trait is not important to anyone's success? Yet, at the same time, how easy it is to forget how important this trait is. It is a rare person who does not have to work—on a daily basis—to maintain a high sense of self-esteem and a positive outlook on life. How easy it is, instead, to slip into being critical of oneself and of others around us, and how easily that criticism can, once again, undermine one's success.

The list goes on: integrity, persistence, a sense of purpose . . . all important factors that have contributed to the success of those people interviewed for this book—and important factors for you to evaluate for your own life.

This book is not a formula for a successful life. But it is a reaffirming of life and what it means to be alive and operating at one's fullest potential.

Dr. Kenneth Blanchard
co-author
THE ONE MINUTE MANAGER

INTRODUCTION

> "I believe the important thing is never to say die until you're dead. It is, as we quickly realize, a short trip. Pack in as much as you're eager to pack in."
>
> — Malcolm Forbes
> Editor-in-Chief and CEO,
> *Forbes* Magazine

What Is Success?

Are there character traits common to most successful people?

What does Malcolm Forbes, owner of *Forbes* business magazine, hot air balloonist, motorcyclist, and fun-loving man have in common with Supreme Court Justice Sandra O'Connor? Is hard work part of their everyday experience, or have they found some way to circumvent it? Were there complicated hurdles they had to surmount? How did someone like Norman Cousins survive a childhood trauma and "tame the beast," as he put it, to become a well-known editor? Do they all have a high energy level? Are riches and notoriety the only rewards of success, or, if their lives were devoid of material trappings, would these men and women still feel a sense of fulfillment and vibrancy? Can individuals who have not been raised in an environment that encouraged them to be high achievers still attain success?

I traveled cross-country over a 12-year period interviewing more than 1,000 succesful individuals to find the answers to these questions. I did not just want to chat with these men and women, as I had when some of them appeared in my TV interviews; rather, I intended to seek out some consistencies—success patterns from which others and I could benefit.

Why did I seek out such a broad range of professional people who seemingly have little in common with one another in terms of life careers? The theory I held was that regardless of what these successful people did professionally—as chief executive officers of a business, writers, sports personalities, television producers, financial executives, even the President of the United States—they all have similar traits and values that propelled them to success.

Why did I undertake such an ambitious project? The quest to help others as well as myself to find our potential has been one of the consuming goals of my life. In my interviews with some of the best known, most highly respected people, I asked them the same basic questions:

- *How do you define success?*
- *What events and people in your childhood helped you succeed?*
- *What traits do you use in your career that further your success?*
- *What are traits of other successful people you've known?*
- *How do you handle difficulty?*
- *How would you like to be remembered?*

Did my original theory hold up after more than 1,000 interviews?

The answer is a resounding YES! There are qualities consistently found in the lives of successful people. I call them MEGATRAITS, a new term coined from the word "megaton," which is described as a unit of explosive force. These traits are indeed explosive because they continue to ignite new areas in the lives of those who take them seriously.

This research may offer some reassurance in this day of the "crazies," with so many new life-styles, philosophies, self-help books, and a prevailing attitude of being encouraged to "do your own thing," that have us wondering if former beliefs are obsolete.

Although some great technical advances are occurring in our world, our personal potential, instead of becoming easier to discover, seems to become more evasive. From my observation, this technology has brought about more opportunities for us to ask the question, "Why was I born?" but it has not helped us find satisfying answers. So we, as our ancestors in ages past, still must take responsibility for answering this question. One of the best ways of discovering how we may achieve success is by examining the lives of others who have been labeled successful.

My first step was identifying what success really means. It is often thought of strictly in financial terms; but does being a millionaire necessarily mean that one is a success? Success, for some, may mean that you stop dropping the bowling ball on your foot or that you reach for an exercise bar instead of another Twinkie. For others it may mean saving a historic building destined for demolition or winning an election.

But these are examples of achieving a single success, and that is very different from leading a successful life, which is a continuing, ongoing process. As Earl Nightingale of Nightingale/Conant puts it in his classic recording, "The Strangest Secret" (which has sold over one million copies): "Success is the progressive realization of a worthy ideal." [1]

Will Durant and his wife, Ariel, well-known philosophers, attribute their long and happy life to having "something to do, someone to love, and something to look forward to." [2] It is a simple philosophy but a noteworthy one.

Kay Koplovitz, President and Chief Executive Officer of USA cable television network, said that while most people define success in terms of how much money one makes, she has a different definition:

> To me, being successful is not only being able to achieve my goals, but being able to use my influence in a way that influences other people in a positive manner. So I give a fair amount of my time to organizations that I think are doing worthwhile things. I think that's important . . . I'm a business person. But that's not a complete person. To me, it's more important to be a part of the whole society in which you live and to contribute something back to it. And to me, that's success.

I had seen Kay use her talents outside the work environment, and I commented with a grin, "I've seen you play tennis . . . fiercely." She responded with a smile in an upbeat tone, "Winning tournaments is also being successful."

Golf champion Chi Chi Rodriguez has had his share of winning tournaments, but he sums up what success is to him in completely different terms:

> Success to me is having peace of mind, not being jealous of anybody, being content. The most successful human being I know was my dad and he never had anything financially.

Some of those I talked with, who had achieved the material rewards and prestige usually associated with success, placed success in relationships above all other criteria. Robert Dedman, who manages approximately 30,000 employees in his two roles as Chief Executive Officer of Club Corporation of America and Chairman of the Texas State Highway and Public Transportation Commission, told me, "I think success in life is primarily a result of the ability to set up win-win relationships personally and professionally."

Jess Hay, Chairman and Chief Executive Officer of Lomas & Nettleton Financial Corporation, also gave high priority to relationships in his definition of success:

> My understanding of what a successful life would be would include development of some very deep and very real relationships with people both in business and otherwise. Development of a sense of community and pursuits, whether they are economic or social or political or

> whatever, I think is very important . . . people that I have most admired and would view as personal successes would be those that are tuned in and sensitive to the needs of the people around them. They are anxious to build something, perhaps for themselves, but they are also people who recognize that those things that are worthwhile normally are built in concert with others. That kind of intangible quality that relates people in a very dynamic and meaningful way to others is, I believe, bottom line, the single most important factor in whether a person can pursue an effective and productive career.

A warning comes from Stanford University President Donald Kennedy, who cautions students not to equate visibility with success. He elaborates by asking the questions "Are we placing too much weight on the glamorous and the distinctive and failing to recognize deeper, more sustained—though perhaps more ordinary—forms of service?" [3]

A profession often considered filled with extremely successful people is the movie industry, but it is not without its pitfalls:

> Many actors and actresses basically are insecure people, unsure of their true identities, in many cases guilt-ridden of success too easily achieved. They are fearful of growing old, or having few true friends, of rejection by an industry in constant search of new, young, sexy personalities. To assuage these fears and incidents of professional and personal rejection, they frequently turn to alcohol . . . They hope it will serve as an escape mechanism for their unhappiness. [4]

After talking with many people who were labeled accomplished, I concluded that *real success is a high degree of fulfillment in several areas: mental, social, physical, spiritual, and emotional.* Success is not static; it is a continuing process of discovering more of one's potential. It is a growing, evolving experience.

Plenty of money is often a common element shared by these people, but it is by no means the only measure of success. In fact, I interviewed some very wealthy people whom I chose not to include in the book because acquiring money was the only thing they seemed to be interested in.

Although those I interviewed were extremely busy people with already full schedules, they took time for these interviews because they were willing to return to the system from which they had been so richly rewarded something of benefit to others.

You may be surprised at the simplicity of what the research uncovered. Sometimes the most obvious is right under our noses. But it is useless information until we choose to recognize it and put it to use. Interviewing these successful people has changed my life. I listened to their stories for 12 years. As a result, each day, when new situations present themselves, I draw upon the lessons I learned from their examples.

I am presenting them here to you in hopes they will enrich your life just as they did mine when these people shared their life experiences, their values, and the many difficult paths they trod to realize their goals. After the interviews, I found myself gripped for days by their poignant stories. By incorporating the principles here into your own lives, and as parents, teachers, managers, and chief executives, inspiring them in others, you may be able to encourage happier, more fulfilled individuals.

The trait I found most consistently in the lives of successful people is:

1. THEY ENJOY THEIR WORK

As real estate magnate Trammell Crow put it, "Work is so much more fun than fun, it is improperly called work."

All the people I spoke with are enthusiastic about their jobs and carry that feeling over to their other activities. Generally they work hard, with total involvement, and then play hard. If interest in their jobs wanes or their values shift, they change careers. This is especially noteworthy in view of the fact that many Americans don't enjoy their jobs.

Says Malcolm Forbes, "The essence of success lies in doing what you enjoy. Otherwise you neither do it well, fully, nor successfully." President Reagan, commenting that his life just keeps getting better and better, believes "The best is yet to come." Florence Chadwick has found successes in various fields—but always ones she enjoys. Early in life she made 16 major channel swims and broke numerous records, then completely switched careers and became a stockbroker. At age 60, although she loved the profession, she was not happy with her stock brokerage firm and changed companies.

2. THEY HAVE HIGH SELF-ESTEEM AND A POSITIVE ATTITUDE

Multi-talented opera producer and director of the Pittsburgh Opera, Tito Copobianca, was so well prepared from a young age in the talents of his chosen profession that he succeeded in the superlative in almost all of its aspects. Who inspired him? His parents and uncle, who served as his mentors, gave him the encouragement and regard from early on that enabled him to do so well. They saw to it that he learned to play a variety of instruments, direct, sing, produce, study lighting, and act. Now when he directs an opera, he knows exactly what he is asking others to do. He has high self-esteem and confidence because of his knowledge and past experiences.

All of these successful people, because they have found and developed their unique qualities and talents, do their jobs with a sense of confidence. This strong sense of fulfillment in their work, in turn, contributes to their self-esteem.

A characteristic that goes hand-in-hand with high self-esteem is a positive attitude. The successful never doubt that they can make it. They expect success rather than failure. As Mary Kay Ash, founder of Mary Kay Cosmetics, Inc., put it, "It never occurred to me I couldn't do it. I always knew that if I worked hard enough, I could."

3. THEY USE NEGATIVE EXPERIENCES TO DISCOVER THEIR STRENGTHS

TV writer/producer Norman Lear revealed that as he grew up observing the marriage of his parents, he "looked at two people who lived at the top of their lungs, on the ragged ends of their nerves. In self-defense, I had to find the humor. In retrospect, this gave me an understanding of the humor in life."

The Reverend Jesse Jackson overcame a heritage of poverty to become a Democratic Presidential candidate: "My mother was a teenaged mother and her mother was a teenaged mother. With scholarships and other help, I managed to get an education. Success to me is being born in a poor or disadvantaged family and making something of yourself."

It was a cruel childhood prank that helped writer/lecturer Norman Cousins develop his skills as a negotiator. While he was in a sanatarium recovering from an illness, some of the young patients took him miles away and left him in the woods in freezing weather. Never again would he fear death. Not only did he find his way back, he learned how to communicate with these boys to gain their acceptance. What could have remained a terrifying experience fortified him with the stamina and special insight to become one of the top U.S. negotiators in major world disputes.

In retrospect, then, many of the successful can actually see how the difficulties they experienced offered them opportunity to discover more of their potential. In some cases, they were able to use traumatic experiences as a means of seeing more options than they had before.

4. THEY ARE DECISIVE, DISCIPLINED GOAL-SETTERS

The successful individuals I interviewed have made clear decisions about what they wanted and then gone after it. *They waste little time once they discover their goals.* Coupled with this decisiveness is the self-discipline to make the desired results achievable.

Florence Chadwick practiced swimming for two years on her own, without telling even her family of her goal to beat Gertrude Ederle's English Channel record. As a child, she got up at 5:30 each morning to swim Mission Bay in San Diego, enduring a water temperature that sometimes reached the low 50°s. Following her first channel swim, she made 15 other major channel crossings, working to support herself at jobs that would not conflict with her first love, swimming.

5. THEY HAVE INTEGRITY AND HELP OTHERS TO SUCCEED

The importance of acting with integrity was emphasized by many of the successful. I think Jess Hay, CEO of Lomas & Nettleton Co., summed it up particularly well:

> I value integrity. I believe that honesty and integrity are the hallmarks of character and essential components of long-term functioning in this or any other society. Integrity involves more than just not lying. It involves being true to yourself and being truly yourself in dealing with others. It involves being you . . .

Many of those I interviewed expressed their beliefs that an important element in success is ensuring that both parties benefit from any transaction or relationship, whether business or personal. They believe success isn't defined by a single act or accomplishment but by repeat business, by long-lasting relationships where everyone wins.

Robert Dedman, Founder and Board Chairman for Club Corporation of America which owns 225 country, city, athletic, and resort clubs, says, "Your ability to set up successful, lasting relationships is the biggest determinant you'll ever have of personal and business success." Ace Greenberg, CEO of Bear, Stearns Securities, sums up his life's motto, "I hope that everybody I have come in contact with feels that they received more than they gave from our relationship—that they never had the feeling of being taken advantage of." Karl Eller, Chairman of the Board for Circle K stores, comments, "With any deal I've ever made, I've been careful that I was fair to the other side—so that both parties were happy."

6. THEY ARE PERSISTENT

Ray Kroc, founder of McDonald's Corporation, was turned down for a $1.5 million bank loan to finance the chain he wanted to build, but he didn't give up. In fact, he enjoyed the challenge, saying, "It's a hell of a lot more fun chasing it than getting it." The successful are often entrepreneurs introducing innovative ideas which have not been tried previously. They must have the courage of their convictions and persist in convincing others of their merit.

7. THEY TAKE RISKS

One overriding trait of the successful is that they believe in their idea, their product, themselves so fully that they are willing to take risks.

Forrest Shumway, as Vice President of the Allied-Signal Companies, Inc., made what others at the time might have considered daring changes but was willing to take risks because, as he says, "In 75 percent of the cases over the course of a lifetime, I will be intuitively correct, and that is a fair percentage."

Often people are unwilling to take risks because they are afraid of making mistakes. McDonald's late founder, Ray Kroc, talked about how he dealt with the possibility of mistakes:

> When I make a mistake I throw it off by saying, "That's why they put mats under cuspidors." You have to overcome your mistakes by making another decision. But I'd a heck of a lot rather see people make mistakes than make nothing. Mistakes are painful when they happen; but years later, a collection of mistakes is what they call life experiences. When you make a mistake, you have to make another decision, and that is good. You are doing something.

It often takes many tries to produce one success, and taking risks is a part of the process.

8. THEY HAVE DEVELOPED GOOD COMMUNICATION AND PROBLEM-SOLVING SKILLS

It is not enough just to create good ideas. One must know how to translate them to other people in order to get the ideas implemented and to "sell" the product.

If they do not already have good communication skills, successful people make an effort to acquire them. Additionally, most make a conscious effort to solicit and listen to communication from others. Many of the top executives mentioned that they have initiated programs in which employees are encouraged to offer suggestions, making communication a two-way process.

Most have the ability, either naturally or by conscious development, of "self-talk." This is the capacity to talk one's way through a problem or decision, weighing the various elements to achieve the most beneficial results. Successful people question previously established norms. They continue asking questions until a new approach becomes apparent.

Sol Price, founder and Chief Executive Officer of the Price Club, used these skills to develop the concept for his chain of stores selling inexpensive wholesale/retail consumer goods. He asked the questions: Why such long hours? Why so many different brands? Why such luxurious surroundings? Why allow credit cards? He then went about solving the problem of charging customers high prices by coming up with a new concept in selling.

9. THEY SURROUND THEMSELVES WITH COMPETENT, REPONSIBLE, SUPPORTIVE PEOPLE

A remark I heard consistently was that no one makes it to the top alone. Regardless of how intelligent, innovative, or creative someone is, he must have others around he can trust.

As Malcolm Forbes says, "No matter how successful your business is, the only real asset is the people you have." [5]

Bob Magness, Chief Executive Officer of Tele-Communications, Inc., believes his ability to delegate responsibility to his competent staff is the most important factor in his success.

In the process of getting to the top, many used the principle of aligning themselves with competent people whom they used as role models or mentors. Mary Cunningham, formerly of Joseph E. Seagram and Sons, Inc. and Bendix and now President of Semper Enterprises, Inc., gave high marks to this practice, saying, "If I had to pick one of the three factors in my career path that has made a difference, it would be that there's always been a mentor in every situation I have participated in." [6]

10. THEY ARE HEALTHY, HAVE HIGH ENERGY, AND SCHEDULE TIME TO RENEW

Many of the successful engage in sports regularly. Charlton Heston and Norman Lear play in pro-celebrity tennis tournaments. General Jimmy Doolittle, World War II Ace, plays tennis in his 80s. Artist Francoise Gilot practices yoga, swims, and has won horseback riding awards.

The successful have a high energy level. Many mentioned that they sleep less than most people. They have busy schedules and, because they have more waking hours, are able to accomplish more.

Most of the successful work hard and then play hard. The changes in rhythm might involve a shift in activity or pace and often a new environment. Revitalizing themselves is crucial enough to them that they actually schedule time for it.

Ann Ruth, paralyzed in a gymnastics accident at age five, sparks up her routine by searching for new surroundings to enjoy with her family. Her latest adventure is parachuting from an airplane—an act most of us with full use of our limbs would not attempt.

11. THEY BELIEVE IN GOD, A HIGHER POWER, AND SOMETIMES JUST PLAIN LUCK

Many of the successful see themselves as co-creators with a "higher power" who has helped guide them. Businessman Charles Woods believes that, in spite of his badly burned face and hands, he is one of the most blessed men. He, like others, finds a great deal of comfort in being able to call upon his Creator's help. President Reagan said, "I have a deep-seated faith that if you ask for help, it will be given." He points to his mother who left her legacy of faith with him.

Some attribute their success to luck, to being born in the right circumstances, being in the right place at the right time, finding partners—spouses and co-workers—who contributed to their achievement.

12. THEY HAVE A SENSE OF PURPOSE AND A DESIRE TO CONTRIBUTE TO SOCIETY

The successful show an inner strength, a "knowing," that enables them to move out of the ordinary at times when they believe the situation calls for it. Not so much a rebellious act, it is the will to inspire a higher level of good in society.

Maria Martinez, a native American potter, though ostracized for it by the members of her tribe, broke tradition by an unheard-of sharing of her pottery secrets with women from other tribes. New skills enabled these women not only to earn money by selling the pots, but to experience a renewed sense of dignity when their talents were recognized. Maria persisted in her cause even though the price was a costly one.

Members of the Kennedy family have a history of dedicating themselves to the service of their country. The political contributions of John, Ted, and Bobby are well known. Equally impressive is the participation of their mother Rose and the Kennedy sisters in their work with physically and mentally handicapped, the arts, and various other volunteer projects.

Other Characteristics of the Successful

There were a number of characteristics the successful didn't talk about as much but which, as an interviewer, I considered important. They were:

Many challenge traditional concepts. Some are "rebels at heart." Sometimes this happens because they are angry at "the system" and dissatisfied with the status quo or with things unjust or wasteful in society.

They are constantly coming up with innovative, fresh ideas—always trying to make their product better. Sol Price, who created a new concept in marketing wholesale and retail merchandise with his successful Price Clubs, says that ideas get old very quickly. Other companies will always use your ideas, and he realized the need to be constantly open to new ways of doing things. He quotes Sachel Paige who said, "Never look around or someone will gain on you."

They are able to shift gears easily. They can move quickly from one project to another and focus on it with their full attention. Many of them are multi-talented and able to perform adeptly in a number of diverse arenas.

Age is not a barrier to their starting new companies. Sol Price started the Price Club at age 60. Ray Kroc started McDonald's at age 52 and never had much money until he was 61. Karl Eller, after selling his companies and leaving Gannett Publishing Co., decided at age 50 to put new companies together and became Chief Executive Officer of Circle K food store chain.

They continue, even in their late years, to be productive, many choosing not to retire until long after the traditional age. International authority on beauty Aida Grey, at nearly 80, continues to actively run her cosmetology business. She makes speeches and frequently visits her 100-plus salons around the world. Businessman Bill Daniels, known as the "father of cable TV," gave up trying to retire. He says, "I moved to Del Mar,

California five years ago and I was going to stay on the beach. I did that for five weeks and got sick of it. I went back to work, and my company is bigger than it's ever been."

Probably one of the most important characteristics I observed was that, although not all of them have college degrees, *they continue to schedule time for their education*. They recognize that there is a wide range of options available for growth and learning outside the traditional formal schooling. Johnston College, which I helped to found at the University of Redlands, was built around the theory often mentioned by key educators in the country that there are more ways of becoming educated than just through the formal traditional university. Many universities, recognizing this fact, now give "life experience" credit as a substitute for formal classroom instruction.

Neil Bergt dropped out of school at age 15, but that didn't prevent him from acquiring the knowledge and skills he needed to become the multi-millionaire Chairman of Alaska International Industries. No one would suspect that award-winning writer/director/producer Norman Lear completed only one year of college. He used his curiosity, ingenuity, and sensitivity to continue to grow and explore new avenues of expression. William Kolender flunked out of high school and had to go to summer school to graduate. Later he attended San Diego State University. Today he not only is San Diego's Chief of Police, but serves as President of the California Community Colleges' Board of Governors.

Businessman Bill Daniels didn't finish college and says, "I've always been self-conscious of my lack of education . . . But I read and I know what's going on." Besides reading the weekly news and business magazines, he reads *four* newspapers a day, including the *Wall Street Journal*. "I want to know what is going on in the business world," he explained, "and you'd be amazed how that pays off when I'm sitting down talking about something, and I can give them some information because I read it the day before."

Now that we've reviewed the overall traits, let's take a look at how the successful men and women have used them in their lives. Later in the book we offer tips on how you might apply them to your own life and encourage them in your children and others.

One of the decisions we had to make in writing this book was how to refer to both genders. Rather than using the cumbersome "he or she," we decided to use the word "he" to refer to both sexes.

THE SUCCESSFUL MAN

For most men, success has traditionally been defined as success in a career. However, since it has been estimated that many Americans do *not* enjoy their jobs, I was particularly interested in what successful men had to say about career fulfillment.

The successful men in this book acknowledge that they are somewhat different from the way they are usually viewed by the outside world. Contacts made through the country club circuit, wealth and prestige are not necessarily success, according to these men. In whatever field they have achieved success, they have one trait in common: *They all enjoy their work.* Work, for them, is not just a way to support themselves, it is a means of fulfillment, a consuming part of their lives. They say their work is often tough, but they enjoy the challenge.

Other common denominators include *integrity, self-discipline, and mutually winning relationships.* A certain *steadfastness of purpose* can also be noted in the assertiveness they manifest in the pursuit of their goals. One has the feeling that, whatever impediments fate places in their way, they have the *stamina, mental as well as physical, to survive and triumph.*

These traits were confirmed in a study I conducted of members of the Professional Men's Club of La Jolla, California. I asked them to list the attributes that had helped them in their achievements. The traits they mentioned most often were: enjoyment of their work, pleasure in working with people, the careful consideration of decisions, and the ability to supervise and stimulate people. They spoke of common sense, dependability, honesty, a willingness to accept responsibility, patience, a capacity for hard work, a search for knowledge, perseverance, self-discipline, and the ability to curb one's temper.

A sense of humor was mentioned frequently, as was the need for a positive outlook. In the words of one executive, "You can't hit the ceiling aiming at the floor." Some said they were motivated by negatives such as fear of failure. An older man said his memory of the Crash of 1929 still gives him his drive today.

Several men credited their wives with a share in their achievment—having the good luck to be in the right place at the right time and marrying a woman who is an intelligent professional, but who doesn't feel she has to tear down her husband to prove herself.

How do the successful acquire these qualities? We'll see later what the individuals I interviewed told me. First, let's take a look at a study conducted by writer and psychoanalyst Erik Erickson. In his book, *Childhood and Society*, he describes the stages of development the healthy man goes through. If he fails to progress through any of these stages, Erikson asserts, he will not become a fully functional, mature adult.

In many cultures, according to Erickson, the grammar school child has already passed through the stages of *basic trust, autonomy, and initiative*. He begins to develop his study skills while keeping his adventurous side under control. As an adolescent, his suppressed emotions resurface, and his identity emerges as he tries to distinguish his beliefs from his parents' beliefs. As a young adult he moves toward close intimate relationship with his peers. From there, he will probably move toward intimacy with a significant other, and if they both choose, will raise children.

If he continues as a healthy individual and has found fulfillment in his job, this man re-focuses his attention on contributing to the outside world. If all these stages are completed, then he experiences the fulfillment of a mature adult. [7]

Harvard psychiatrist George E. Vaillant used Erickson's stages of development in the important Grant study which he directed involving successful men. He described how the best and brightest Harvard men came of age and how each man responded to challenge and change.

A comparison of the "best and worst outcomes" in the Grant study shows clearly how the best outcomes had been positively affected in their career choices by identification with their fathers. Their own children's outcome was also described as good or excellent.

The worst outcomes seemed to have had the poorest childhood environments, were dominated by their mothers in adult life, failed to marry by age thirty, held grave self-doubts, by age fifty could recall no genuine friendships, and held few jobs of supervisory responsibility.

According to the study, the effect of childhood upon later adjustment was unmistakable. Men with unhappy childhoods tend to be: 1) unable to play, 2) independent and lacking in trust, 3) more likely to be labeled mentally ill, 4) without friends. Adolescents who were considered "asocial" were least likely to be labeled best outcomes, while adolescents who were seen as well-integrated, practical, and organized were best adapted by age 50. [8]

Now let's take a look at some of the successful and see what stands out for them in the early years. One of the traits I found was the isolation some of them experienced in their childhood. They used this period of isolation to question and explore creative thoughts that would not have been possible if their days had been filled with planned activities.

Former three-star general Jimmy Doolittle, who earlier in his life was an engineer and then a businessman, said his parents left him pretty much on his own as a child. They believed there wasn't too much trouble a young lad could get into in the remote town of Nome, Alaska with only 200 to 500 people. He described the effects that his early childhood had on his later life:

> I felt some lacks—and it created a desire to fill those vacuums—in my own personal life . . . My dad gave me a kit of tools when I was very small and that, I think, filled a creative desire to do something. And then the restraints of a small town left another vacuum—that was to see more of the world. Those were the two things very early in life that caused me to be an engineer.
>
> . . . I think one of the problems today is that people don't determine what their destiny is to be until quite late in life. This is one of the fortunate things that happened to me—an objective early in life.

Like many of the successful, General Doolittle discovered his leadership qualities at an early age:

> I remember as a very young kid noticing that some boys had ideas and that others didn't. The boys with ideas were leaders. I found that it was very easy if they were interesting and different ideas to get people to follow you. And so the idea of being a leader was developed in my mind very young, and I found that achieving excellence and being a leader went hand in hand. My mother was a typical frontier woman. My father, as a carpenter, was an adventurer. I think I inherited from both of them, but I don't think either one of them made any effort to direct my destiny.

Ronald Reagan also grew up in a small town. Of his home in Illinois he said, "I never saw a key to our front door." Without benefit of the private lessons and planned activities found in big cities, he created his own fun. "There were adventures to be found . . . we'd take off to the river that ran through our town, down the river, out into the woods, out into the countryside." From this childhood experience he developed the creativity and resourcefulness, as well as the deep love for the outdoors, that remain with him today.

Parents might take note that, when I asked actor Jimmy Stewart, who has played many tough and yet gentle roles in movies, the main factor in his attainment of success, he said his father had been his role model. In addition, Jimmy appreciated the values he had gained from the small town in Pennsylvania where he was raised.

Many of the men talked about how their parents had influenced them. Senator Ted Kennedy spoke of the effect his mother, Rose, had on him as a child:

> I think she was an educator in the broadest sense, to all of us. She was constantly challenging our minds. Whether it was in the area of history or public life or just in reading about this country, about the world, about people, about the injustices that exist in our society. And I think that was something she did that was very powerful. And then obviously she was an enormous resource for both love and attention. I described her as the "safe haven in the family." Whenever any child, or even a grownup had a problem, she was always the source of enormous strength.

Tim Hansel, a professor, writer, and Christian "survival school" director acquired the ability to work hard and persevere early in his childhood. Because his father worked long hours, his brother was given the task of filling that role. He learned to cope from his mother who said, "Don't cry until the blood runs."

Tim attended a strict high school and his teachers, coaches and parents all stressed the importance of excellence. His family encouraged him to take risks, which he had to remind them of when they objected to his year-long sail around the world after college.

Tim's survival school would not exist if he hadn't learned the value of taking risks. He believes self-respect leads to respecting others and encourages his students and his children to gain a high self-esteem by conquering challenges.

What about the adult years of these men? I went back to the Grant study to see if its findings correlated with mine. The study points out that successful Harvard men tended to become specialists. The ego ideals they had acknowledged at nineteen were abandoned and replaced by "mentors" in young adulthood. The mentor became a father figure. After 40, mentors ceased to be important.

According to the study, the forties were a time of reordering the real truth about adolescence and young adulthood; these men became explorers of their inner worlds. If they were depressed, it was often because they were "no longer satisfied with their careers . . . They now wanted to be of service rather than forge ahead for their own benefits." Thus, a common denominator most successful men share by the age of 40, is the development of a social consciousness, which is shown in a willingness to donate time and effort to charitable endeavors.

Many of the successful men I interviewed indeed showed this social consciousness. For some it was in the form of patriotism. They expressed a deep appreciation for the opportunities America has provided them in the free enterprise system. Others exhibited it in their spirituality.

Former pro basketball player, John Block, credits Christianity with encouraging him to do something more with his life than just play basketball in Chicago. His social consciousness drives him to direct children and young people in athletics. He talked about his work with a country church camp:

> I really believe God has called me to try to put this thing together and have kids learn their skills, in basketball or tennis or any other sport we're able to have, and that camp and family life should go together so we can have family camps and see families enriched and growing together strong . . . I believe that families, adults and kids alike, can find a new life with God and see more purpose in their lives.

Tim Hansel puts his spiritual principles into action in the survival school he developed to help people see "the remarkable things that ordinary people can do in all areas of life when God is in control." As a former teacher, he moved out of the classroom and now pushes students to expand their potential in four outdoor environments: the mountains, the desert, the ocean, and the city. He has made a film called "Holy Sweat," because "Holy reminds us of our highest calling . . . Sweat is what it takes to get there."

In his early 40s, Adam Osbourne, author of leading books on computers and Chief Executive Officer of a computer company, began his quest for spiritual answers. Although he doesn't believe in a fundamental Judeo-Christian religion, he says he is convinced of the existence of a soul. In fact, he is so consumed by his conviction that he translated his ideas on spirituality into a novel—a far cry from the world of computers and text books with which he was formerly engrossed.

Another trait the men I interviewed shared was that they chose to turn failures or mistakes into learning experiences. As Circle K's Chairman of the Board, Karl Eller says, "I've learned only from my failures. I don't learn from my successes."

Bill Galt, founder of The Good Earth restaurants, and now President of Galt International, also takes a philosophical approach when things don't turn out as planned. He said, "Our culture defines individuals as winners or losers . . . I'd much rather see the situation defined as winners and *learners*."

These men have the insight and the courage, when their jobs are no longer fulfilling or when they see something more rewarding, to make a change. In some cases this may mean moving from a position of outward financial success toward a more rewarding job at a lower salary. This can happen when a man no longer sees the excitement and challenge he once did in his job, because his values have changed, he is no longer willing to put up with the stress, possible heart attacks, ulcers, and sometimes even boredom.

It takes a gutsy man to sacrifice the prestige and material comforts of a lifestyle to which he and his family were accustomed, but more and more men are doing just that. Because his family also experiences the lowering of lifestyle, it is crucial to have their support before making such a change.

Businessman David Brucker had the courage to change careers four times, which earned him the envy of many of his contemporaries. "It wasn't courage," he said, "I was merely trying to survive." He went on to say, "When I am unhappy, I do something about it."

Television and film producer Ed Scherick, who organized the "Wide World of Sports" series, talked about the importance of people finding their own special area that he calls the "itch."

> The "itch" for me was that every time I walked into a remote truck doing a basketball or football game, the little hairs on the back of my neck stood up. Just the idea that out of that small arena could come pictures that would be telegraphed all over the world because we brought cameras in there, gave me that thrill.

Many of us know Grant Tinker best for the numerous television programs he put together under the MTM Company. Formerly Chairman and Chief Executive Officer of NBC, he is currently President of GTG Entertainment. He formed this company with Gannett Company, publisher of *USA Today*, to parlay the paper's print success into a video series. When I asked him what he considered to be the most rewarding endeavors, he listed his work in building MTM as well as the challenge he met in turning the NBC network around over a five-year period. In his surprisingly humble style, he claimed that his success has come, not from any special talents, but because he truly enjoyed what he was doing.

> How did my success come about? Certainly not through any particular ability. In fact, I think of myself as a guy with no skills or talents at all. I think it is due to the fact that I simply enjoy what I do, and really look forward to it—almost running to the office, if you will—because

> I enjoy what I do when I get there. I think if you enjoy it enough, you inevitably do it fairly well.

Pride is often a motivating factor for the successful man. William E. Murray is a lawyer, businessman, and philanthropist who restored Drayton Hall and three city blocks in downtown Charleston to its original ante-bellum state. He talked to me about pride, saying he believes it is a double-edged sword: "One of the biggest motivators for success can also bring about the decline of one's success." He said:

> The successful are not simply working for the essential elements of earning enough money to make mortgage payments and pay for food, cars, and education of children and things like that. Most of the major business transactions are conducted by people who already have money and status. It's all a game, a hobby. If more people realized that the way to appeal to a lot of people is to appeal to their desire for status, they would find that it is easier to negotiate with them.

He points out the negative side of pride when people pursue a losing venture in a futile attempt to save face in spite of their judgment to abandon it.

Another issue the successful man must deal with is the effect that his career has on his home life. Corporate life has certainly been destructive to many lives. David Rockefeller, President of the Chase Manhattan Bank, is quoted in a book called *Corporate Wives, Corporate Casualties,* as asking for a social audit to the contributions and costs of business practices to human welfare. He goes on to say, "We know that many men have grown rich and powerful. At the same time, we have been conscious of how many wives and children were destroyed in the process." [9]

Which brings up another point: What type of women do these successful men pick? The women they have chosen as wives are usually supportive of their husbands' goals. When I spoke to a group of forty-five members of a Young Presidents Organization (men who are millionaires before they are 40) all were married but one—and he was looking! This suggests the need these men have for this special person who can share their lives in a close, confidential way.

Males in America have long been judged with the yardstick of a strong John Wayne character, or more recently, "Rocky," "Rambo," and Clint Eastwood. Ian Fleming's 007 is an intelligent, cool, calculating, and womanizing agent. He does his job efficiently, survives, and quickly drops his gorgeous playmate after a torrid affair. These Walter Mitty-type fantasies have long governed the American male's self-concept.

A new era is upon us, precipitated largely by the change in women. It is bringing with it great changes in relationships on the job and in the home.

The new man. What characteristics does he have? He is a successful man who expresses one quality in particular—"chutzpah," a quality of daring, an extra scintilla of verve. Chutzpah literally means "he who owns his own spurs." Dr. Warren Farrell, in *The Liberated Man*, describes this new man.

> Becoming a liberated man, then, is achieving new freedoms—freedom beyond proving oneself; beyond worrying about appearances, on the playing field or in the office; in earned degrees or in job titles . . . It is getting beyond condescension and contempt towards women, needing to be in control and have an answer to all problems at all times: beyond specializing, needing to become the expert, . . . It is learning how to listen rather than dominate or self-listen; to be personal as well as intellectual; to be vulnerable rather than construct facades of infallibility; to be emotional rather than emotionally constipated; to be dependent as well as independent; to value internal, human rewards as well as external rewards . . . It is working toward new dimensions of self while not rebelling against the best of the old self. [10]

A nice image, but not necessarily easy to attain. Becoming the liberated male involves a great deal of self-searching and evaluating, a task that some men just don't take time to do.

The new man has pre-eminently the grit to be himself, which presumes considerable awareness on his part. Confident of his virility, he can view masculinity in broader terms. He does not have to stereotype a woman in a specific sex role as wife, mother, or housewife. Nor does he have to put his love object on a pedestal. He can encourage his youngsters to cry when they feel hurt, instead of inhibiting them. He remains in touch with his feelings and will cry if he needs to.

Many men have a hero side to their personality. By that, I mean they enjoy saving and protecting people and causes, as the crusaders who fought for worthy ideals. The legend of King Arthur and his Knights of the Round Table underlines this heroic aspect. Today, this personality trait still exists, and America has a great share of such men, although the characteristic often goes unrecognized.

One man who has long championed causes is Bob Hope. In addition to his career as actor and comedian, Bob is well known for entertaining the troops near and far. He chooses to do this during holidays to the exclusion of his safety and comfort. Now at eighty-plus years, when most people have retired, Bob is embarking on a new project called "Hope for a Drug-Free

America." He introduced the program during the 1988 Super Bowl Weekend. Bob brought into an hour-long television special, Charlton Heston and Walter Cronkite, as well as astronauts, pro-football players, and his good friend Jimmy Stewart.

Jimmy Stewart has, of course, long been regarded as a hero by people all over the world. To me, he has been a forerunner of the "New Man." He manages to exude a masculine strength while typifying the true meaning of the word *gentle*man. At the benefit he gave his definition of a hero:

> What is a hero?
>
> *Real* heroes come in all shapes and sizes and from all
> walks of life. But they all have a few things in common:
>
> They are never so big
> that they can't bend down to help someone else.
>
> They are never so wise
> that they don't remember who taught them.
>
> They are never so strong
> that they can't be gentle.
>
> They are never so gifted
> that they won't share their skills with others.
>
> They are never so fearless
> that they don't play by the rules and live by the law.
>
> And they are never such big winners
> that they forget what it feels like to lose.

In these fast-changing days, when both women and men are re-examining the traditional roles of the sexes, concepts about what it is to be a successful man or a successful woman, are being questioned to encompass a broader range of the personality.

What emerges out of the words and lives of the successful men and women profiled in this book is the new concept of "androgyny." The idea is that all people possess characteristics associated with both the sexes. Men can be gentle and flexible; women can be assertive, nonflexible, and judgmental when the situation calls for it.

Interestingly enough, Greek men who fought all day in the heat of battle were seen returning to their homes at night crying openly as they walked down the street. It is as though they had proven their masculinity in battle and had earned the right to cry.

In our modern society there is less actual need for men to demonstrate their physical prowess. They have, of course, the opportunity of choosing their own means of expressing their masculinity, such as in sports, hunting, and fishing. However, if there is not a constructive avenue for this expression, it may surface in a negative macho behavior. This often displays itself in the form of an overly inflated ego, making it impossible for men to show their true feelings.

One view of the need to change the masculine image was expressed by California Representative John Vasconcellos, head of the state Ways and Means Committee. He believes we have all been raised in our society strictly from the male viewpoint, and that we need to incorporate more feeling into our cultural perspective.

> I think that Western culture, particularly men, have been conditioned to view the world through the eyes and brain only . . . Men should learn to be models for one another in tender relationships, and women should learn to expect men to be tender and to welcome this. Women should take responsibility for their own growth and look at the constraint and repression around them. The mythology of the male and female in its contemporary social stereotypes is frankly crazy.

According to Sandra Lipsitz Bern, a psychology professor from Stanford, "The research points out the fact that traditional roles of masculinity and femininity do hold a person back in important ways. Androgyny, in contrast, allows an individual to be both independent and tender, assertive and yielding, masculine and feminine. As a result, androgyny makes it possible for a wider range of behavior for everyone." [11]

Walter Payton, running back for the Chicago Bears, holds the all-time record for number of yards run. We might assume that, when asked what was the most memorable moment in his life, he would describe one of his football achievements. Not so. His response on the Oprah Winfrey Show was, "What was the biggest thrill in my life? Being there to see my son and daughter smile for the first time."

The impact that our fast-changing society has had on men has been, perhaps, even more profound on women. In the next chapter we'll look at the opportunity and challenges successful women of this era have met.

THE SUCCESSFUL WOMAN

A new woman is emerging.

Just as it takes "gutsy" men to reach the top, so women have exhibited their own form of "pluck" in order to succeed as the resourceful, talented women in these chapters have done. Being willing to show strength while retaining their femininity is not an easy task, but most of these successful women have done just that, with powerful results.

I asked television writer/producer Norman Lear what he would say to men who are now coming to terms with this new woman, and he replied:

> . . . how would you feel if you were standing on the beach and the radio was telling you a tidal wave was coming and then you started to see it loom on the horizon? Would you stand there and ask somebody to bring you an encyclopedia so that you could understand how tidal waves work, or would you run in the same direction as the wave so as to prevent yourself from being drowned? . . .

A wave of successful women. It is happening, and any opposition will soon be drowned out by the cheers.

A survey I conducted of men and women has evoked descriptions of this new gutsy woman: *Independent, realistic, honest, open, self-assertive, not afraid to show how she feels, feminine, warm, and willing to stand up or speak out for what she believes. She may be disliked because she's willing to stand out on her own. A lady who possesses dignity, she does not compromise personal beliefs under pressure, does not quit when the going gets tough. She is comfortable in a leadership role, even in a normally all-male organization.*

How were the women I interviewed similar to the men in these chapters? Like the men, many of them learned self-reliance at an early age. Despite deprivations as a child, Mary Kay Ash learned, while her mother worked to support the family, to care for her invalid father via the telephone. ("Honey, now listen to me . . . you do this first and then you do this . . ."); Sandra Day O'Connor learned resourcefulness, ". . . living out on a ranch in a remote area . . . you had to solve all the problems yourself."

A characteristic that appeared even more strongly in the women I interviewed than in the men was a strong belief in a power higher than themselves.

Xernona Clayton, a corporate Vice President at Turner Broadcasting Corp., says: "I can tell you that I believe strongly that your life is guided by a force. I think it's God."

The effects of the Women's Movement are not seen as totally favorable by all women. I asked veteran actress Helen Hayes for her viewpoint, and she said:

> Well, I suppose it's a good idea, but we must do it gradually, because we can't just plunge in and demand it of men. I think that there is a little bit more unhappiness and marriage has gone down, they say. Marriages have tapered off and divorces are still on the uphill. I think that's so sad, because you can get awfully lonely without it.

She went on to express a viewpoint about sex objects that might seem surprising coming from this family-oriented woman well into her 80s:

> I think that we mustn't ever lose our femininity, my goodness. And this business of being thought of as a sex object—I love to look back on the days, for instance, where our picture stars, our film stars, were great sex objects. Greta Garbo, Norma Sheer, and Joan Crawford—that was so exciting and glamorous to all of us. And we like to pattern ourselves after them. The same thing on the stage. Also, have you noticed that more films and plays were written for women in those days than they are now, because you can't write women as sex objects, and that's when we're best.

Syndicated columnist and humorist Art Buchwald says the Women's Movement has created an identity crisis for some:

> They don't know what their identity is. They're still supposed to be all the things that they were before, but they're supposed to add one dimension, a career. It's much harder on women than men in this world.

These women inherited other dilemmas that did not touch the men, such as *the guilt factor*. Were they neglecting their homes and families? Did they have to make an irreconcilable choice between career and husband?

Women have had to fight this legacy of guilt. In *Why Do I Feel So Bad?* authors Cleiaia Halas and Roberta Matteson point out that paradoxes still exist: "I've done so well, why do I feel so bad?" . . . "I don't see it the way you do, so I must be wrong." ". . . I mustn't upset anyone." [12]

These women have had to rise above the negative connotation some have given to powerful women with terms such as gutsy, harsh, pushy, demanding, and overbearing.

Women are the only group in society that characteristically blame themselves for failures. Consider these differences between 3,000 women and 2,000 men studied by Drs. Hennig and Jardim of Simmons College:

> When things go wrong, men usually blame the boss, the business climate, the circumstances, the "system." Women tend to blame themselves.
>
> Men assume they are competent and set out to see that somebody important finds out about it; women fear they are not yet good enough and spend more of their time on self-improvement.
>
> Men set priorities; women try to do everything equally well.
>
> Men take risks to get what they want; women are more likely to play it safe . . .
>
> Men decide on a goal and go after it; women wait to be chosen. [13]

Besides overcoming the guilt factor, another issue successful, powerful women must deal with is the threat they may pose to men. They are careful not to compete with their mates at home as they might with males on the job. In their careers, how could they be less threatening to their male colleagues if that threat keeps them from reaching their goals?

Mary Cunningham became the target of male envy and resentment at Bendix, when she was frequently with the corporation's president in her job as his assistant. As one of her male co-workers put it: ". . . a person being mentored walks around with a bull's-eye on his back the whole time . . . [she therefore had to] bend over backward not to allow that resentment or hostility to get the best of [her] . . ." [14]

Novelist Abigail McCarthy, now separated from husband Senator Eugene McCarthy, talked about the division between the sexes and the fact that men often feel threatened by women:

> I feel men and women are very separate in America now. The culture separates men and women anyway; this is quite clear in the history

> of men escaping from women all through American history. The movement west . . . cowboys and soldiers and men escaping into their hunting clubs and so on . . .
>
> I think we are really quite separate in our enjoyment of one another, and I would like to see us discover one another very soon. I think it's possible. I see it with younger men. I do see men who have changed completely. Unfortunately, it usually is with a new wife or after leaving another relationship behind that is somehow not resolved. I feel women need to better understand men's fears and how threatened men are, as women in a one-on-one relationship discover.
>
> What we learned as young women was how to manipulate men: listen to them, admire them, learn to talk football. Most wives, because they looked on their marriages as their livelihoods, learned to press the right triggers [to get what they want].

Women have had to overcome active discouragement by males in careers and even in some colleges. Dr. Joyce Brothers was nearly dissuaded from becoming a medical intern by an advisor who believed she would be taking the position away from some male student. Sitting on the U.S. Supreme Court was an all-male privilege for 191 years, until Sandra Day O'Connor was appointed as the first woman Justice.

Pamela Fiori, Editor-in-Chief of *Travel and Leisure* was told to go into secretarial work by her high school counselor. But one day she went with a friend who was going to Italy to do some work. The trip sounded more interesting than the direction of her career. She enjoyed the experience so much that she began writing travel articles for a living and is now heading a group of writers at the American Express travel magazine.

Even among women there has been discrimination and discouragement, as demonstrated by many women's opposition to the Equal Rights Amendment. Psychologists have called this "identification with the aggressor." Research shows, in fact, that in the past, when given the choice between working for a man at a lower salary or working for a woman at a higher salary, women have chosen the male boss. And, interestingly, studies show that when women think an article is written by a man, it is accorded greater authority; when informed the article is written by a woman, they rate it less competent and valuable. These women, in short, do not support their "sisters," and the bottom line is they often think less well of *themselves* than they do of men.

The successful women I interviewed, in contrast, are so aware of the ladder they have climbed by dint of hard work and talent, that they do not put women down; rather, they stand and applaud their advancement. They have found their fulfillment and are not threatened by women or men.

However much we are locked into sexual stereotypes by society, the term "androgynous" is coming into frequent use. We are realizing that, while the average woman is 51 percent or more feminine in nature, she has some masculine traits; similarly, the average man is 51 percent or more masculine, yet has some feminine traits. Androgyny is the balance of these traits within one human being.

Psychology Today published studies which demonstrated that people who were androgynous could learn a variety of skills with greater speed. It is evident that if one has learned a new task and isn't held back by traditional sex stereotypes, he is more free to respond spontaneously.[15]

Women are establishing that, in addition to the usual description of themselves as "caring," "nurturing," "loving," they are now earning titles that in the past have applied to males: "leader," "adventurous." Women such as Katharine Hepburn, Clare Booth Luce, and Mary McLeod Bethune have long been admired for their ability to be ladies without sacrificing their strength.

The successful women I interviewed exhibit this exquisite balance of traits, so that they are assertive without being aggressive, businesslike without being harsh, and they emphasize the importance of dressing professionally without being masculine. They are used to competing with men in a non-threatening way. Financial corporate executive Venita Van Caspel explains how she manages this:

> I have a fairly logical mind that men, on the whole, respect. I never wear masculine looking clothes; I think that's a mistake. I try to wear soft colors and speak in a soft voice and when I open my mouth, have something to say . . . If I were to march in with my little pin-striped suit and a loud voice, it might be a problem . . . this idea of dressing . . . like miniature men . . . if I had come in and been a militaristic woman, there would not be the respect.

Well-known artist Francoise Gilot (who lived with Pablo Picasso for ten years and is now married to Jonas Salk) says women have always created, then nurtured; men have created, then burned. Today, she states, women are learning to burn what is no longer needed, and men are learning to be more nurturing.

The women in these chapters have been able to break into what was often formerly male-dominated territories by using their lesser-developed sides when necessary to be more rigid, judgmental, and able to throw out what is no longer needed. Men, on the other hand, are learning to use their lesser-developed sides to become more flexible, nurturing, feeling, and are better able to express that.

How have these women been able to break barriers? Mary Cunningham, President of Semper Enterprises, Inc., sums it up succinctly, "By working harder." She, like the others I interviewed, finds it easy to do this because she totally enjoys, totally immerses herself in whatever venture she is working on. Francoise Gilot admits, "I am obsessed with my work . . . it becomes number one." Venita Van Caspel, after the death of her first husband, commented:

> I dreaded the weekend . . . that's one of the reasons I became successful . . . I worked so hard that it blotted out anything else . . . do that long enough in the right direction, and you're going to be successful . . . I never did quit!

Supreme Court Justice Sandra Day O'Connor says she was "blessed with a high energy level," as were the men in these chapters. Mary Kay Ash learned that "three early risings make an extra day . . . and six would [make] a nine-day week."

When I asked Myrna Blyth, Editor-in-Chief and Publishing Director of the *Ladies Home Journal*, what she considered the most important traits to her career, she replied, "The ability to get a lot done, to be productive, to be able to make decisions, to get along with people." She elaborated on the importance of being personable:

> Being personable means pleasant—pleasant enough to get along with people, to make people do things for you, to make people feel that they want to contribute to what you're doing . . . to motivate people.

Hard work has also paid off for Kay Koplovitz. As President and Chief Executive Officer of USA Cable TV network, she holds the highest position of any woman in the television industry. She was a television producer before starting her own network in 1977. She said:

> It's been a long climb, but I think we're really coming into our own. We air and deliver into about half the homes in America, so we're growing rather nicely.

Kay makes a difference and exhibits a concern for important projects, like other successful women. She spoke about the one-hour special USA Cable was airing on Bob Hope's "Hope for a Drug-Free America":

> I think it has been a really special event for us to be able to offer the Bob Hope special this evening. I personally am involved with several of the drug-free programs in the country and I have a personal commitment to it. We felt it was a good thing for our network to do.

Another woman who has broken into the top echelons of the media industry is Katharine Graham, Chairman of the Board of *The Washington Post*. She emphasizes quality as a prime ingredient of success. The company's investment in quality, she claims, was the number one factor that enabled the newspaper "to rise from fifth place in a five-newspaper town, to number one today—with the highest market penetration of any major-city newspaper." She also credits the emphasis on quality for the fact that *Newsweek*, which the company owns, has grown from a small publication for businessmen to a major magazine with a worldwide circulation of more than 23 million readers. In a speech to the National Association of Television Program Executives, she reminded the audience that it was *The Washington Post's* dedication to quality that enabled them, during the Nixon administration, to withstand the pressures encountered in their exposure of the Watergate story. She talked about the ingredients of quality:

> Quality requires infinite patience, demands a willingness to take risks, and compels acceptance of failure. It takes courage to take risks and be willing to fail and try again.
>
> Quality also needs money, but money certainly doesn't guarantee quality . . . Quality is a constant struggle. But it's worth it. I believe that real quality ultimately pays off. You have to be profitable to be able to invest in the product.

Women traditionally have found their identity in areas of service. Now they are finding a wider range of opportunities. Gutsy women can use their considerable talents at work and at home alike. Today they are living affirmations of Betty Friedan's statement in *The Feminine Mystique*: A woman's place is not necessarily "in the home among the pots and pans." [16]

How do husbands feel about having their wives away from the house so much? The mayor of a small town outside of Dallas was only partially joking when he commented on the effects the changes in women's roles have had on their marriage:

> It's driving me crazy, my wife is. I can't get her to cook any more. She is *the* changing woman. Three years ago she was happy to stay home and watch a little TV with me in the evenings. She would always cook my dinner. Now she's all wrapped up in other things. She's president of a charity group this year, and when she's not doing that she's off decorating some office. I hardly see her any more. She's a different lady altogether.

On a more serious vein, he went on to acknowledge the positive aspects of the new situation:

> I think she has a lot more self-esteem. She feels a lot better about herself. Our family unit is still solid. As a matter of fact, I enjoy it. I used to take her for granted, and now I enjoy her when I'm around her.

Many women successfully combine home and career, especially with the help of a supportive family. Sandra Day O'Connor says her husband's help was "fabulous." Mary Kay Ash put it, "My childhood negates all this business about how working mothers can't influence their children. My mother was gone all the time . . ."

Publishing Director Myrna Blyth is another who has successfully managed a busy career while raising a family. She is married to a British journalist and they have two teenage sons. I asked her how she managed to handle her responsibilities at the *Ladies Home Journal,* in addition to writing books and serving on boards and committees, and still have time and energy for her family. She replied:

> Just the way millions of women in the United States are doing. Millions of women in this country work, have children, and manage both things. It's not an extraordinary thing to do at all. It's probably the most typical lifestyle for most women in America today.

I asked her if the subject of conversation, when she gets together with her professional women friends, has changed over the years because of today's emphasis on careers. She said, "No. We talk about our children, our husbands, clothes, and getting older."

What about the women who choose to stay at home? With so many more women opting for career roles—partly because of the increased opportunity and partly because today's economics often require two salaries to meet the mortgage payment—many homemakers are beginning to feel pressured. And, as Art Buchwald points out, that pressure often comes from other women. He says when a career woman asks a homemaker, " 'What do you do?' and you say, 'I'm a housewife,' they just don't talk to you any more. A housewife is not an honorable profession as far as their peers go any more."

Regardless of how the role of homemaker is viewed it is still an important one. For years, psychologists have said that the first five years of a child's life are the most critical in determining his character and the direction the rest of his life will take. Parents who use child care need to consider this carefully and check out the education the child will receive. Is the child being taught values and behavioral traits which are in alignment with the parents' philosophies? My experience is that the Montessori schools use a method of self-discovery which seems to be very effective in helping the child learn new skills as well as in building a sense of self-esteem.

The Russians have made the child-care industry highly respected. It has a reputation as a bona fide profession, and those working in it take their jobs very seriously. We in this country should put similar emphasis on this important position that affects the early education of our future generation.

For the mother who chooses and is able to stay in the home, society should recognize the contribution she is making—not only as a nurturer, but as an educator, a mentor, a teacher, and an imparter of beliefs and values. She can take pride in the contribution she is making to our most important natural resource. Mother Theresa, upon receiving the Nobel Peace Prize, was asked what people could do for world peace. She said, "Go home and love your family."

For many women, working in the home has been more than living "among the pots and pans," as shown by their strong roles as teachers and facilitators. One example is of a young mother of three children who had an interest in sculpting. Taking lessons from a professional one morning a week, she would rush home to develop her own style. But the children got into the clay and other art supplies, and there was a free-for-all. So she hit upon the idea of sharing her clay and tools with them; the result was three young artists apprenticed to a master craftswoman. She established her identity while showing the children that mothers have interests and needs too.

Drs. Hennig and Jardim performed a study of 25 top women executives to discover factors they had in common. The majority of these women were the "only child" or the first born. They were extremely close to their fathers, who encouraged them, and they came out of childhood with a "tremendous sense of self-esteem." From their fathers, they learned yet another key ingredient of success which other women are not taught—*strategy.* [17]

In an article in *New West,* "Goal Consciousness: You have to Have a Strategy," Ruth Mehrtans Galvin writes, "Knowing what you want and planning the strategy to get it are more important for women now, perhaps, than ever." Galvin states that many women do not understand the necessity of game [team] playing. In the past, they did not learn to play sports, to play hard and win or lose hard, to cooperate in winning, and in sharing the glory and defeat. They were not taught to be "buddies" in the ways that men have been. [18]

Mary Kay Ash understands and uses this concept well. Encouraging her people to submit creative ideas, she rewarded, in particular, one woman who came up with the idea of team leaders wearing red jackets to symbolize the team spirit.

Florence Chadwick, who learned about teamwork with men when she was a competitive swimmer, encourages men in her stockbrokerage firm to share financial magazines she leaves for them on her desk.

Research reveals a surprising fact: Women also have had to struggle against their own fear of success. It is often an unconscious behavior. This monster rears its head in frustrating ways such as: just before the success is finally achieved, women sometimes drop their projects, become mentally diffused and confused, choose an easier way out, defer to somebody else, apologize for their inadequacies, get sick, go on a vacation, give everyone else the credit.

The successful woman belongs to a comparatively new breed with few traditions upon which to draw. However, she is gradually developing a concept similar to the "old boy system," which enables men to cement their corporate power by virtue of sports, club, or university connections previously nonexistent for women. A system of *networking* is gaining status as women learn to support each other through an exchange of information and strategies.

Jewell Jackson McCabe founded the National Coalition of 100 Black Women to help women gain political and economic power. The aim of the Coalition is to further develop leadership in the black community by finding, showcasing, and networking talented black women. Since its inception in 1981, the Coalition has grown to 6,000 members, and Jewell says she is "not going to be happy until it's in 100 cities."

An important part of networking is knowledgeable women instructing and learning from each other. Mary Cunningham extended a helping hand to women at Seagrams. ". . . Each day over lunch, for seven days in a row, I took a group of middle-management women and taught them . . . core concepts . . . of business . . . jokingly named 'Harvard Business School in Seven Days.' "

In another type of support group, my women students have discussed their concerns in areas such as: how to be assertive without being aggressive, getting rid of guilt, establishing identities, setting career goals, and how to handle the compulsion for perfection and trying to please everyone. They explore their fears: how to express anger, aloneness versus loneliness, "super-momism," and sexuality.

It is good for women to talk together. The isolated family of today does not provide the exposure to long-term close relations with aunts, uncles, and other relatives who, in the past, enabled individuals to see their strengths and pitfalls. Previously, American society has said, "Don't complain. You are the most advantaged women in the world," which only compounded the loneliness without providing an opportunity for women to develop and use their skills.

Today's generation has responded with a new dimension to help women cope with problems and discouraging situations. There is a whole system of support and self-help groups—drug-free programs, Alcoholics Anonymous, and other twelve-step programs and many, many others—to substitute for the guidance formerly provided by the family.

In addition to outside support, successful women look to their inner voices for affirmation and a sense of self-worth. In the words of Norman Lear, they tell themselves, "Good fellow, you said you were going to [do this] . . . and you did." Venita Van Caspel expressed her philosophy, "It never occurred to me that I wouldn't do it."

A new woman is evolving in our world: a Diane Sawyer or a Nancy Reagan, one who finds softness and gentleness totally compatible with strength and self-assertion. She is constructively competitive on the job and is comfortable about her success.

As the successful woman grows in numbers and her dynamism shatters the myths, she:

- Defines her own role at home or on the job.
- Is a team player; she competes only with her best self, not against male or female co-workers, to get the job done.
- Has a high energy level and puts in long hours of *quality* work well beyond the norm.
- Has a high degree of optimism and an "I can do it" approach.
- Retains her womanliness as she pursues her established goals.

- Can be flexible when needed and knows how to negotiate.
- Sees the total picture and weighs the consequences of an action from many angles.
- Often asks herself early in life, in the words of Mary Cunningham, "Am I making a lasting contribution? Am I living up to my fullest potential in all dimensions of my life?" (In contrast to successful men, who often first establish a strong professional and financial base and *then* look for ways to be helpful to society.)

Venita Van Caspel sums it up:

> They suddenly discovered women . . . and you know there are not very many of them [whose talents are yet recognized] so that's the reason I'm on so many boards, and I'm quite aware of this.
>
> I'm glad there are women who have taken an active role. I think they've done a lot for many women . . . although it's not my nature to be a Betty Friedan . . .
>
> I think the pendulum had to swing very far in order to get to the middle, and I see that I'm benefiting greatly from it . . .

Venita is concerned, as are other successful women, about her contribution to society. Her goal was to help older citizens become financially independent so they could retire with dignity. Mary Kay Ash wants the women who work for her ". . . to be everything God created them to be."

Acknowledging the strong support Americans are now giving women for their achievements, Sandra Day O'Connor commented on the reaction to her appointment to the Supreme Court:

> The most moving part of the whole event has been the outpouring of joy and support I have received from people all over the country . . . It is this outpouring of common humanity and the feelings that we all share . . . [that is] the most remarkable aspect of the nomination.

These women are making a difference. And it is being felt economically as well as socially and culturally. According to a government study released in January of 1988, the gap between the salaries of men and women is steadily narrowing, but my feeling is that this change is coming all too slowly. In 1979, when the Bureau of Labor and Statistics first began collecting data, the median earnings of working women was 62.5 percent that of men. In 1987 that figure had risen to 70 percent. [19] Many people believe that this inequality in salaries keeps women from the real power base and decision-making roles in America.

There is no question that women have made tremendous strides in the recent past. But there is still much room for improvement. Supreme Court Justice Sandra Day O'Connor once again pointed out at a conference on Women and the Constitution that less than 5 percent of Congress and the judiciary are women. She added that justice "moves slowly, so we usually arrive on the scene some years late. But once there, we must usually linger for a while." She foresees sex bias cases continuing through this century. [20]

I asked Senator Ted Kennedy what he sees as the primary areas of concern for women today. He pointed out the headway that has been made by legislation dealing with discrimination against women in employment and education. However, he said:

> There is still extraordinary *feminization of poverty*, for example, in our society . . . There is continued discrimination in our pensions. There is discrimination in Social Security . . . So although there has been some progress made in some important areas, areas in which I've tried to move forward, there is still a very great distance to go. And even if we pass laws, there is always the issue and question of whether those laws are actually being enforced.

He encourages women to take a more active role in the issues with which they are concerned: war and peace, nuclear arms, housing, health care, and education, saying women are "an enormous political source which hasn't been tapped to date nearly enough and which certainly needs to be if we're going to find solutions to the problems we are facing in our society."

As the stories in the women's chapters which follow point out, we can take heart that there is a "wave of women" capable of doing just that—women who are continually reaching out for new successes for themselves and, as in ages past, improving the quality of life of those around them.

Like their male counterparts, these women are individuals of vision who are able to see beyond the status quo—have the insight to recognize a need, the resourcefulness to find a way to fill it, and the gumption to meet their goals, regardless of what others around them are saying.

Let's take a closer, more personal look at the lives of these successful men and women to find out exactly how they have attained their achievements.

"Now you can do it, you can do it. . . . If I had the choice to give my children a gift of a million dollars or to think positively, I would choose the latter."

MARY KAY ASH

Founder and Chairman of the Board, Mary Kay Cosmetics, Inc.

Born in Hutwells, Texas May 12. Attended the University of Houston, 1943-44. Unit Manager of Stanley Home Products, 1938-52. Officer, World Gift Co., 1952-63.

Mary Kay Ash, chairperson and founder of Mary Kay Cosmetics, Inc., began her career in utter poverty. When she was two years old, her family moved to Houston so Mary Kay's mother could find work to support her family. Her father, an invalid with tuberculosis, depended on Mary Kay for all his needs, since her mother worked 14 hours a day managing a restaurant.

At the age of ten, Mary Kay was entirely independent. She bought her own clothes, cooked, and shopped for herself and her father. I asked Mary Kay to expound upon this stage of her childhood. She said that her mother was her greatest influence and added:

> My mother always worked. She got up at 5:00 in the morning and came home at 9:00 at night. So you can understand that during many of my earlier years, I was asleep when she left and asleep when she came home. My childhood defeats all these theories about how working mothers can't influence their children. My mother was gone all the time. She never was there to do the little things for me that needed to be done physically, like teaching me how to tie my shoes from a very early age or . . . how to cook or how to take care of a house or how to do anything, but fortunately, the telephone had been invented, and she told me by phone what I needed to know. Because she was the manager of the restaurant that she worked in, she was available to talk to me when I needed her. I would call her ten times a day and I'd say, "Mother, I don't know how to do this." And she'd say, "Okay honey, now listen to me. Now you do this first and then you do this and then you do this. *Now you can do it, you can do it.*"

It seemed as though Mary Kay's mother tried to encourage her daughter's self-confidence at an early age. Mary Kay commented:

> Well, I think it was primarily because she couldn't come and do it for me that she had to tell me that I could do it. She often said you can do anything in this world you want to do if you want to do it bad enough and if you're willing to pay the price. And yes, you can sell the most tickets to the event and yes, you can do this and yes, you can do that. So her attitude toward me—you can do it—was probably the guiding influence in my life . . . Pleasing her was another thing I especially wanted to do. She would not settle for an A; it needed to be an A+. Whatever I got into, I had to do it better than anybody else.

I asked Mary Kay if the responsibility she shouldered at such a young age felt burdensome to her at that time. She replied:

> No, I never knew that anybody else had to live another way . . . We never had any of that "you have to do these things." I did everything out of love and because I wanted to do it. Especially with my father. I wanted to take care of him and I wanted to please him, and I would call up and I would say, "Mother, Daddy wants potato soup. How do you fix potato soup? What do you do?" And she'd say, "O.K., now listen carefully and I'll tell you. Now jot this down. You use about two potatoes, and you should use one onion, and you should use this and that. Do you have all those things? Well, run down to the store to Scardino's [it was . . . a little store around the corner from us] and get whatever you need." She had an account there. And all I had to do was run down there, and I would charge the groceries. I would get whatever I needed, and I would come home and fix the soup or whatever it was he wanted. My mother taught me to cook on the telephone.

"And you did it because you thought you were pleasing him?" I asked.

> It was pleasing him and it was fulfilling to me that I was able to do it, and that I didn't ruin it. Of course, I did ruin some things, naturally. Even today we ruin some things—but most of the time it was edible and acceptable.

Mary Kay said she didn't resent the fact that she was given more responsibility than other children at such a young age. In fact she wasn't even aware that she was raised differently:

> You see I was so busy that I had very little time to visit around with other children. Dorothy was my best friend. She was really my only contact.

Mary Kay had brothers and sisters, but they were older and had left home when she was growing up. She said:

> Nobody was home but me. I was the last one. I had very little time to play. In fact, I don't remember doing much of that. I came straight home from school and I had to do the things for my father, cook his dinner, study my lessons, etc.

I asked her if, having missed the experience of playing as a child, she had learned how to play later in life. She replied:

> I've never learned how to play. I still don't know how to play. I almost feel it's a waste of time. For instance I see people going to ball games and doing all these things and I think how can they just sit there and look at a dumb football game. I just don't understand that. I think it's such a waste. We have a box at the stadium and I hardly ever go—but when I do, I take something to do while I'm there. I just can't stand sitting there not doing something . . . I get much more enjoyment out of work. I go home at night and I invariably have stacks of things that I need to read, and so I spend my time catching up on all the business that comes across my desk that I don't have time to read at the office. Usually the whole evening is spent that way.

She went on to say that work has always been her play and that this is true even today.

After finishing high school, Mary Kay married. Faced with financial difficulties, she and her husband moved into her mother's home. The couple had two children. Although Mary Kay worked seven days a week as a typist at her church to supplement the family income, they barely had enough money to put food on the table. She also served, without a salary, as a superintendent of the beginners classes for all the Baptist churches in Houston.

A post-war divorce left Mary Kay with three children to support. In desperate need of substantial income, Mary Kay became a dealer for

Stanley Home Products, a direct sales party plan company. This position enabled her to earn money and still spend time with her children who were being looked after by neighbors.

After three weeks of receiving average sales of only $7 worth of products per party, Mary Kay attended a sales convention. At this convention, she determined to one day be crowned "Queen" for selling the most Stanley Products. Mary Kay won the crown the following year, and she stayed with Stanley Home Products for 13 years before joining World Gifts, a company selling decorative accessories in the home. She advanced to National Training Director in a relatively short period.

In 1962, Mary Kay suffered from a rare form of paralysis on one side of her face. After surgery and a couple of months in the hospital, she resumed her normal routine without any definitive setbacks.

In 1963, she retired from World Gifts. Mary Kay pondered the idea of starting her own direct sales company with her husband. He could administrate and she could oversee sales.

One month before she planned to open, her husband died of a heart attack. Mary Kay's son decided to help her, and on Friday, September 13, 1963, with nine people and one shelf filled with cosmetics, the company opened.

By 1968, the company had grown enough to have stock traded on the over-the-counter market. The company's stock was listed on the New York Stock Exchange in August 1976.

Today, Mary Kay Cosmetics, Inc., is an international organization with more than 150,000 independent beauty consultants throughout the United States, its territories, Australia, Canada, West Germany, and Argentina.

I asked Mary Kay to describe the years as a single parent supporting three children, working with Stanley Home Products, Inc. Up to that point in her career, she had always had just enough income to provide the bare necessities, she said:

> . . . it never occurred to me I couldn't do it. I always knew that if you worked hard enough you could [make it], and at least in sales we don't have any ceilings. The way you get a raise is you hold an extra Stanley party or an extra show and I always just figured how many I had to have for next week to make ends meet and go out and book it and hold it—and you had the money. So it was not like a structured job where you're going to make $10,000 this year, or whatever, and there's no way you can get beyond it. It wasn't that way. If you needed $15,000, you just worked harder. So, I worked harder.

Never feeling that she had limitations imposed on her, she took full advantage of her enthusiasm and initiative. I asked what skills she had learned from "living on a shoestring" when she was working for Stanley, and she replied:

> Well, first you have to learn how to organize your time and realize that even the President of the United States has the same 24 hours you do.
>
> How do you get more time? You can't, except that I learned that three early risings make an extra day and when I read that I thought, gee whiz, if three would make an extra day, six would give me a nine-day week and I need that. I have a thing we call in the company the 5 o'clock club and I discovered that by getting up at 5 o'clock in the morning before the phone begins to ring, before the dog begins to bark, before all the annoyances and interruptions that come later, you have two or three uninterrupted hours to really work and you can get out three times as much as you can get done after 8 o'clock. That means I go to bed fairly early—at 10:30, after the news.

Mary Kay schedules her calendar carefully, saying she turns down 90 percent of the invitations she receives. "Most of them are apt to be these things where a table is a thousand dollars, you know, and I would rather give the thousand dollars to charity."

I asked why it was so important to her to encourage the women working for her to develop their full potential, and she answered:

> Well, I guess I'm kind of like a mother who wants her children to have what she didn't have and I struggled so hard against male situations where, "a woman couldn't hold that job—that belongs to a man." In that last company my supervisor thought that the sales manager had to be a man. Now my title was "National Training Director," which paid half as much as Sales Manager. I had to train the man who eventually became my superior, when I had taught him how. And then suddenly he was given the title for twice as much money as I was making. Now that doesn't really make good sense.
>
> In this organization, we have women who could be on the front of *Vogue* magazine. Not one or two but hundreds of them who fit that picture . . . I want them to be feminine; I want them to be ultra successful. I want them to be everything God created. See, I don't

want that female competitiveness to get to the point where they're scratching somebody else's eyes out to get where they want to go. So, from the beginning, since that was a problem in other companies I worked with, where people would step on each other to get some place, and I didn't want that in this company—we put all our prizes on plateaus. Everybody who does $120,000 wholesale wins a Cadillac. So you don't have to step on anybody to get it. When we have contests on a monthly basis, everybody who does "X" number of dollars wholesale wins a ring, or whatever we are giving. Nobody has to compete with anybody but *themselves*. The only place that we depart from that is at the annual awards and seminar in January. Somebody has to be the queen.

. . . when we started the company, my objective was to help women become the beautiful creatures I knew God had created. In my own case I have constantly been told, even when I got on the board with World Gifts, "Mary Kay, you're thinking like a woman." What else? Considering we were dealing with women; they should have listened . . . it irked me . . .

Mary Kay has a sense of trust in the people she hires. This was put to the test when the staff of the TV program "Sixty Minutes" showed up at her door unannounced. "In a split second I had to make a decision," she said. "We have 1,000 people in these two buildings. They could be making opium over there, for all I know." Deciding she could count on her employees, she said, "I instantly rolled out the red carpet."

Mary Kay's financial success only complements the great personal success which she has achieved. Through poverty, her father's sickness, her mother's physical absence during her waking hours, divorce, and the death of a husband, she encountered hardship. Yet, she consistently approached her crises as opportunities to show greater resourcefulness. Even when she worked seven days each week, she volunteered her time and skills to the Baptist community.

She has brought to a skeptical, male-dominated system a business structure built on earned rewards, community spirit, sharing, and creativity. She pressed on when others said she would not succeed. Mary Kay has truly made a uniquely feminine contribution to the masculine business world both in her product and by her example.

Through self-confidence and diligence learned early in life, she primed herself in skills required for her later accomplishments. Certainly, her love for her work and her sense of fulfilled destiny contribute to her happiness.

"Take some risks. If you are only going to go for the certain proposition, you'll miss half your life."

PHILIP CALDWELL

Former Chief Executive Officer and Chairman of the Board, Ford Motor Company

Born 1920 in Bourneville, Ohio. B.A. in Economics, Muskingum College. MBA in Industrial Management, Harvard. Navy: 1946-53. Worked in 15 different positions at Ford before becoming top executive. Currently Senior Managing Director, Shearson Lehman Brothers, Inc.

On October 1, 1979, Philip Caldwell succeeded Henry Ford II as President and Chief Executive of Ford Motor Company. Shortly thereafter he was named Chairman of the Board as well. This was the first time someone outside the Ford family had ever held this position. To find out more about Philip Caldwell, I went to Dearborn, Michigan, the heart of the automotive industry, to talk with him.

Arriving at the front door of the international Ford headquarters, I was struck by the immensity of the structure the Ford company occupies. Upon entering the building, I saw a large display of shining Ford Motor cars representing a range of styles and years.

I felt somewhat intimidated upon being greeted by a group of male vice presidents who ushered me into the elevator for our ride to the executive floor at the top of the building. The entourage escorted me to the executive reception room, where we awaited the arrival of Mr. Caldwell.

Philip Caldwell is, I found, a somewhat reserved man but one who gives out practical logic with a homespun warmth. I knew him not only as Chief Executive Officer of Ford Motor Company but also as a graduate of Muskingum, a small Ohio liberal arts college which we both attended. The competence which he emanated I had expected to find in a man of his position, but I was surprised and pleased to find it tempered with a genuine friendliness that may have been a product of his small-town upbringing.

As the interview began, I soon lost concern for the imposing audience as I focused in on the wisdom and insight of this talented man. He described his definition of the role of a chief executive:

> The job of a Chief Executive Officer is to know when to come in and when to stay out. It's important that you remain detached. You can't be in the middle of the battle and be running the general staff at the same time. There's a great temptation to want to get involved in all of it, but there's nothing worse for an organization than somebody who tries to do all the masterminding for the organization.

Philip is heralded for having turned his company around, bringing it out of one of the most difficult times in its history. Under his leadership, Ford moved from a loss of $685 million in 1982 to a 20 percent increase in sales, earning over $40 billion, with a profit of $1.8 billion in 1983.

Caldwell came to Ford with a well-established record for achievement. He was the top civilian professional in Navy procurement. In 1950, he was the first recipient of the William A. Jump Memorial award given to the most outstanding young federal government employee in the executive, legislative, or judicial branch in public administration.

He began his career at Ford in 1953 and in 1968 was elected a vice president and appointed general manager of truck operations for North America. He worked in 13 other capacities before succeeding Henry Ford II as chief executive in 1979.

I asked him what the situation was when he took over, and he said:

> The problems really were more operational than policy problems. Our products had tended to not be as strong as they should have been, both in concept and, above all, in quality; and of course the external factors were pressing in on us from at home and abroad. There was an inadequate planning process. So we had plenty of work to do.

He told me the approach he had used to help Ford regain its flagging reputation and sales was "going back to the basics." I asked him what that meant, and he replied:

> What are the basics? Products with integrity. Products that are what they are represented to be, what you advertise them to be: reliable, dependable. Product integrity. That's a pretty big word with us around here. We had slipped quite a lot.

He told me that one of the ways he was able to accomplish this was through long-range planning, an element that was missing when he assumed command. He and his staff take time to make "a serious, thoughtful statement of the objective" they are trying to accomplish. He said they:

> Discuss it, debate it, analyze it first. Then everyone agrees on what we are trying to do. It's easy to assess it at that point. Things that are going well, we spend no time on. Things that aren't going so well, we spend whatever time is necessary. It's important to get agreement on what you're trying to do first.

Philip considers one of the most important functions of a Chief Executive Officer is selecting the top executives. He said, "The only way you can multiply yourself is to work through others." I asked him what traits he looks for, and he said, "I guess I would start with one simple premise: There is no substitute for brains. You're going against the brightest and best." He also said he finds curiosity an important quality. He went on to say that he likes his management team to be whole people not "sunflowers." He explained:

> Consider the shape of the sunflower plant. As it grows, it has a stalk that is tall and thin and no branches. When the head comes on and the seeds develop, it has a very big head. At some stage, you'll notice the head kind of drops. We would rather have oak trees with many branches and strengths so that when you get to the top there is a lot to draw on.
>
> You cannot do that if you have been in one function all your life. So, for our managers, we would like to see people in different disciplines, in different geographical areas, dealing with assignments that have different priorities. We want to grow whole people, not sunflowers.

In order to support employees' growth, as well as utilize the ideas of all employees, Mr. Caldwell instituted a policy he calls "employee involvement." "We've gone to a policy of cooperation rather than confrontation," he said. "We trust each other, we want to communicate with each other because we believe that everybody has a contribution to make."

When confronting a difficult problem, his formula for dealing with it is to make sure that everything that can be done is done and then he puts it out of his mind:

> I guess you have to decide how high you're going to set that bar in the high jump. If you've set it as high as you know how to set it, there's no point in worrying about it afterwards. If you know and you see others are not setting the bar as high as they should, that's a time to be very restless. That's when I have sleepless nights.

I asked Philip what advice he would give young managers. He said he would caution them not to be so eager for advancement that performance in their current positions suffers:

> Do the job at hand as well as you possibly know how. Be interested in the next job and what's over the hill, but don't spend all the time on the job you're on trying to get to the next job . . . People aren't effective when they do that and they're hurting themselves. They should spend time thinking how they can do their job better than anyone else. That is the biggest key I know to opening the next door.

He said he thinks it is important to stick with a task until the end no matter how tough it becomes. "People who run away from difficult assignments," he said, "will keep on running away forever."

He also recommended that people not "be afraid to be torn up a bit. Get out in the world. Have a lot of experiences. Be curious. Ask." He continued:

> Accept assignments when you can't fill in all the blanks. Take some risks. If you are only going to go for the certain proposition, you'll miss half your life. If I had studied any offer I had too much, I probably would have said no. And if I had said no to any of those jobs, there probably wouldn't have been the next one.

Caldwell thought it important to define a mission, find a way to make a contribution not only to oneself but to mankind. "Try to give as well as take away from every situation. As you become more experienced and more successful over the years, give more and take less."

He makes contributions in a number of areas of society. He serves on the board of directors for Chase Manhattan Bank, Digital Equipment Corporation, and Harvard University Associates of Business School. His efforts were also recognized by Brigham Young University when they named him International Executive of the Year.

His personal mission at Ford was to leave his company stronger and better than when he took over his assignment. "While we are not the best regarded company in the U.S., we've taken a major step forward from where it was. I'm proud of that," he said. "I would like to feel that a generation from now, I will have done something that made it possible for the company to prosper." Wanting to share this sense of pride, he worked to help all Ford employees feel proud of their company, and he believes the majority are.

What about the end of the day? Where does he go for rest and relaxation? Philip Caldwell said his home life gives him the opportunity for recharging. Noting that one of the characteristics of jobs everywhere is the loneliness, he said it helps to have peace inside when he has to make decisions. "My home situation provides that serenity," he added.

By all indicators, Philip Caldwell accomplished his mission at Ford. In recent years, the company has made record sales. It was with a sense of pride that he retired at age 65 from one job and moved to New York to the position of Senior Managing Director of Shearson Lehman Brothers. This is a man who has continued to find a mission in life and to make a contribution. [21]

"My first race, I came in last, and that really motivated me. I wanted to learn to swim more than if I had won."

FLORENCE CHADWICK

World Record-Breaking Channel Swimmer; Senior Account Executive, Smith, Barney, Harris, Upham & Co.

Born 1918, San Diego, California. Attended several colleges. Won over 100 swimming trophies, broke 16 world records, two of which were previously held by men. Had a role in the movie, "Bathing Beauty." Aquatic director, who put on shows, trained and taught students. In her late 40s became a stockbroker.

On August 8, 1950, Florence Chadwick established a new record for a woman swimming the English Channel, breaking the 1926 record set by Gertrude Ederle.

It is remarkable that Florence, in her 70s, an age when most people are retired, is still hard at work. She is up at 4:00 a.m. and in the office working at 6:30. She usually puts in 12- or 13-hour workdays at the San Diego investment firm of Smith, Barney, Harris Upham & Co., where most of her co-workers are men half her age. Weekends are sometimes work days for her, too. Most nights she is in bed by 8 p.m.

What kind of a woman is Florence Chadwick? What traits does a person need to spend the necessary long, exhausting hours of training for those grueling long-distance swims and to enable her to work such long hours even now? These were questions I asked myself as I was welcomed into her home surrounded by a spectacular rose garden overlooking the Pacific.

Four large boards holding awards and ribbons looked interesting, and I assumed they were Florence's from earlier days. "No," she said, "they were my mother's. She won them for her prizewinning roses."

I found out from Florence that her medals and trophies were displayed in various places in the country—the International Hall of Fame of Swimming in Fort Lauderdale, Florida and in the Balboa Park museum in her hometown of San Diego.

Florence has been swimming since she was six. At ten she was the first child to swim the San Diego Bay Channel. Her father was a detective and a narcotics agent. After his retirement, her parents operated a restaurant. Florence attributes her involvement in swimming to her family, particularly her uncle:

"He's the one that started me swimming. My father took a lot of interest in it too, and my mother used to drive me around to swimming meets and to the bay at 5:30 a.m. to practice. So you have to have encouragement at home too."

Florence was excited whan she entered her first race at age six, the girls' championship for twelve and under. She invited all of her uncles and aunts to this event because she was sure she would do well. She did not win first place but came in last, and she was very embarrassed. She learned a big lesson from that experience, "Don't blow your horn until you have something to blow it about."

I asked her what traits or personal qualities helped her to do those long swims. "I think it's mostly dedication and ambition," she said.

"At six you had a lot of ambition?" I asked.

> I think so. My first race, I came in last and that really motivated me. I wanted to learn to swim more than if I had won. I practiced real hard for a whole year for my second race.
>
> All I wanted to learn to do was swim. When I was seven I had my second race, and . . . I did a little better. I was just next to last. I stopped to pick up my chewing gum. I had the gum in my mouth when I was racing and when I turned my head to get a breath, it came out, so I stopped to pick it up. I learned right there, in competition you don't stop for anything. Once the race is on, you keep going.

Swimming always came first for Florence. She described how she arranged all her activities, even as a young child, to develop her swimming abilities:

> I remember when I was just a little girl and my mother wanted me to take piano lessons. I didn't like piano. I practiced an hour because I was told I had to, but I'd have the clock right in front of me to make sure it wasn't 30 seconds over an hour. I focused everything in those days on my swimming, which I did like, so I said I wanted saxophone lessons. I was told that it would help develop my lungs. I took private saxophone lessons for about seven years.

Florence trained hard, in and out of the water, and she received a lot of encouragement from her parents:

> I could swim up and down the bay with temperatures down to 50 degrees. I think that all helped toughen me up a little bit for my long-distance swimming later on.
>
> When I was 13, I went to Mr. Gunther and he coached me the rest of my career. He's the one that decided I should build myself up physically. He and my father used to encourage me to work out in the gymnasium as well as in the water.
>
> My father and my coach, Henry Gunther, put up a good gymnasium in our garage at home. I would get out there every day and work out on pulley weights and chin myself and saw wood. I did everything I could to develop my shoulders so it would enable me to swim better. Florence Chambers was my first coach. When I was just a little girl she had me hold onto the side of the wall for a whole half hour. Well, when I was ten years old that used to seem like a lot of kicking, but I was told that this is what you have to do.

Gunther was a hard taskmaster. She recalled a backstroke race at the San Diego County Championship in which she came in first with a time that should have broken the Pacific Coast record. However, she said, when she got out of the water, beaming with pride:

> Henry Gunther said, "Wipe that smile off your face. You made a bad turn down there. You broke your form." I was disqualified for making a bad turn. There was no excuse for breaking my form, according to him, so again he drummed that form, form, form into me.
>
> The first year I worked with him he took me out of competition for one whole year. That almost broke my heart because I always wanted to race. And he used to say, "Girl, until you learn to swim, how are you going to race?" I had already been racing for five or six years.
>
> I thought I was doing well. His theory was, "how can you swim a mile right if you can't swim one length correctly?" Finally, he let me start racing. Then in training, most of the time I would be swimming against boys.

I asked Florence how she became a world champion. She said it wasn't a goal she had when she first started swimming—that it was an inclination that developed gradually as she began winning.

As Florence got older she kept competing. She became champion of San Diego, then San Diego County, then Pacific Coast, and then Far Western Champion. In 1948 she became professional. She also worked in a movie called "Bathing Beauty" with former swimming teammate Esther Williams.

The first of Florence's 16 Channel swims was in 1950. She swam the English Channel four times between 1950 and 1956, the first time from France to England and the other three times in the opposite direction.

I asked why, once she had "conquered" it, she had gone back to do it again. She said:

> Each time it was to go back and try to lower the record. I would get the men's world record and someone would come along and break that, then I'd go back and try to get it back again.

Florence swam the Catalina Channel in California in 1950, 1951, and 1952. She went on to swim the Strait of Gibraltar in Spain, the Bosporos and the Dardanelles in Turkey, and the channel between England and Wales.

Florence explained why she didn't complete the Irish Sea crossing. Despite coating herself with lanolin to preserve her body heat, the cold water numbed her, and she was pulled out with only a mile and a half to go.

I asked her what she considered to be the most important trait she had acquired in childhood. She said her father had told her from the time she was a little girl to always try to be a little bit better than average. She reflected that a lot of people hear that but don't put it into practice.

Florence learned at an early age that being "a little bit better" meant making some sacrifices. Her rigorous training schedule left her little time for social activities:

> I remember in 1936 when I graduated from high school, I had to skip the prom. I was too busy training. And I skipped the baccalaureate services and ditched the "ditch day activities." The only thing I attended was graduation, and I left for the Eastern Swim Meet the very next morning. I've been used to it all my life—giving up things because swimming was my life.

She has no regrets about what she missed out on as a child but believes it was worth it:

> I'd do it all over again. You have to make sacrifices to reach a goal

> if that's what it takes. I was never allowed to stay overnight at someone's house because I had to get up early and train the next morning. The girls nowadays make the same sacrifices if they're serious about their sport. You sacrifice in some things, but it balances out, because we do things that normally we wouldn't have a chance to do if we hadn't gotten into this type of career.

Travel was one of the added bonuses Florence got from her swimming program. Her competition and training have taken her all over the world. She spent two years in Saudi Arabia working to sponsor herself in her first channel swim. She didn't tell anyone of her plans until she was ready to leave for home by way of France, trying the swim along the way:

> I wrote a letter to my parents a couple of weeks before I left and said, "You know, I told you that I had been doing a lot of swimming over here. Now I can tell you why." I said, "On my way home, I'm going to stop and try the English Channel." As the plane was getting ready to taxi down the runway, I saw this little errand boy come out waving a letter up in the air, and the airplane stopped and they opened the door and handed me a letter. It was from my father. He said he would come over to help me if that's what I wanted to do. He was with me on my first swim, accompanying me in a boat.

Florence used the Australian crawl to make the swim because it is the fastest stroke, and her goal was to break the record. Although the Channel is 19 miles straight across, she estimates she had to cover 24 miles because of the currents. She completed the swim in 13 hours and 20 minutes. I commented that she must have been exhausted, but she said:

> No, because I trained hard to get used to that—staying in motion for so many hours. But I was always wondering if I was swimming fast enough to break the world record. Gertrude Ederle was my idol, and that was my ambition eventually—to break her record.

Florence's coach and father kept her informed and gave her encouragement from the boat. At the end she got caught in strong currents, which kept her in one spot quite a while. She had experienced swimming against the current as a child when she swam in the bay. Conquering the currents requires not only physical strength but the inner fortitude to persevere, as well. She had to call upon her internal voice, which she called her "inner coach," to keep going: "If I said to myself once, I said to myself

15 million times, stay with it, stay with it. Gradually I came through the currents."

She commented, "When I finished, my father leaned over and put his arms around me and said something about 'nice work, Babe, a new world record.' I always said that was the biggest thrill of my sports career. That was the first time I realized I had broken the record."

Later, Florence was asked to promote swimming suits for different manufacturers. She toured the United States, making appearances on radio, television, and in department stores. She kept up her training schedule while doing this. "It meant sometimes getting up and in the water at 4 o'clock in the morning because I still had to go to work," she remembers.

She went on to become an aquatic director for several years, putting on shows and training and teaching. I asked why she had changed careers, and she replied:

> My swimming career was over. There comes a time, because of age, that you have to say "Well this is it, it's time to hang up the bathing suit." I had done what I wanted to do; now let's see how I can do at something else.
>
> I came back to San Diego and opened a swimming school. I was doing well except that I was killing myself. Everybody that came in wanted me to teach them to swim. I would be in the water 14 hours a day. And then at the end of the month I wouldn't have enough money to warrant having worked that hard. So I decided that I would try to do something else.

The "something else" was becoming a stockbroker. She not only tried it but became very successful. Noting that selling stocks is a far cry from swimming channels, I asked Florence if there were any traits from her earlier life that helped in her new career. She replied, "*Hard work*. I'm used to working hard. This is anything but an eight-hour job, and it's very highly competitive."

But competing doesn't bother Florence. She has been doing it all her life. I asked for her view on women in competition, and she said:

> I think a lot of women aren't used to competition. They've never been exposed to it. For the last five years I was the only woman broker with Kidder Peabody in the San Diego office, but it didn't bother me. It's just a highly competitive field and you have to get used to it. Racing

against men all the time made it easy to do this. I think I've learned teamwork. I've been on teams all my life.

I asked Florence if she had a daughter, what she would want for her. She replied:

> First of all, I would want to know what she's primarily interested in. Is she interested in sports? And if she is, I would try to help her. If she's interested in dancing or whatever, I would try to help her. But you can't put it there if it's not there. They have to want it very badly to make the sacrifices that are necessary to get to the top.
>
> I think no matter what anybody chooses to do—work, play, whatever, my answer is "give it all you've got," because anybody can be average. Everybody can't be number one and everyone can't be number two and number three. But you go after whatever you do want and do it to the best of your ability.

I commented that she still has remarkable energy. Her response was, "I always think you're as old as you feel. There are old people at 24 and young people at 70." I asked if she was planning to retire. She said she had planned to retire at 70, but was getting so much pleasure from her work that she will probably wait until 75 before quitting to travel, tend her 180 rose bushes, and swim.

Florence has always worked hard and diligently for the things she's loved to do. Like many others who excel at their professions, Florence used her childhood failures as an impetus to do better.

Pursuing athletics naturally made health and exercise a premium commitment for Florence. And now she continues to set her marks high and "give it all she's got!" Even after retirement she plans to continue to find new adventurous pursuits. She told me, "I hope someday to sail around the world. I don't even know how to sail, but by the time I decide to retire, I will have learned how."

I have no doubt that she will do just that.

"I'm a person who aims high. I think big. I just believe that anything I set out to do, I'm going to do."

XERNONA CLAYTON

Corporate Vice President of Urban Affairs, Turner Broadcasting Corporation

Born 1930 in Muskogee, Oklahoma. B.A. with honors, Tennessee State University. Serves on boards of Trustees of Martin Luther King Center for Non-Violent Social Change, Multiple Sclerosis Society, and NAACP. Previously host of WAGA-TV Atlanta's "Xernona Clayton Show" as well as other weekly shows at Turner Broadcasting. Named one of America's Top 100 Black Business & Professional Women by *Dollars and Sense* magazine. 1984 Black Georgian of the Year.

Xernona Clayton, Vice President of Public Affairs, holds the highest female position at Turner Broadcasting Systems. Earlier, she was the first black person in the South to have her own TV show. This striking woman is obviously intelligent, creative, and capable. But the competition is fierce at this level, and Ted Turner does not take lightly the choosing of his executives. What special qualities brought her to this powerful position? I asked Xernona that question and she replied that she considered self-esteem to be her greatest asset. She explained that this was one of the two basic lessons that her father, a Baptist minister, had taught her that had guided her through life:

> One lesson was I have no control over the things that make me look the way I look. I didn't choose to be a female. I didn't choose to be black. I didn't choose my height or my physical makeup. He said that none of those are things I should put a lot of emphasis on, feeling no pride nor no sorrow in any of that. But put all my emphasis on how I can control the things that I can control. That is, your thinking and your attitude . . . how you feel about yourself and your fellow man.

Being kind to your fellow man, she went on to say, was her father's second basic lesson. And, she said, he didn't make a distinction between people. "He didn't say, 'Be kind to black people.' He said, 'Be kind to all people.' He said your fellow man, and he meant *all* men."

She grew up in a small town, Muskogee, Oklahoma, where her father was well-respected and his counsel often sought. Since Oklahoma has a large Indian population, he often consulted about Indian affairs as well as with the white city officials. Because of this early association with various races, coupled with her father's attitude, race was not an issue for her. She said:

> We saw Indians coming in and out of our house and white people coming in and out of our house. Our friends and neighbors were black. So black people came in and out of our house. We really saw all kinds of people all the time. We never felt inferior. We never felt insecure.

She said, in fact, that her father did not dwell on their race but emphasized developing personal self-esteem:

> I remember I never had to worry about that feeling of black pride when the country was saying "Feel proud. Be proud of your blackness." I've been black all my life. He taught me to feel good about myself because that's something I can control.

This quality has also helped her hold her head up and move on even when dealing with bigoted people. "I had the strength inwardly to not feel inferior," she said. "If someone told me I was dumb because I was black or I stank because I was black, I didn't believe it."

She said that, despite the advantages of holding a good position, being married to a late, prominent writer for *Ebony* and *Jet* and enjoying what she terms "economic comforts," she still calls upon her positive attitude to help her cope with racial prejudice. She mentioned that at times she has been denied housing in certain locations because of her race. She said Atlanta, where she lives now, is "a deep Southern city steeped in a tradition of segregation, discrimination, and hatred. I think if I had not been a strong person, I would have fallen along the way and become entrapped with the hatred and the bigotry."

Because of her positive attitude and desire to overcome prejudged ideas and bigotry, she took the bold step of going to see Calvin Craig, the former Grand Dragon of the Ku Klux Klan:

> I never accepted the fact the he really did hate everybody who looked like me. And yet I had read that. So I set out to have a one-on-one relationship to change his attitude. I know he's happier today because he got rid of a lot of baseless bigotry. I had a part in that. I took the time to get "the rest of the story."

Her experience with people prejudging her has caused her to be extremely sensitive about prejudging others. She makes it a point not to act until she has heard both sides of the story. "I would hope that in all of my dealings with everything I've done, that people saw some fairness in what I did or what I tried to do," she said.

Xernona posesses an unusual combination of personal qualities. She is highly professional (she lists being prompt as a high priority for herself), has a reputation for getting things done efficiently, and yet she exudes a genuine warmth and wonderful sense of humor.

I believe the reputation Xernona has acquired for efficiently getting the job done on time is due partly to the fact that her ego is not constantly on the line. Her high esteem and positive attitude allow her to help make people all around her "winners." She motivates her staff through constant encouragement and recognition of their individual strengths. She is also quick to acknowledge the support of her colleagues.

Her self-confidence has not only brought her success but has enabled her to learn from and overcome situations that made her uncomfortable. She told me:

> There were times when I was ill-prepared. Those times encouraged me to learn more. Once you've prepared yourself, you don't feel fearful anymore . . . I have sense enough to know where I am weak and then gain knowledge in that area. Read and find out what you don't know.

Xernona came to Turner from a CBS affiliate where she had her own show. She won an Emmy for her first project at TBS, a feature about the black community in Atlanta. The favorable publicity led to other opportunities and successes, and she was asked to fill in one night as host for a public affairs program. The public response was so overwhelming that she became the regular substitute host and, eventually, host/producer. After that, she said:

> Then Ted gave me assignments that didn't fit into any description of a job category that I was fulfilling. And he flattered me by saying that I was the person who got a job done and got it done expeditiously. That really set me out on a course of doing lots of things, and from there I was made vice president.

Xernona's ability to get the job done was exhibited in her ambitious plans for commemorating "Black History Month" in February 1988. She wanted to celebrate it to the maximum by airing a "Minute-a-Day" feature every day of the month but had to convince Ted Turner. "I realized that was a big request," she said, "but I think big. And so does he."

He was reluctant, commenting that it would amount to nearly 30 minutes of air time, but Xernona persisted:

> "You're right," I said. "But 30 minutes in a month for a group of Americans who have been shut out, contributing to the richness of this America, occupying the missing pages of our history, persevering against all odds, is a small price to pay." And he went for it.

Xernona was a teacher before getting into the broadcasting field, and she uses skills acquired in that profession today to help people with their problems. Because people trust her and open up to her, she has become a confidante to some prominent members of society including the late Martin Luther King and his wife, Cloretta Scott King. Xernona was, in fact, one of the last people to see him, having driven him to the airport for his flight to Memphis, where he ultimately died. She was with his wife when he called later that day. He is said to have told Xernona that he had a premonition, and, for the first time ever in his life, he was frightened. History records that he was shot and killed that day.

Xernona has a high regard for the late Dr. King and referred to him along with her boss, Ted Turner, when I asked her what traits she saw in successful people. She spoke first of Turner's qualities:

> I think Ted is a man who is keenly sensitive to the existence of people and things. He is keenly sensitive to animals. He is keenly sensitive to the environment, the trees. I would say when a person is keenly sensitive to a wide range of important areas that it shows me he has a high character.
>
> Dr. King was also successful. I had a chance to know him privately and deeply. He was a man who was so committed to what he was trying to do. I've learned that so many people really don't have the commitment that is required to do a job well. That's why I think a lot of people fail at what they do. You have to have a commitment. It's a word that's tossed around a lot, but the commitment that I'm speaking of is a genuine, deep serious concern for what it is you want to do.

She explained that she believes she has a special destiny that has put her together with such powerful people who were motivated by such high ideals as Dr. King and Ted Turner. That led me to ask her about her religious beliefs:

> I can tell you that I believe strongly that your life is guided by a force. I think it's God, but I choose to say it differently because sometimes people want to call it something else, and I don't want to leave them out . . . My faith and my teachings in the Sunday School of my youth said to me "He does lead you."

It was Xernona's deep love of children which led to her first profession as a teacher, for which she received citations of excellence from two Boards of Education. For a time she regretted not having children of her own. Then she became involved with helping disadvantaged children, black and Mexican members of Los Angeles gangs. She organized a project called Volunteers for Dropouts, which was called to the special attention of President John F. Kennedy. Of this experience, she said, "I was able to devote a lot of time giving some guidance to them and being the mother hen. I got a lot of them back to school who had dropped out. I think if I had my own children, I probably would not have had time."

Time is something Xernona uses to the fullest, to the benefit of a range of worthwhile organizations. She has served on the Board of Multiple Sclerosis Society and in 1985 was president of the National Association of Media Women. She does volunteer work for such groups as Society for the Blind, as well as orphanages and nursing homes. She is a member of the boards of the NAACP and the Martin Luther King Center for Non-Violent Social Change. Truly her father's daughter, she has a strong interest in people of all races and cultures. While living in Chicago, she developed an interest in and appreciation for the Jewish culture, which many of her neighbors followed. In 1969, Hadassah Women planted a tree in her honor in Israel's Freedom Forest.

I asked her which of the dozens of honors and awards she had received meant the most to her. Given her love of children and her driving desire to help overcome cultural and racial prejudices, it was not surprising that she considered the highest honor to be having a scholarship named after her by the American Intercultural Student Exchange. She said:

> Knowing that, in my name, a student is going to have an exchange experience with another culture just outranks anything I've ever had happen to me. I think it's almost selfish if people who are looked upon as having success or achievement don't do anything to influence young people. If it can't be transferred, I don't think it has any influence.

I asked Xernona if there were any other attributes she felt had helped her. She told me:

> I'm a person who aims high. I think big. I just believe that anything I set out to do, I'm going to do. I believe that so strongly that I never even think of failing. I don't know if I've succeeded at everything, but I certainly have that attitude in anything I do. My husband tells me now that every project I go after or go into, whether it's a volunteer assignment on some committee or whatever, he says I do it as if I'm going on a White House assignment.

Later that day, after our interview, I observed these principles in action. Xernona was in Los Angeles to host the premier of "Black America '88," a one-hour TBS television special highlighting achievement of blacks. She reiterated the philosophy she had learned from her father: that her strength came from her attitude, not from her gender or race. She added that she tried to "put a lid on pomposity" and focus on her thoughts and her treatment of people. She warmly and personally acknowledged each of her staff, as well as the celebrities, for their contributions to the program. It was with genuine appreciation of people, so characteristic of Xernona, that she included the audience of 300 as part of the energy for producing the program.

She later took the highly-acclaimed show to Chicago and New York, where she again created that sense of being a member of a winning team. When Xernona aims high, she hits the mark resoundingly—to the benefit of all concerned.

"Success, I guess, is only temporary until the last day, and then you measure all of your successes. Somebody else is going to have to be the judge of that."

PETER H. COORS

President, Brewing Division, Adolph Coors Co.

Born 1946 in Denver, Colorado. BA in Industrial Engineering from Cornell. MBA in Business from University of Denver. Chairman of the Board, Ducks Unlimited. Member, Board of Directors, Colorado Outward Bound School.

When Peter Coors said he and his brothers received a "special heritage" from their great-grandfather, he was referring to more than the well-known brewery. Jokingly describing Adolph Coors as "an illegal immigrant," Peter said he was a stowaway from Germany, arriving in America in the 1800s without papers, without a passport, and without a penny. From that unlikely beginning, he developed a brewery that has thrived for over 100 years, surviving Prohibition, to be handed through four generations of Coors.

That legacy of starting from the bottom has been carried on. Although far from penniless, Peter and his four brothers all had to work their way up to the management jobs they now have in the company.

After earning an Engineering Degree at Cornell and a Masters Degree in Business at the University of Denver, Peter was handed a broom and a shovel for his first job as a trainee in the Coors waste treatment plant. "And I don't mean as a management trainee. I mean a worker." At first he was disappointed at his lowly position, but he later came to appreciate the philosophy his father and uncle were using. He explained:

> When you graduate from college and you're young and full of energy and ideas, you have a hard time seeing yourself in a position where you're using a broom or a shovel. I wanted to go and tell them how to run the company. I think what my dad and uncle were wisely trying to tell me was that there isn't any place or job in this plant that isn't important, and there aren't any people in this company that aren't important. I think that's the key to the way we operate here.

We were sitting in Peter's unpretentious office in Golden, Colorado, overlooking the mountains, with the sound of the moving railroad cars that carry Coors beer across the country. Rather than send a secretary to meet me in the reception room, Peter had come out himself, smiling and shirt-sleeved. I immediately sensed his warmth and throughout the interview got a deep feeling of what a humane, caring person I was talking to. Pictures of his wife and children grace his desk, and it was clear I was in the presence of a man who has a high regard for his family, his job, and, he made clear, his God.

Peter carried to a new level the belief that all employees of the company are important by creating an environment where all workers are encouraged to present their ideas. Through the Coors Employee Involvement Teams, similar to the quality circles originated in Japan, nearly 1,500 employees regularly get together with their supervisors, managers, and officers to give input on issues that affect them. Peter said:

> We don't want to wait for somebody to be here 20 years and get into management before we start listening to them, because the likelihood is that those ideas are 20 years old, 20 years too late. We need to temper the new ideas with the experience and knowledge of our management team. People at the entry level see things in a totally different light than someone who has been doing the job for a long time.

He wants to encourage those on the job to assume responsibility and accountability rather than having every decision made by top management. Peter attributes the difference in management style between this generation and previous ones primarily to the changing times:

> Fifty years ago an autocratic kind of environment was the standard. The Industrial Revolution was built on strong leadership and employees who were just told to do the job. It has been a relatively slow transition to recognizing the importance of the individual employee in the whole picture.

Feeling a responsibility to educate the drinking customer, Coors has an active alcohol education program with a full-time staff. "We've taken the approach that alcohol is not the enemy; it's the abuse of alcohol that is the enemy," added Peter. Their approach is to identify and treat the cause of alcoholism, which he believes is generally stress-related.

Another service the company provides is a wellness program, with a fitness room where employees can work out as well as take classes on diet, nutrition, cooking, and smoking cessation. A major part of the program is rehabilitation, both physical and psychological, of employees who are on disability because of back injuries or cardiac problems. "The toughest thing after six months of a disability is to come back psychologically. That's much more difficult than the physical aspect. With our rehabilitation program, we can reduce the time of disability up to 50 percent simply because we have eliminated the psychological barrier," Coors said.

Peter has a long heritage of success to draw on in terms of both his family and his company. When his great grandfather started the brewery in Golden, Colorado in the 1870s there were 4,000 or 5,000 other breweries in the U.S. That number decreased to 2,000 just before Prohibition, and of the 700 breweries that started up when Prohibition ended, only 350 survived. Despite Coors' small size, it managed to survive and become one of the five largest in the U.S.

One of the policies that has helped the company thrive is avoiding long-term debts. The Coors family choose to reinvest money in the business rather than diluting it. Peter points to the time when interest rates rose to 20 percent, endangering many companies who were highly leveraged. He said Coors has "been able to weather a lot of storms just because we have the financial strength to get through."

Recently the company expanded, with a $100 million facility in Virginia, as well as a $30 million expansion to the Golden brewery. They accomplished this without having to borrow money, an unusual practice for a large company today.

I asked Peter what he believes is the most important trait or experience he received from his childhood that has helped him today. He said he couldn't point to a single item or issue:

> I think it's more what I got from my mother and father in terms of their involvement in the community and their very high principles. Dad has always been firm in his convictions. He may be wrong but you know where he stands. There is never any question about that. I think that, as much as anything, contributed to my development. We also got a lot of love in our family, and I think that was very important.

He spoke with the same sense of pride about his uncle William and said, "I can't emulate him, but his style is something that I work toward. His style is that he is always totally honest. He says what he believes and that's not always popular."

The Coors family is active politically. Peter's mother was involved in the Reagan campaign, and his father was credited as one of the designers of President Reagan's "Kitchen Cabinet."

Peter, himself, took part in the 1976 Republican Convention. As his role at Coors has grown, he has had to limit his political activities. Most recently his key involvement outside the company has been with the national Ducks Unlimited organization, the largest conservation organization in the world, with over 600,000 members. He was president for two years before being "booted upstairs" to his position as Chairman of the Board. He finds being a manager of a large, non-profit organization to be a growing experience. He enjoys the contribution he makes by helping preserve wetland habitats throughout North America.

Coors loves the outdoors, even more than hunting, and said he enjoys watching birds and entertaining hunters at the family's ranch—a goose refuge on the South Platte River. The area sometimes attracts as many as 2,000 geese.

Peter is on the Board of Directors of Colorado Outward Bound School, an organization he became involved with as a result of a community service project his company developed and participated in for several years. The purpose of the program was to help young, disadvantaged people in Denver's inner city learn skills and develop self-esteem and to get them into productive employment.

Coors hired the young people, some of them ex-convicts and people with hardcore, difficult histories, gave them a week of exercise, training, and orientation to the company, and then took them on a three-week Outward Bound experience.

Here they faced challenges, such as rappelling off cliffs at the end of a rope and forging rivers, which they survived only by helping and being helped by others. They then returned to Coors to work at jobs in the salvage yard, where they learned to use heavy equipment. Since most of them couldn't afford cars, Coors bussed them to and from work until they were eligible for car loans.

Peter said the program was very effective and explained the concept of using Outward Bound:

> The real advantage was to get them away from a dependency on themselves, which basically is the idea in the inner city. Everybody is out for themselves, struggling for survival. Outward Bound puts them in an experience where they are dependent on others and others are dependent on them. It was relatively effective in training them to accept the fact that they need to be able to work with a group in

accomplishing the goals of this company and in terms of getting the job done.

I asked Peter what success meant to him. He divided it into the three areas of his life that are important to him: God, marriage and family, and his company and its employees:

> Success for me is pretty basic. First, when my life is completed, success would be standing in front of God and feeling that, although I've made some mistakes, I've always had Him at the center of my life.
>
> Secondly, success for me is having a successful family and a successful marriage. That's a very important part of my life.
>
> Thirdly, success to me is, after my tenure with the company is complete, being able to say that I contributed something to it and didn't simply ride along until it was someone else's turn. I'd like to be able to feel that some of the things I did helped not only the company but the individual employee.

He said he thinks success is an ongoing process, a series of challenges met. "I think part of success is never losing the feeling that you're being challenged or that you can challenge yourself to do just a little bit better and a little bit more." He cited the example of the difficult negotiations he conducted for Coors with the Coalition of Black Organizations and the Coalition of Hispanic Organizations.

> We went through hours of negotiation and compromise and some soul-searching of our philosophy, and it was a challenge. When we finally signed those agreements, I had a feeling that this was a great accomplishment for the company and for the community. We no sooner signed them than we realized we had an obligation and now we needed to do some things to make it happen. So the challenges just keep coming. There are some gratifying points along the way, but the challenges just keep right on coming.

Peter is a family man who speaks fondly of his wife and six children. When asked what he wants for his children he said:

> I hope that they will learn basically to be good, decent people who recognize the importance of other people, and that they learn to

grow up with a lot of love. We have a Christian home, and that's very important to us.

Saying he hopes his children won't feel that they have to go into the business, he intends to provide them with the same opportunity that he and his brothers received. "I also hope we'll have the same attitude that other generations have had, giving them a start which shows them that things aren't automatic here at Coors. My brothers all have children," he continued, adding, with a twinkle in his eye, "and we can use the help."

When we finished the interview, Peter arranged for me to take a tour of the brewery. As I left the building after the tour, I ran into Peter again. It was lunch time and he was walking, athletic bag in hand, to the exercise room for a workout. It was refreshing to see that Peter not only talks enthusiastically about fitness and the importance of interacting with all levels of the work force, but he also puts those ideas into action.

"Choose POSITIVE EMOTIONS. They help to combat illness and serve as an effective blocker to disease. Love, Hope, Faith, a Will to Live, Creativity, Festivity, Laughter, Determination, Purpose, Confidence are divine powers!"

NORMAN COUSINS

Author: Best-Seller, Anatomy of an Illness; Diplomat; Senior Lecturer, UCLA Medical School

At age 28, appointed editor of *Saturday Review of Literature*. Held position for 35 years. Author of 20 books including *Healing Heart* and *Pathology of Power*. Sent on diplomatic missions by Presidents Eisenhower, Kennedy, and Johnson. One of the founders of public television. Honorary degrees in science, law, and medicine from 53 colleges and universities. President, World Federalist Association. Board of Directors, Mothers Embracing Nuclear Disarmament. Prizewinning photographer.

Norman Cousins is widely known as a great humanitarian. He arranged for the plastic surgery of the horribly disfigured "Hiroshima Maidens" who were scarred during the dropping of the bombs on Hiroshima. He did this so they might have some chance at a better life. He is also a noted writer, critic, and photographer. Formerly an editor, he now teaches humanities to medical school students, one of the first such courses to be taught at a medical college. His interviews, conducted over two sessions, proved to be not only enlightening but helpful in assessing the characteristics of success.

He is known for his diplomatic missions, and I asked him how he happened to enter the world of government. He told me:

> In 1963 I was preparing to leave the *Saturday Review* for a job in Washington. I had represented Kennedy in the test ban negotiations and helped with his American University speech. He invited me to work with him. I asked for six more months to clean up my affairs at the *Saturday Review*. Then came Kennedy's death on November 22, 1963. So that was the end of that particular aspiration.
>
> For a long time before that, I had flirted with the notion of going into government, but I saw no way of disengaging myself from the magazine.

> It wasn't that I considered myself indispensable or vital, it was just that the founders of the magazine had taken me on faith, and that we had a program I wanted to carry out. By 1963 I felt free, finally, and so I accepted the President's invitation. The death of the President had a devastating effect. It was almost as though you could see all of the programs that would be deferred—almost as though you could see the Vietnam war as a reality.

Cousins served as diplomatic emissary for three successive presidents, going on missions to help negotiate with foreign governments. Because he was privileged to work closely with these men, he gained insights into their character which few of us have the opportunity to see. He believes Kennedy's death was a terrible loss because it changed the direction our country might have gone. He says:

> I had the feeling that Kennedy had gone through a Gethsemene. The Presidency is a juggling act of competing pressures. The one thing you learn very fast is that you've got to reconcile these pressures somehow. A great President can deal with these pressures without making them primary. I had a sense that Kennedy knew that every man, whether President or pressman, had to define the circumstances under which he might become expendable, and in the process, accomplish great purpose. And so he discovered that if he didn't allow the pressures to dictate what went on inside his soul, he might be able to do that which was most needed for this country—put it on the road to lasting peace.

I asked Cousins what special traits he believed Kennedy had that made him so successful. He said:

> *The ability to grow*. He was not the same man in 1963 that he was in 1960. He could accept responsibility; he wasn't intimidated by it, and he didn't panic. He didn't flail; he didn't grab for advice; he had a remarkable sense of calm; he could put different pieces together. He was not quite Plato's idea of the philosopher-king. He was still very much a political animal, but he didn't shirk the obligations of the Presidency and was measuring up to those obligations very rapidly, I thought.

Another president Cousins served was Lyndon Baines Johnson, who called upon him to perform diplomatic missions as well as for personal council.

In fact, Cousins said, "He surprised me by taking my criticism of Vietnam with good grace."

Johnson asked him to go to the Far East to persuade Hanoi to enter negotiations. From Cousins' involvement with such projects, Johnson asked him to be Co-Chairman of the International Cooperation Year. I asked for his impressions of President Johnson:

> Johnson also grew in the presidency; despite all the criticism of him, he was extraordinarily conscientious. He's been accused of being a poor listener, but I don't think that was true. His mind worked very rapidly.

President Johnson, like every other President, worked long and hard in his decisions about what to do. As Cousins says, "The Vietnam War was tearing the country apart and Johnson was part of the fabric that was being torn."

Cousins pointed out the reality that Johnson had the responsibility of taking care of our domestic business in addition to trying to win an unpopular war—and that was a big order.

Cousins said he believes that, no matter how many small successes a President may achieve, the job itself is overwhelming as it is structured:

> The Presidency of the United States is an impossible job. I don't think the Presidency is manageable. Too many things in motion that you can't reverse. Too many agencies creating momentum in certain directions. Too many systems. Too many political pressures. It takes a man like FDR who, because of his infirmity, perhaps, could think of nothing else. Or someone with great ambition and cupidity. But for men of good will, the Wilson or Kennedy type, it's a rough one. You want a President to be intelligent, humane, sensitive, courageous. You want him to have a vision and yet everything in the job militates against it.

I asked Cousins what or who encouraged him as a child to develop his own talents, and he told me of an amazing experience he had in his youth:

> In my ninth year, going into my tenth birthday, I was pretty sickly and was sent away to a public sanitarium in New Jersey. It seems to me incredible that I was there for the short time that I was. It was only six or seven months, but if I were to take blocks from my life, that would be one of them and it would be the equivalent of a ten-year span in respect to other things. I did an awful lot of growing up in

> that sanitarium. Kids can be pretty rough. The second or third night I was there, in the middle of a very cold winter, I was lifted out of my bed without a blanket and dumped far out in the woods at night and warned not to follow them back. Kids can be cruel.
>
> Then I learned how to tame "the beast" within the boys. The new kids who were coming in were being beaten and tossed out too, and I just figured out a way of dealing with these kids that gave them satisfaction in being decent. They were all very lonely and insecure. These were not intellectual realizations at that time, however. I learned a great deal about gang warfare and the ease with which kids can slide into violence and how they can win each other's esteem in terms of the cruelty they can vent. I also learned a lot about illness at that time and how important it is not to panic. That's the great multiplier of illness. Illness, severe though it may be, becomes hellish when accompanied by panic and deep apprehension.

I asked him how he was able to avoid letting physical disease handicap him. He responded:

> Those experiences in the sanitarium taught me that the human body is amazingly resilient. There were some kids who didn't come through that experience. Some were carried out. But after I made it through that, I knew nothing again would scare me.

Cousins remembered this experience and drew on it later when, at age 39, he was diagnosed as having a "silent coronary." He said he got word from the doctors that:

> I had 18 months to live if I were very careful and gave up my job and gave up sports. I decided not to tell Ellen about it. My little girls came running up to me to be thrown in the air—at that moment I looked down two roads. One was the road where I would throw my girls into the air. The other road was where I would do what the insurance doctors told me to do and would live 18 months like a vegetable. I threw the girls up in the air. The next day I went out and played three sets of singles.

Cousins used these experiences and his recovery from a later illness as the basis for his long-time best seller, *Anatomy of an Illness*. Many people remember that, when diagnosed with a serious illness in which he was told he had one chance in 500 of surviving, he used his own special therapy to recover. He checked out of the hospital, checked into a hotel, and watched Groucho Marx movies and other comedies. According to Cousins, laughing caused his body to circulate the endorphins that were so needed for his recovery. Watching the movies also enabled him to sleep for two or three hours at a time to allow the body to use its healing process without the pain-killing pills that he believed prolonged the recovery period.

Norman attributes a lot of his success to luck. He learned some lessons in it from the man who launched him in his 35-year career as editor of the *Saturday Review of Literature*. He reflected:

> I was especially lucky in meeting Evertte Lee DeGolyer who understood luck and backed me in the *Saturday Review* . . . He came up the hard way . . . This kid became a millionaire before he graduated from the college he was working his way through. But he never forgot what it was like to be poor.
>
> Evertte was a natural partner for me when I came along. He was lucky and he wanted everyone else to be lucky too. He once hired an honors graduate in geology from Princeton who knew everything there was to know about petroleum geology, but he fired him. I asked why, and he said, "Because he wasn't lucky." He said, "Luck is being where you have to be at precisely the time that it's good for you to be there."

Referring to his backer, Cousins commented, "He was the best thing that ever happened to me." He became philosophical about his life, and said:

> I was lucky when I came through my illness as a kid . . . I was lucky in the friends that I made . . . I was lucky in the woman that I married . . . I was lucky in my children . . . I was lucky to be able to change my career at the age of 63. There are many more people who are more deserving, who are more talented.

Next, I questioned him on what he believed about the changing roles of the sexes today. He said, "I just hope that men will feel foolish in holding their macho viewpoints. Ridicule is a common source of change." He said he believes that once the more educated men in our society begin to take women seriously, the others will follow suit in re-thinking their prejudices, in part so as not to look foolish.

What has made Norman Cousins the courageous, successful man that he is today, engaged in a totally new career? Norman has consistently driven himself toward personal growth. Be it as a child locked out of the sanitarium or as a heart attack victim, he has taken responsibility for himself in crisis, working with his weakness to see his tragedy produce a positive outcome. He exercised decisiveness and leadership competency from an early age, later, in his editorial position with the *Saturday Review*, and continuing as a chief negotiator for United States diplomatic relations.

Although several times it seemed the odds were against him, Norman never succumbed to the limitations others imposed on him. He has listened to a different drummer, and to a beat which sounds of compassion and excellence. Combined, that adds up to real strength.

"Humanizing business means treating human beings as the single most important element in any business equation, and if you treat them that way, they will begin to behave that way."

MARY ELIZABETH CUNNINGHAM

President, Semper Enterprises; Best-selling Author; Founder and Executive Director, The Nurturing Network, Inc.

Born 1951 in Hanover, New Hampshire. Graduated Magna cum Laude and Phi Beta Kappa, Wellesley College. M.B.A. with honors, Harvard Business School. Formerly Executive Assistant to Chairman, Bendix Corp. Promoted to Vice President of Strategic Planning. Later became Executive Vice President and CEO, Semper Enterprises, Inc., a Venture Capital and Strategy Consulting Firm. Author: *Powerplay*.

"Growth is a constant process of eliminating labels, definitions, parameters, and patterns," says Mary Cunningham, and a look at the list of achievements of this bright young businesswoman shows that she is doing just that. She has worn a variety of hats in her short but dynamic business career.

A Magna cum Laude graduate of Wellesley, she was elected to Phi Beta Kappa. She started her professional career as a legal assistant with a New York law firm and later became one of the youngest Assistant Treasurers at Chase Manhattan Bank before leaving to enter Harvard Business School. With masters degree in hand, she joined Bendix Corporation as Executive Assistant to the Chairman and was promoted to Vice President of Strategic Planning, with responsibility for $450 million divestitures. Later, as Vice President of Joseph E. Seagram and Sons, Inc., the strategic marketing plan she developed to market and distribute wines in 23 countries worldwide resulted in her promotion to Executive Vice President and the establishment of the first international wine group.

Her latest career is as a venture capitalist in partnership with her husband, Bill Agee. Their corporation, Semper Enterprises, has invested in 15 companies in which they actively participate either as board members or as management consultants. Another major area of involvement for Mary is The Nurturing Network, a charitable organization she founded, which offers support and services to women with crisis pregnancies. Mary started this after the birth of the first of her two children.

I flew to their Cape Cod home for an interview with her for an audiocassette album in the Nightingale/Conant, "This I Believe" Series.[22] Her spacious and cheery home, a delightful blend of simplicity and elegance, reflects her warmth and charm. The house overlooks a duck reserve, and we could see ducks diving kamikaze-style as we talked. It seemed so very, very far from the hubbub of downtown New York City, where she conducts much of her business. I was curious to discover some of the secrets that had contributed to her impressive profile, so impressive that World Almanac voted her one of the "25 Most Influential Women in America" for two consecutive years. Mary credits a series of mentors for helping her get where she is today:

> If I had to pick one of the three factors in my career path that have made a difference, it would be that there's always been a mentor in every situation I have participated in.
>
> A mentor really is a teacher. But he or she is more than an academic teacher; a mentor is a practical teacher—someone who knows the ropes—someone who knows whose desk to put the memo on, whose name to put on a copy list, what time to set the meeting because John Smith doesn't like morning meetings or Jane Doe is not good after lunch. That is a mentor.
>
> A mentor is a very practical person who has been down that road before and wants to help you to avoid some of the land mines—not all the land mines, because no one can anticipate all of them.

If a mentor doesn't volunteer, Mary feels it is important to seek one out.

> Mentorship is a very delicate thing. It's a little like friendship. You can seek out friendship; you can't mandate that it occur. You earn a mentorship to some extent. It's like earning respect.

To show both sides of the coin, however, she cautions people about some of the drawbacks of having a mentor. First, if an individual works too closely or too long with just one person, there is the possibility that his power will rise and fall with that of the other individual. She recommends changing mentors every 12 to 18 months so the employee can establish his own power base. She also warns that people need to be aware that this "special relationship" may cause resentment among co-workers, and she advises not to allow too much insulation from the rest of the organization.

This advice comes from her experience at Bendix. Her mentorship by then-Chairman and President William Agee created a negative political situation with her co-workers. Resentment built when, after a year-and-a-half, she was promoted to Vice President of Strategic Planning. Although the entire Bendix board recognized her talent for the job, the isolation that her role with her mentor created led to the tension, jealousy, and suspicion among fellow workers that ultimately contributed to her feeling forced to resign. Because of this experience, as well as her positive experiences both with and as a mentor at Seagrams, she is much wiser in the politics of business. She teaches this to young, aspiring business people, particularly women, who might be most vulnerable to similar traps.

Mary herself has often served as a mentor throughout her various careers. She frequently gives speeches, particularly to women's groups, encouraging and inspiring them. During lunch hours while at Seagrams, she held workshops which she jokingly called "Harvard Business School in Seven Days." Her goal was to give middle management women the benefit of what she had learned at Harvard. Realizing she couldn't teach two years of material in seven lunch hours, she nevertheless wanted to encapsulate the seven or eight major business principles she studied at Harvard.

Mary has a long list of foundations, colleges, and charities for which she is a board member or advisor. She serves on the board of advisors of The Journal of Business Strategy and of the Strategic Planning Committee of The Conference Board. Her interest in women's affairs has prompted her to serve on the advisory board for the National Organization for Women and as a member of The Women's Equity Action League and The Women's Forum. She is an advisor to the Committee for National Security and serves as a Chairman's Advisor for the U.S. Congressional Advisory Board.

With Mary's busy schedule and the high level of responsibility she has had in her various positions, I asked her if there had ever been times when she felt she had taken on more than she could handle, and she said yes:

> We've all had that moment when it feels like this is the one; this is too big; I can't handle it. The important thing to do is get a good night's sleep, look at the situation fresh the next day, and don't extrapolate from your low moment. Give yourself another 24 hours—maybe even another 48 hours—look at the problem fresh, and really identify what it is that is so awesome about this task . . . The chances are it won't look quite so awesome after a good night's sleep and with a fresh perspective brought to bear on it.

I asked Mary if she had a business philosophy, a single guiding creed she could summarize. She told me she had two. The first was what she called "humanizing business."

> Humanizing business means treating human beings as the single most important element in any business equation, and if you treat them that way, they will begin to behave that way. It is important not to just treat them that way but to believe it, because people have an uncanny capacity to understand when something is sincere and when it isn't.
>
> It's a little like trust. You have to give people the chance to demonstrate that they can be trusted in order to foster that in them. If you don't give people a chance to show that they are deserving of this kind of humanistic behavior—if you don't show them trust, if you don't show them candor, if you don't show them respect—then you're going to probably end up in situations where you're not receiving much of that either.

She believes it is important for everyone in an organization to know how his work fits into the goals and accomplishments of the company. She says a number of corporations are becoming aware of this and are instituting programs to encourage communication among all levels of management and employees. In addition to the programs, it is important for management to set an example and practice it consistently. Mary believes in using an incentive system to motivate employees—a system to financially reward or censure employees based on their performance.

Her second philosophy is to blend the practical with the ideal:

> There is a frightening tendency to polarize idealists from pragmatists—to think there's something antithetical between being idealistic and being practical. I have found in business that those two are not at all antithetical—that the best business people are people who know how to blend the very practical elements of any issue with certain values, certain ideals. When you bring those two together, you have a formidable force.
>
> Most of the failures I've seen in business have been failures where people have gone too far to one extreme or the other. Either they've been fabulous idealists with great beliefs about mankind and a great desire to make a contribution, but lost it on the practical side—they didn't know how to get it done, or they were fabulous pragmatists—they had all the shrewd advice and techniques and know-how that you need to have, but lost it on the level of values.
>
> The practical and the ideal should be brought together on any given business problem or issue.

Mary said her view of success is different from "climbing up the corporate ladder." Success to her is an ongoing process, which involves fulfilling one's potential to the maximum:

> Success is not as static as having climbed a ladder . . . It's a continual process that will probably—and maybe even hopefully—take place in many different environments.
>
> But in the end, success is really measured by how well you have realized your God-given talents—how well you have fulfilled your potential and done so in a way that makes a contribution to mankind.
>
> It may well be that there are individuals at the bottom rung of the ladder who are far more successful, by my definition, than people at the very top rung of the ladder.

She said her definition of success provides her with ongoing motivation and will help prevent her from burning out at age 45:

> It goes beyond title and money and into the area of "Am I making a lasting contribution? Am I living up to my fullest potential in all dimensions of my life?" And the answer to that may well be yes even at times when the outside world may be telling you that you have failed.

The most recent way Mary has found to use her potential and contribute her talents to the world is as a nurturer. Herself the mother of two young children, Mary created and heads up a national support organization called "The Nurturing Network," which helps college and working women with unplanned pregnancies. The non-profit consortium, consisting of doctors, counselors, nurturing homes, colleges, and employees, offers mothers-to-be a positive alternative to abortion. Because of her deep concern for these women and her strong ability to organize and motivate, she has turned this into a nationwide project that is bridging the chasm between pro-life and pro-choice extremes. By offering the life-supporting services of The Nurturing Network within the context of "choice," her organization has already been able to reach hundreds of women who previously had believed abortion was their only alternative.

Mary Cunningham is a remarkable woman who puts her philosophy into action. Never resting on the laurels of one success, she moves on to new areas that offer opportunities for growth and contribution. She is, indeed, continually "eliminating labels, definitions, parameters, and patterns."

"I was born to very, very poor parents . . . They were . . . 'too poor to paint but too proud to whitewash.' Their combination of poverty and pride caused them to have an attitude that the best place to find a helping hand is at the end of your own arm."

ROBERT H. DEDMAN

Founder & Chairman of the Board, Club Corporation of America which includes 225 country, city, athletic, and resort clubs

Born 1926, Rison, Arkansas. Holds four degrees from Southern Methodist University and Texas University. Lawyer. Philanthropist, having donated $45 million to education. Dedman College and Dedman Center for Lifetime Sports at Southern Methodist University are named for Mr. and Mrs. Dedman. Trustee and Board., SMU. Chairman, Texas State Highway and Public Transportation Commission. 1976 Texas Entrepreneur of the year. 1980 Humanitarian of the year.

How is success defined by an entrepreneur who quotes poetry, decorates Texas highways with wildflowers and, from a childhood of abject poverty, has accumulated a fortune estimated by *Forbes* magazine at over $600 million? [23] I asked Robert Dedman that question as I sat in his understatedly elegant office in one of Dallas' most prestigious office buildings.

"I think you define success as living all the facets of your life successfully. Not just your business life or your public life. But every facet of your life. And that's your married life. Your love life. Your sex life." He had a twinkle in his eye as he added, "And obviously if all three of those are the same, it saves a lot of time." He continued:

> Of course, you also need to look after your athletic life, your church life, your civic life, your cultural life, and obviously your business life. When most people talk about success, they are usually just referring to their business life. And I think that's a mistake. I think success in life is primarily a result of the ability to set up win-win relationships personally and professionally.

There is no question that Robert Dedman meets those criteria for success. He is an amazing, multi-faceted, multi-talented man who participates fully in life and gives to it generously. His relationships are testimony to his personal and business success:

> I'm still married to the first woman I ever married—for 35 years now. We have really good relationships with our children, who are 32 and 30, and we see them all the time. I've had my own business for 30 years, and the first employee I ever had is still with me. We have lots and lots of people who have been with the company for 20, 25, or 28 years. And so I feel that we've all won together. I feel good about basically being a success.

Dedman said he feels strongly about the need to create win-win relationships:

> A lot of people believe, and sometimes they're taught this in school, that those who are the most successful are the most dog-eat-dog, competitive people who want to win at any cost. You win; someone else loses. Your successes are almost directly proportional to someone else's losses. I think that's a mistake, because that's not really true in life at all. In any relationship—personal or business—anytime one partner wins at the expense of the other, the relationship is not going to endure. The loser will terminate it.
>
> The only thing you should do in any relationship is to try to be the most giving partner. As a rule, you'll prosper in direct proportion to how the relationship prospers. There are some situations where if you win, someone has to lose. In athletics there are winners and losers. In cards there are winners and losers. Sometimes in business, if you get the business, maybe someone else doesn't, but that doesn't really mean they're losers. That's not the determinant of success or failure in life.
>
> It's repeat business; it's enduring relationships that are the real determinants of success. Your ability to set up successful, lasting, win-win relationships, in my own judgment, is the biggest determinant of personal and professional success.

A positive mental attitude is another factor Robert Dedman believes has contributed to his success, and he thanks his mother for helping him develop it:

> I was born to very, very poor parents, back in Rison, Arkansas. They were the living incarnation of the term "too poor to paint but too

> proud to whitewash." Their combination of poverty and pride caused them to have an attitude that the best place to find a helping hand is at the end of your own arm. My mother thought I was great, as most mothers do. I think it was that combination of poverty and pride and that very positive mental attitude she had that encouraged me to have a positive mental attitude. We very much work for that in our company in everything we do. We often say, "If you don't have a positive mental attitude, get one!"

Dedman is a man who truly enjoys helping people, and he believes he benefits in the process:

> You'll only do well in direct proportion to the number of people you help. If you'll just enable other people to achieve their goals, it's incredible what you can achieve. There's nothing little about it. You win personally by building others.

He has a keen sense of sizing people up, finding out their strengths and needs in order to best utilize their skills and help them develop:

> You have to be able to assess people to know which type you need. Then you have to be able to attract and keep them. You need to know how to organize them together to get the most out of them individually and collectively as a team. The euphemism is "put the square pegs in the square holes and the round pegs in the round holes." Everybody doesn't need to be a quarterback or a runner or a blocker or a tackle. You need a whole team of different talents. Seeing those talents and getting them organized together is the trick. And then obviously you need to motivate them to do as well as they know how and coach them to do better than they know how to do. We want to always be helping our people grow, and through them, our company grows.

Like many of the successful people I interviewed, Dedman said he believes in giving back to the system that has treated him so well:

> I'm very proud of having made a lot of money, but I'm a lot more proud of knowing what to do with it—and plowing it back into the system. I enjoy the thrill of "giving while living" and trying to serve as a little bit of a pump primer to get others to turn loose of some of their resources while they're still alive.

Education is an area in which Dedman generously contributes money, as well as his time and energy. His interest in education is not surprising, considering he graduated from Southern Methodist University and Texas University with a total of four degrees.

He and his wife Nancy have donated more than $45 million to educational institutions. Their gifts of over $25 million to Southern Methodist University caused the Dedman College and the Dedman Center for Lifetime Sports to be named in their honor. At the University of Texas in Austin, where they have donated $10 million, 3,200 Dedman Scholars carry their name. A frequent speaker to students, Dedman is especially fond of visiting his old alma mater to give talks on his philosophy of life.

He has spoken not only to students but to many other varied groups, sharing his philosophy on the need for balance in life and how this has contributed to his success. In his presentations, he often uses something as basic as a chair to illustrate his point about balance. Members of the audience become spellbound by his simple but poignant remarks. He mesmerizes them as he goes from Dedman, the tough business man, to Dedman, the sensitive man quoting poetry from memory to emphasize a point. As people connect his ideas to their own lives, there is often a reflective silence after he has finished, followed by a standing ovation.

Dedman also takes an active role in improving the environment and finds particular delight in decorating the state with wildflowers. As Chairman of the Texas State Highway and Public Transportation Commission, he has initiated a wildflower program to beautify Texas highways. He recently built a country club in Temple, Texas around the concept of wildflowers aptly named The Wildflower Country Club. Excited at the prospect of getting the entire community thinking in terms of wildflowers, he said, "It's like a smile on your face!"

Robert Dedman, like most of those I interviewed, works hard. His average work week is 60 to 80 hours. And, like the others I talked to, he loves whatever he is doing. I asked him how he found time to lead a balanced life when he spent so much time working. What did he do to relax? He said:

> Well, I enjoy my wife and my children and my grandbaby. I immensely enjoy playing golf and tennis. I love to travel. Whenever I can, I watch TV or a movie. So I have a lot of fun in life. I have a ball. And, of course, everything I'm doing all day long at work is a ball, too.

This zest for life, energy, and balance is a trait shared by Robert and his wife Nancy, who also graduated from SMU and is a Phi Beta Kappa.

An attractive couple, they are the picture of health and vitality. Nancy, a petite, youthful, energetic woman, told me she often exercises twice a day. Robert's well-groomed, thick white hair and physically fit physique contribute to his striking, distinguished appearance. He exudes confidence without a trace of arrogance. He said he finds time to stay in shape by combining exercise with business, often conducting meetings with his country club managers on the golf courses they manage.

Another of Dedman's hobbies woven into various aspects of his life is poetry. He has a vast reservoir of verses memorized years ago in school, which he quotes frequently in speeches, in conversation, and to himself when he needs a philosophical pick-me-up. He recited a poem to me during our interview, and he even quotes it on the golf courses, sometimes to the frustration of his colleagues. One of his golf companions complained that, in the midst of a very tough hole, Dedman will take time out to quote poetry to break the tension.

I asked him how he dealt with difficult times. He told me:

> I try to always focus back on the good things and put whatever bad times there are in perspective and say, "Now you know, this is not that big a deal—as tough as it is. However bad it looks, it's not as bad as it seems."
>
> I try to remember to make the best of it when I have tough times. I have a whole flock of philosophies about turning adversities into advantage. I tell a lot of jokes—to myself and others.
>
> And so you do that and you quote to yourself and then you cry a little bit. And you get up the next day and start again. Usually sleep helps a lot. You know the familiar quote, "Sleep knits the raveled sleeve of care, the balm of each day's hurt wounds." That's a beautiful line. So I go to sleep and get up and face another day and try to get a change of perspective. You start every day with a new life. I think it's super!

Robert Dedman has created that super life. And he has touched an incredible number of people, improving the quality of their lives as well. Through his belief in a win-win philosophy and his generosity, he has contributed to the successes of countless individuals, while thoroughly enjoying himself, his family, his work, and his hobbies.

"I've learned only from my failures. I don't learn from my successes."

KARL ELLER

Chairman of the Board, Circle K convenience stores

Born in Chicago, Illinois in 1928. Graduate, Business Administration, University of Arizona. Former Chief Executive Officer, Eller Outdoor Advertising Company, and Combined Communications Corp. Founder, University of Arizona's Karl Eller Entrepreneurial Center.

It was 6:15 in the morning when I met Karl for our interview. He wanted to start early so he would have time to play tennis before beginning his work day. We entered the living room of his home, and I was surprised to see it decorated with 50 T-shirts, each with a different design or slogan. Karl told me that he had given them to his wife the night before for her 50th birthday to show her that 50 could be fun.

Showing loving support of his family, rising early, and working hard are traits Karl acquired early in life. At the age of three, his parents divorced, and at age six, he was washing dishes and cleaning for his mother who had a boarding house and worked in a jewelry store in Tucson, Arizona. A few years later, he would awaken at 4:00 a.m. to deliver newspapers, thus establishing an early rising routine which has continued throughout his life.

Honesty and a sense of fair play are also qualities which he expressed early in childhood and which have characterized his business perspective ever since. He recalls:

> When I was seven or eight, we stopped at a gas station on the way to visit relatives in Chicago. About 15 miles later, I figured out my mother had received about a dollar too much in change. I couldn't understand why she wouldn't drive back and give the attendant the money. A dollar was a lot of money in those days, and I didn't want to cheat the attendant. I remember raising such a stink about it that they finally went back and gave him the dollar . . .

> With any deal I've ever made, I've been careful that I was fair to the other side—so that both parties were happy. I would say that 99.9 percent of the incidents have happened that way. There have been some sad things, but at least honesty has always been there.

Karl has always taken full advantage of every opportunity. After high school, he served two years with the Army, in Japan, where he played as fullback for the 8th Army league and was the driver for General Eichelberger. At times he would drive both him and General MacArthur. Eichelberger was a Phi Gamma and encouraged Karl to become one also, which he did, upon entering the University of Arizona on a football scholarship.

Of his college years he recalled, "I was a bigger entrepreneur in college than anything else." I asked him to relay some of his college business experience:

> I had to foot my own way through college. By that time my mother was living back in Chicago and I'd been sending her all my money from the days in the Army. So I had to support myself through school. I lived at a judge's house and did his lawn so I could earn my room. I ended up getting my board free from the scholarship deal, and all my books and tuition.

> I was so interested in advertising, even in those days, that I ended up being the Advertising Manager for the newspaper and the football program, and so I started selling advertising back in college. Then one day I had all the hashers unionized in a way that they all had to come to me to get jobs. I made sure that there would be hashers at all the sorority houses. I had all the concessions: sandwiches, coke, candy, etc., at all the fraternity houses.

Another entrepreneurial project developed when he took a required Humanities course his sophomore year:

> It was a tough course—a lot of reading and things like that. There were 700-800 kids that took it every year. I sat next to a girl that took copious notes, and I watched her really getting everything down. She had everything categorized and I used to borrow the notes from her so I could keep up on the class.

At the end of the year, realizing what a difficult course it was and how good her notes were, Karl suggested that they print the notes and sell them:

She said, "I'll be happy to type them if you want to get them printed." So I said, "Why don't we go 50-50. You type the notes up on stencils and I'll mimeograph them."

In those days we didn't have any fancy Xerox machines. I went down to the old Army ROTC headquarters. They had one of those crank mimeograph machines. And so I went out and bought the cheapest paper I could buy, which was yellow canary paper. I started cranking the stencils. We cranked out 400 pages of those Humanities notes.

All of his friends laughed at him as he walked around his kitchen table, putting the sets together. No one thought the idea would work. And at first it seemed they were right

We hardly sold a one. I was very discouraged. I thought, "Well geez, maybe we blew this one." And then one of the professors said, "Any of you kids that have those yellow Humanities notes will not pass the course just from reading them. You're not going to get what you want to get out of the course." That did it! It took reverse psychology. We started selling them like hotcakes.

I'll bet we sold 400 or 500 a semester for the next 10 years. I finally willed them to the fraternity house. I made enough money off of that to buy my wife an engagement ring and get married when we graduated.

I did all kinds of other things to be an entrepreneur in college . . . I rented out the empty lots and used them as parking lots for football games. I was always an organizer of sorts. I got our fraternity guys elected to the student body. I guess I was always the guy that was promoting and organizing.

I asked Karl what was the single most important thing he learned in college, and he said:

I would say probably the best thing I learned was how to be an entrepreneur. And that I could do it on my own. I didn't need to have anybody. I could think up the idea, implement it, and get it done. I learned how to sell . . .

And I guess I had a rare combination of things that make an entrepreneur. I was always a hard worker. I never slept much. I still

> only sleep three or four hours a night . . . I learned how to gauge my time. I learned how to work and do three or four things at one time. I can keep all those things catalogued in my mind. I guess I've got a good memory. I always had a goal to be rich. I had a goal in my mind that I was going to be the richest guy around, and I loved to read books about rich people. So I think that probably was the goal in back of everything: to make money and be wealthy and have everything I wanted to have.

I asked him if his business sense was intuitive versus intellectual. He answered:

> I think it's a combination of intellectual and intuitive, but it really becomes a confidence in your judgment. You become confident of your ability to get into a situation, analyze it, figure out what the downside risks are, what the upside potentials are, and then make a judgment decision whether to go or not. Your intuition and experience contribute to your confidence in your ability to make that judgment.
>
> I think that most people who fail or are not able to take a risk are people who don't have any assurance of their judgment in making that strategic decision—they depend on somebody else to make that decision for them. But I've never done that.
>
> I've depended on other people for input so that I could make that judgment. I get as many facts as possible in front of me . . . But I really think the key thing is the assurance of your own judgment. When you want to grow and really become big, then you have to make some judgment decisions that are very risky.

That combination of willingness to take risks, confidence in his judgment, and perseverance helped Eller succeed at his first post-college entrepreneurial endeavor in 1962. He was working for an advertising agency in Chicago when he received a call asking if he wanted to buy an outdoor advertising company in Phoenix. Eller was from Arizona and liked the idea of returning. He asked the price and was told $3.5 million.

> And I said, "I don't know whether I could raise that kind of money. I don't have that kind of money. But I'd sure like to try."
>
> That was probably an intuitive situation. Anybody else might have said,

"No, I can't do that." I mean I didn't have any backing or anything. So I said, "Well, I'd like to try." The man who made the offer said, "I'll give you 30 days."

From then on, everything I did was something that I probably wouldn't have done if I'd have known how tough it was going to be.

I went to every bank in Chicago and tried to sell them on the idea of borrowing money. I went through the pitch, and finally, I thought I was down the tubes because nobody understood the billboard business or the financing of a billboard company in those days. They thought it was too risky. And they didn't know about me because I was just another advertising guy.

Finally, one night, I wrote down all my assets on a piece of yellow paper. I even included my wife and my kids. I went to a guy at the Harris Bank and I said, "Bill, I'm willing to pledge everything I own because I believe this thing is going to work." And that did it! Once I was willing to pledge everything I owned, the bank said, "We've got to loan you this money. But we're only going to loan you half of it. You've got to find some other partners for the other half."

He was able to convince another investor, who knew the outdoor advertising business, to provide the remainder. Karl and his family moved to Phoenix and began his first business; Eller Outdoor Advertising Company.

As his company flourished, Karl looked for further ways to expand his company's assets. In 1968 he became a diversified communications company as he joined forces with KTAR Broadcasting. The new company, called Combined Communications Corporation, went public in 1969. Ten years later, it owned outdoor advertising companies in 27 cities in the United States and Canada, had two newspapers, seven TV stations, 13 radio stations, and was making nearly $400 million a year in profits.

Karl went from there to Gannett Company, Inc., publisher of *U.S.A. Today*, and then to Columbia Pictures.

In 1983 he became Chairman of the Board at Circle K. Since that time, Circle K has grown from 1,000 to 3,500 stores and has expanded to the Far East, Europe, and other international markets.

Karl feels a sense of responsibility to contribute to society—particularly through education. Because Circle K sells beer and wine, he initiated a program to educate employees on using judgment about alcohol.

The Karl Eller Entrepreneurial Center, which he founded at the

University of Arizona, provides graduate students the opportunity to work on their own business plans while earning their Masters in Business Administration. Students divide up into groups of two or three to develop entrepreneurial ideas, many of which they later take out into the business world and successfully market to venture capitalists. I asked Karl if he thought you could actually teach people to become entrepreneurs:

> You can't teach anybody to be an entrepreneur, but you can create an environment and let them absorb what has to be done if they have an idea or want to do certain things. They know a little more how to go about it, and I think that's probably what we've tried to accomplish. I think we've accomplished it.

I asked Karl if there were anything he would do differently if he had it to do over again. He replied:

> I feel blessed with my life and my career. I mean I wouldn't change it one iota for the rest of the world. I just feel so blessed that I was able to do what I have done and have all the experiences I've had. I've learned only from my failures. I don't learn from my successes.

". . . to me the trait to spot or find in a new CEO is that there's heart in equal measure to brains. A 'cold' brain will seldom have the feel of a marketplace. He will not be tuned into the people who are making the product or performing the service . . ."

MALCOLM STEVENSON FORBES

Editor-in-Chief & Chief Executive Officer, Forbes Magazine

Born 1919, New York City. B.A., Princeton University. Publisher. New Jersey State Senator, 1952-58. Republican candidate for Governor, New Jersey, 1957. Author, *The Sayings of Malcolm Forbes, Around the World on Hot Air and Two Wheels, Global Hunger: A Look at the Problem and Potential Solutions,* and *What a Way to Go.* President, Forbes Trinchera. Chairman, Fiji Forbes.

I met this personification of the gutsy male on a warm spring day in New York City. It was an early morning appointment for my crew and me, but Malcolm Forbes had already been at his desk since 7:30, opening mail he had not had time to answer the day before. Malcolm has friends all over the world and his mail is his tie to them.

The walls leading to his office showed his recent acquisitions from the art auctions he often attends. His taste in art runs from Winslow Homer to his world famous collection of lead soldiers, most of which are housed in a special museum in Morocco. He has made some of his art available to public viewing in a museum on the first floor of the Forbes building.

A letter by Thomas Jefferson and honorary doctoral hoods, presented to him by various universities, adorn his office walls. A memento from one of his granddaughters graces his desk, along with one of his prize Faberge eggs and an elegant green serpentine dish, which holds his pens. Malcolm believes not only in having fine art, but in using it, as well.

Throughout our entire six-hour interview, Malcolm responded in the highly energetic manner with which he has accomplished everything, be it business deals, art collecting, or cross-country motorcycle tours.

Curious about the natural dynamism of this man, I asked: Where do you go to get your new, fresh ideas? Where do you charge your batteries? He replied:

> Well, I believe that your battery should be charging on the job. Otherwise, you're not giving it full measure. I find it a charge to come down to this desk at 7:30 every morning—earlier some mornings. I'm looking forward to the stuff that's left from yesterday—the mail that's been sorted out that wasn't tackled during the day . . . I very often don't get to read the morning papers until I go to bed at night . . . So for me the battery is on charge all the time because I'm not parked. I'm not in the garage. It's on all the time and it's not arduous.
>
> Half the time the notes I'm making might have to do with where we're going to go on the next motorcycle trip. Have reservations been made? Who's willing to go along? Which son can I hook or persuade to go . . . or will be as excited as I am about it? Not all of it has to do with the bread and butter of our business. But the battery is always doing its thing.

I asked Forbes if he had a single guiding business philosophy. He replied:

> I would say I have a philosophy of life that is probably reflected in the way I conduct this business. And that is, if you're not doing something you enjoy, you won't do it well. You can put your heart only into something that's *there* for you. So my basic business philosophy, I suppose, is not a single guideline. It's just that the essence of success lies in doing what you enjoy. Otherwise you neither do it well, fully, nor successfully.

I asked him how he specifically applied that philosophy to his own business, and he replied:

> At Forbes we do have guidelines in terms of what we see as the magazine's mission. Our advertising slogan is "The Capitalist Tool." And by that, I don't mean that we are a tool of capitalism. But by being, literally and figuratively, probably the foremost critic of corporate management, of the performance of the people with the company steering wheel—by measuring their performance, by being critical when criticism is needed, by making comparisons, patting backs, searching out the achievers—we fill out management's report card.

I asked Forbes if he believed his magazine was a catalyst for change. He said it did have an impact on the corporate world:

> It exposes a weakness that either enables management to make changes or stockholders to bail out before it's too late. They can't ignore a criticism that is rational and makes sense. They set about the business of correcting the error of their ways, or they get booted out.

I asked Forbes what distinguished his magazine from its competitors. He replied that *Forbes'* main focus was the human element of business. It evaluates the people who run businesses, particularly the chief executives, and he said he believes that is the most accurate method of measuring a company. *Forbes* editors take chief executives out to lunch three to four times a week—off the record—just to get a feel for the "people at the top," the way they conduct business and the way they relate to others.

I asked Malcolm what traits he looks for in a Chief Executive Officer that are indicators that the company is likely to move ahead. He replied:

> Well, surprisingly, to me the trait most important to spot or find in a new CEO is that there's heart in equal measure to brains. A "cold" brain will seldom have the feel of a marketplace. He will not be tuned in to the people who are making the product or performing the service—the people who are carrying out the mission.

He went on to say that the element of having "computer" brilliance is important, but it is not the final word for the head of the company. "The element of heart in successful management is seldom referred to and is just as essential as it is to being alive in a healthy way."

I was curious to see how he combines "heart and brains" with his employees. He said he believes in backing his verbal expressions of gratitude with higher paychecks. In addition, *Forbes* offers its employees the day off on Forbes' birthday. He recently enhanced the company's physical fitness program by putting a 3,500 square-foot gymnasium in the penthouse of his office building, a very expensive investment in view of the price of New York's 5th Avenue real estate. He reflected on the value he places on his employees: "The human resource, to me, is the single most fragile, most valuable asset any company has."

Forbes talked about the trials and eventual success of his company, which was founded by his father in 1917. At that point, *Forbes* was the only business magazine in America. In 1929 *Business Week* appeared on the market, and a year later *Fortune* competed for their readers' time as well. The competition, along with the recession, nearly closed *Forbes* in 1933.

Malcolm's father, a widely syndicated business columnist, funded *Forbes* magazine from the profit his articles incurred. Gradually, after the war, *Forbes* regained its financial footing. How? Through Malcolm's cultivation and appreciation of "the human resource." Through the years he gathered a staff of committed, hard-working professionals who cared about producing a top quality publication. Now the competition is eyeing *Forbes*.

Shifting to the businesses he writes about, I asked him what "makes or breaks" a company. He commented:

> The successful don't lose their enthusiasm. They don't lose their zest for what they're doing . . . failure is very seldom dramatic. It's a gradual process—fewer and fewer customers, fewer and fewer innovations, a little less capital, a little less sense of risk. The heart's gone out of the heartbeat of the guy with the wheel. So it's generally a loss of the zest for the business by those responsible for conducting it.

The father of five, now divorced, Forbes is the epitome of adventure. He packs his life to the fullest. As he said, "The only thing I'd like that I don't have is more time." [24]

He is a frequent host at his string of homes, which includes a palace in Morocco, the Chateau Balleroy in France, a mansion in London, a ranch in Colorado, and his own island in Fiji. His yacht Highlander V is equipped with a helicopter and Harley-Davidson motorcycles.

Forbes lives on the cutting edge—not only in business but in sports and travel as well. He took up motorcycle riding at approximately 50 years of age and has cycled extensively in this country, the USSR, and China. A world record-breaking hot air balloonist, he also enjoys collecting antiques, paintings, and historical letters and artifacts. He has one of the world's largest collections of toy soldiers displayed in his villa, and he recently made a $1 million addition to his collection of Fabergé eggs, which surpasses the royal collection in Moscow.

I asked him to give a few words of encouragement to individuals who are trying to expand their personal lives and interests. His advice was:

> . . . I believe the important thing is never to say die until you're dead. It is, as we quickly realize, a short trip. Pack in as much as you're eager to pack in. To spend this life preparing for the next one is a form of optimism that I don't have.

He advised parents to encourage their children in the same manner. If a child shows an interest in art, reading, music, or sports, he should be helped to investigate that inclination. If a child does not know what he wants to do, encourage him to try several different fields.

I mentioned to Forbes that, like most successful Chief Executive Officers I have interviewed, he had an air of seriousness and confidence, but he also had a refreshing sense of humor. He commented:

> You have to be serious to succeed in most businesses. I would say you have to be serious but not . . . too much . . . developing a sense of humor can be done, and it's important to do . . . You can learn to see the ridiculousness of a frustration. It does make life one heck of a lot easier.

I asked what he would most want to be remembered for at Forbes, Inc. He replied:

> By operating the business in a way that as many people here as possible got to do their thing. That's what is making us successful . . . I'd like to be remembered as the boss who didn't find it necessary to be a boss.

Malcolm Forbes has proven himself a most successful boss. He has gathered a group of hard-working professionals and encouraged them to work at their creative best. He inspires them toward balance by making available opportunities for physical fitness and cultural activities. Malcolm has established a colorful balance in his own life, as well, between the workday pressures of running Forbes, Inc., and recreation. From collecting antiques to motorcycle touring to hot air ballooning, Forbes has demonstrated that one can reach for what one wants at any age. His "battery is always charged" because, whether in the office or on tour, Malcolm is doing what he enjoys.

His road to success has not been easy, particularly during the recession, when the magazine was not even self-supporting. He has worked long hours, but his persistence has paid off. Truly a seasoned businessman with a lust for adventure, millionaire Malcolm Forbes enjoys his success to the fullest.[25]

"My prescription for success means hard work, in the first place. An inquisitive mind is second. Responsiveness to an educational opportunity . . . a broad view of the personal contribution that an individual can make, not only for his own welfare but for the welfare of others."

GERALD RUDOLPH FORD, JR.

Thirty-eighth President of the United States

Born 1913, Omaha, Nebraska. A.B., University of Michigan. L.L.B., Yale. L.L.O., Michigan State University. Boxing coach, Yale University. Ensign in U.S. Navy. Lawyer. Member, House of Representatives. Elected Minority Leader, 1965. Vice President of United States 1973-1974. President of the United States 1974-1977.

On August 9, 1974, Gerald Ford took the oath of office as the thirty-eighth President of the United States. He filled the vacancy created by the resignation of Richard M. Nixon amidst the Watergate scandal.

As a result, one of his goals was to have an "open Presidency." He believed it was his task to restore confidence in the executive branch of government.

What was this man's childhood like? In his early life, he saw his parents take part in community projects and, especially, activities of their Episcopal Church. Gerald had an authoritarian father who believed in the values of discipline, education, and hard work.

There seems to be a strong carry-over from his childhood when he speaks out later. Ford is a greatly sought after keynote speaker throughout the country. In addition to his political views, he expresses his philosophy of life.

In an expression of faith, he challenged 800 delegates to a North American Congress of the Laity "to make discipleship in Christ the foundation for all we do in our secular lives." He saw devotion to justice and practical service as part of what this discipleship involved. In a strong public statement, Ford said:

> On both the right and left of our political system, there is now a growing sense that the major issues of our time—human freedom, peace,

> economic progress, and the opportunity for personal fulfillment—all involve personal morality. [26]

Like other successful men, Ford reiterated the co-partnership he felt with his creator, ". . . much remains to be done and we cannot do it alone. It is God's work as well as ours. We must be instruments in His hands."

Again the influence of his father and his early training came through when I asked him a question during a press conference on the campus of the University of California at San Diego. I said, "You are obviously concerned about students, Mr. President. What traits do you think are most important for young men and women to have in order to succeed in today's world?" He responded:

> I think each one of us has a little different prescription for that. My prescription for success means hard work in the first place. An inquisitive mind is second. Responsiveness to an educational opportunity, the university, and its professors. A broad view of the personal contribution that an individual can make, not only for his own welfare but for the welfare of others. Put those things all together and I think you have it, at least from my point of view. Anyway, it is a healthy perspective as to what a young student can use today.

But what is the former president like on his time away from the public? The Fords have a home, not only in Rancho Mirage, right off the golf course, but also a large home in Beaver Creek near Vail, Colorado. Their whole family gets together at regular intervals for rest and relaxation.

Ford is probably one of the most athletic men ever to occupy the White House. He says, "I'm very healthy." He weighs less than when he was playing football for the University of Michigan in the Rose Bowl. He has some difficulty with two bad knees, a result of a football injury that is at times troublesome. One of his frequent golfing buddies is Bob Hope. The two together are quite a pair and often "dress" to the hilt for their audiences. If Bob is the comic, Gerald Ford is certainly his sidekick.

Being at home for Ford does not necessarily mean relaxing. Next to his home in Rancho Mirage is the building that houses his office with a big desk holding documents, letters, and a briefcase with more work. According to his staff, "He works as hard here as he did at 1600 Pennsylvania Avenue." His only break seems to be watching special television programs. "But he still works at the desk at the same time," said Penny Circle, his staff chief.

When asked why he doesn't slow down and take it easy, he responded, "I couldn't sit around here all the time and play golf in the beautiful climate of Palm Springs. I'd go stark raving mad. Nobody would be able to stand me." He concluded, "I can't sit back and watch things going on and not be a part of it." [27]

Even in our short interview, Ford's desire to be fully involved was apparent. He encapsulated what others were saying about morals and values.

Ford is known as a strong family man. He and Betty have been married 40 years and have three sons and a daughter. The family members are respected for their openness and support of one another. The country was surprised and greatly touched by the President's and his family's support of Betty when she called a press conference to make a statement about her encounter with cancer. Later, they again showed a strong support when she announced that she was entering into treatment for substance abuse.

Because of her courage in dealing with and talking about the problem, and through the Betty Ford Foundation, she has helped countless other people put their lives back together. A frequent speaker, she offers inspiration and encouragement to groups across the country. By her example, she has inspired other well-known personalities and celebrities to speak out about their problems, which in the past have usually been kept secret. Rather than detracting from her popularity, the openness with which Betty and her family responded actually increased the respect people had for them.

Gerald Ford exhibits the social consciousness that is a common denominator among successful men after age 40. Self-discipline, a sense of morality, a devotion to family, and a strong spirituality are his trademarks.

What has this growing spirituality to do with success? It is perhaps indicative of a growing social consciousness which expands the interest and perspective of the individual so that he does not immerse himself in the lifelong series of self-gratifying episodes which are found in the lives of unsuccessful people. Even in "retirement," Ford continues to lead a full, productive, balanced life.

"I never thought of art or painting as a game. There was some mystery and glory to it . . . to me painting is an overall state of being, a total involvement . . . it is a continual learning process."

FRANCOISE GILOT

Internationally Known Artist; Poet; Co-Author: Life with Picasso

Born 1921 in Paris. Studied at the Sorbonne and Cambridge. Illustrator of a number of books; author of six, including *Interface, The Painter and His Mask, The Fugitive Eye,* and her latest, *Francoise Gilot: An Artist's Journey.* Her paintings are on permanent display in over 12 museums in France and the United States and have been exhibited throughout Europe, Canada, Australia, and the United States. Married to Dr. Jonas Salk, 1970.

Francoise Gilot was an internationally known artist when she first came to the United States to become a permanent resident. She settled in La Jolla, California, for part of the year with her husband, Dr. Jonas Salk, discoverer of the Salk Vaccine and founder and first Director of the Salk Institute. The rest of the year she spends in New York and her native Paris.

Francoise studied art in the studios of Andre Rozsda, the Academy Julian, and the Academy Section d'Or. She also holds degrees from the Sorbonne, where she studied philosophy and law and Cambridge University, where she studied English literature. She has two children, Paloma and Claude, from her life with Pablo Picasso and a third child, Aurelia, from her marriage to Luc Simon. Her work can be found in the finest private art collections and museums around the world.

Of her early environment she said, "My father was a chemist, a businessman, and a correspondent for the Natural History Museum in Paris. It was an environment which naturally stimulated interest in the arts." Her mother was also a painter before her marriage.

"I am too obsessed with my painting," Francoise commented. "I think all artists, writers, scientists, and all creative people are obsessed with their work. It becomes number one." Of her personal life and her marriage to Dr. Salk in relationship to her work, she has said, "I think each of us never thought we would marry again . . . who could put up with our life-styles?" But they did marry and have been married for 17 years. She spoke of her art:

> I never thought of art or painting as a game. There was some mystery and glory to it . . . to me painting is an overall state of being, a total involvement . . . it is a continual learning process. And I find that though I know what not to do, I never know what I should actually do.

Gilot said she believes communication with other artists is important. "In Europe, artists work all day and then go to cafes to talk about it, which is really idiotic, since their paintings aren't with them. But indirectly, it's beneficial because it's part of their discovering themselves in art."

Like most painters, Francoise is also an art collector. "When becoming an art lover, you must not be inhibited. The taste of a collector is a form of art in itself, an affirmation of the artist in someone." Her workday is formidably long: "I put in some 12 hours a day on my painting. Some is good; some is not. If you are always there, your mind is like a mirror ready to catch what comes along."

She speaks of her profession as an artist much as a priest might speak of his religious profession:

> I was wondering how to start a drawing or painting, because I thought that things had no beginning and no end. They existed in a continuum. Therefore it was difficult to focus on what to choose and what to eliminate. I started mostly by drawing animals, people, still life. I came to landscape later on; it was for me, maybe, a deeper understanding, because now, later on in my life, I have become very much a nature lover. But it took me longer. It was a secondary imprint.

Francoise's family played a great role in the formation of her art interests. I asked if her interest had started at an early age, and she replied:

> Oh, yes, I can remember when I was five I already expressed interest toward painting and sculpture. I didn't go to school until I was ten. I had a teacher who came to our home because my father had his own ideas about what education was, and I was a clever child. Once a week when I was five, I spent an afternoon with my teacher and was exposed to a lot of art. I was also able to start drawing, but as I remember, I was told what I shouldn't do but left free to invent. My mother and father said there's no such thing as scribbling. If you hold a pencil in your hand, it's something very important and there's a mystery and that mystery is called "art." And if you are going to hold a pencil for something else than writing, that other thing is art. And therefore I feared the pencil because I thought "aha, if I hold it like a magic wand,

then something will happen between my paper and the pencil and myself."

What were the parents of such a gifted child like, and did they influence her attitudes? I asked. She told me:

> My father thought that a child should not be treated like a child. I couldn't say, "Daddy," I had to say, "Father." If I wanted to draw, it was fine; if I wanted to paint, it was fine; but then I was given the tools of an adult, the artist. I could do what I felt, but I had to do it with the right tools and use them in a certain way. Later when I was eight, I was given a box of watercolors, fine English watercolors, the extremely delicate pastels, like olive green and other colors the like of which I had not even imagined in my head. When I saw those colors, I said, "But what are you supposed to do with them?" They are not bright. And then my mother said to me, "Color is not yellow, red, or blue. Color for an artist is relationship of different tones; it's putting them together and that creates color." I noticed there was a hue of yellow ochre that I found an ugly color because I looked at it in the tube. She said, "Not at all, because in relationship it becomes gold and if you are an artist with that ugly earth color, you are going to create gold." It's almost like Zen Buddhism. You are not given the lessons directly, but in indirect fashion.

"Do you think a woman can be successful and still be feminine or have you had to compromise yourself in order to become successful?" I asked.

> In the past, women could not express themselves in any other way except in having large families because so many infants died. Now that the families are smaller than they used to be, there's no reason why a woman who has two children cannot handle a career. For example, I used to work until two days before the birth of my children and I was up again fifteen days afterward. Pregnancy didn't stop anything. It seems to me motherhood is an experience that brings a lot of inspiration. I also think that one can be completely fulfilled without being a mother, but if you happen to be, it does not necessarily mean you can't be fulfilled in your career as well.

Francoise has been associated with two very strong men in her life, Picasso and Salk, yet she has maintained her unique individuality. "How did you do it?" I queried. She answered:

> A strong man knows very well who he is, like so many gifted geniuses. Since he knows very well who he is, he is not likely to hinder the gifts and talents and growth of the person who lives with him, because he is not fearful. When someone is married to a person who is not quite sure of himself, the man will try to impede the woman. I would say that a woman is safe with a man who is secure within himself.
>
> That, I think, is absolutely true because I lived with Pablo Picasso who was older than myself by 40 years. I was 21 when we met, and at that time there was not a boy of my age who could stand me. I could never have married any of them, even though I liked some of them. I think the relationship is much better when at least one person in a couple knows who he is and can handle a relationship better.
>
> When I look at modern couples, I often see that one is leaning on or strangling the other because there is a fear. The fear is, "Maybe I'm not as good as the other one, and he will outgrow me." Fear is the key to that deadlock. Once a person has enough confidence in his own gifts and potential, it doesn't really matter. In painting, it doesn't really matter if you are Rembrandt or not because it is better to be yourself. You don't measure in terms of quantity; you measure in terms of quality. Two human beings are or should be equal in quality.

Next I asked Gilot about the healing qualities of art. Did she believe it can achieve therapeutic results? She said:

> . . . art is healing for the artist . . . I'm sure that if I would not create, both in writing and in painting, I would be very neurotic, because I would be blocked.
>
> In ancient Greece, there was a sanctuary dedicated to Aesculapius. Medicine was a sacred art. It was not considered a science. People with a skin disease would come to Aesculapius, which was a place with special spring waters, both to drink and to bathe in. They were also taking herbs, etc. They had a treatment that we would now call strictly medical.
>
> At the same time, they had to stay there for three to six months according to the nature of their disease. They had to attend the theatre three times a week to watch tragedies and comedies. It was part of the cure. Art was believed to cure the human soul as was the body

by medical means. Music was also included in the treatments. They wanted to put the body in harmony again. Because, for them, illness was falling out of harmony. And health was returning to harmony.

"To me, painting is an overall state of being, a total involvement," Francoise said. That is why I see her pieces are so profound and successful. Her paintings express a splendid harmony of the intellectual and intuitive energies.

In the introduction to her newest book, *Francoise Gilot: An Artist's Journey*, Barbara Haskel stated:

> Francoise Gilot has worked for over 40 years as a painter wresting from form and color a visual statement which is at once personal and universal. She works intuitively, almost as if in a trance, in order to allow meanings to emerge of which she herself may not yet be fully cognizant. She is not content with the known; she views her task as an artist to transform and extend perceptions and to stimulate viewers toward insights and experiences they might not otherwise obtain. [28]

Long, disciplined hours and a deep love for her work also contribute to the skillful beauty of her craft. Francoise's discipline spills over into other areas of living, too: competitive horseback riding, swimming, and yoga, to mention a few.

Francoise's ability to have lived with two very accomplished, strong-willed men without losing her own sense of individuality reflects her well-developed self-respect and confidence.

She has given the world a unique gift in her art. Through her symbols, it seems that Francoise has expressed her spiritual perspective of life, a continuity with past and future generations, and an appreciation for the creative potential of the present moment.

"I find it's hard for anybody to be a great success who doesn't love coming to work and doesn't look forward to his job."

ALAN COURTNEY (ACE) GREENBERG

Chief Executive Officer and Chairman of the Board, Bear, Stearns & Company, Wall Street Investment Firm.

Born Wichita, Kansas 1927. Raised in Oklahoma City. B.A. in Business, University of Missouri. National bridge player. Hunts big game in Africa with a bow and arrow.

Ace Greenberg's advice for working on Wall Street: "Be born smart." Looking for employees, he does not necessarily go for the Harvard MBAs or Ph.D.s, but prefers what he calls "PSDs": people who are POOR, SMART, and have a DEEP DESIRE to become rich.

Greenberg is a most unpretentious, unaffected man, says an employee. He doesn't have the usual trappings of Chief Executive Officers: no private plane, no limousines, no frills. Greenberg comes alive when he goes into the trading room, where he rubs elbows with the other "regular guys" on a daily basis. He has a small, functional office, which he rarely uses. He prefers to orchestrate business from the raised dais on the trading floor.

He seems to have little use for Wall Street's politics or handshaking with government officials. Long-term planning and committee meetings bore him. When the firm's executives get together for their weekly meetings, the time is usually brief.

He works hard all day and then may leave at 4 p.m. for a bridge game with some of his cronies, such as CBS Chief Executive Lawrence Tisch.

Greenberg seems to thrive on risk, as long as he has a way of controlling it or making a profit from it. One of the earmarks of Bear, Stearns is its willingness to commit capital where other houses might be afraid to invest. All of the partners are hooked into the fate of the firm: They either share in the riches or watch their personal net worths dwindle when losses come along.

Greenberg has surrounded himself with a staff of bright, sharp entrepreneurs who are self-motivated. It is a firm where individuals who make money for the company are rewarded. Salaries are modest but performance compensation is high. Many of the employees come from humble backgrounds and may even boast about how they became rich despite a lack of social contacts, family wealth, and even education.

I walked into the Bear, Stearns offices for our interview. Sitting on a huge dais overlooking the stockbrokers busily working in the huge room below was the smiling, shirt-sleeved Ace Greenberg. He sat on his special perch conducting the business of the day while his female assistant answered the phones and handed him messages. His relaxed manner seemed almost out of place amidst the hustle and bustle of Wall Street activity.

He greeted me warmly and I immediately had a sense of a man who is sincere, fair, intelligent, and who has a zest for living. We established a rapport within 30 seconds, which is typical of his direct, open style. Throughout the interview he succinctly answered each of my questions, often with a subtle wit. His answers came so quickly I had difficulty, at times, coming up with questions fast enough. I was relieved when we were interrupted two or three times for pressing phone calls, and I had time to regroup and organize the next set of questions.

I asked him what from his childhood had helped him to do what he was doing now. He told me, with a grin, that being born smart is a great advantage:

> I'm a great believer in genes. I think if you have a smart mother and father, you're well ahead of the game. I obviously had no control over that.

Greenberg's executive position at Bear, Stearns was by no means handed to him. He started out with the company in 1949 putting pins on a map to locate oil wells. Nine years later he was made a partner and in 1978 became Chief Executive Officer and Chairman of the Board. He told me everyone who works at Bear, Stearns is rewarded and promoted solely on the basis of performance:

> It's a complete meritocracy. Nobody can work at Bear, Stearns if they're related to an employee or to one of the partners or anything like that. No families. No nepotism. If two people work here and get married, one of them has to leave. We don't care who, but one has to go.

He said he encouraged growth—both of the company and of his staff. I asked what kind of a role model he set up to encourage that growth:

> I love neatness. I encourage neatness. I like our people to show up on time, return calls on time, treat the customers right. I like the

secretaries to answer the phone in a bright voice, not like they're "doom and gloom." I think there are certain ways you run a business, and I call it being neat and clean.

Ace's line of work calls for conducting frequent negotiations. I asked if he had a standard method of negotiating, and he replied:

No, I don't. I'm usually very direct. I certainly don't want to waste their time, so I usually get right to the point and see if there's a possibility of doing something. I like to be fair to everybody, including me.

I commented that he really seemed to enjoy life. "I always have," he told me. "I've always been busy from morning to night and loved every minute of it—at 5 years of age or 55."

I asked him what he did as a child in the area of business.

Nothing. But I was always building things. I was very athletic. I spent a lot of time playing football or running or building airplanes or building cars. Not miniature cars, but cars that I could get into.

I commented that his approach to life seems so casual and yet seems to be so efficient and to work well for him. "Is that because you have a sense of organization?" I asked. His reply was:

I don't know. My wife says that I'm the greatest allocator of time she's ever met in her life . . . If I'm on a bus or an airplane, I've got things to do. I don't do a lot of just sitting and staring.

"Your policy at Bear, Stearns is similar to that philosophy," I said. "You're pretty short on meetings in terms of time allotted. How did that philosophy come about?" He answered:

There's some question in my mind about how important all the meetings are that so many people schedule. I know they have to get together with associates to make decisions sometimes, but it doesn't have to be a meeting with 10 or 12 people. It can be a meeting of one or two people. These big get-togethers to rehash and talk about the future, I'm not so sure that's a very good way of doing business.

"You're not like the average CEO," I said. "You don't have your own private plane, your own limousine, or the other luxuries. Why?" He answered:

> Well, in the first place, I think it sets a lousy example for the rest of the firm. In the second place, anything that I or we can do to improve our bottom line by cutting expenses would benefit me. I'm a big owner of the common stock—very big—and I would rather have the common stock earnings go up than stay the same or go down. So it's self-serving. Besides, if I want a limousine, I can afford not to have the stockholders pay for it.

We talked about the bonus he received, which brought his total earnings for the year ending April 1987 to $5,712,000. I had heard that he returned a portion of the bonus because he thought it was setting too high a precedent. I asked him if that wasn't unusual, and he replied:

> I'm told it's unusual. But keep in mind I have the lowest base salary of any chief executive now on Wall Street—or almost the lowest. Last year my base salary was $200,000.

The reality is that his bonus comes from company money. He turns his bonuses back into the company. If the company does not do well, he might get just $200,000 a year.

"Becoming rich, what does that mean to you?" I asked. "Does that really make a difference in your life?" He said:

> Well, there are a lot of things you can do with money, whether you want to give it away or buy horses. I find it's hard for anybody to be a great success who doesn't love coming to work and doesn't look forward to his job. I just can't believe anyone who hates his work can be successful there. I also think that a very high percentage of people who work at this company love coming to work. They love the way they're treated, and I think they like working for a place that promotes strictly on merit.
>
> Our company policy is that each of the managing directors has to give away four percent of his income, but most of them give away a lot more. My personal policy is that I'm probably going to give away whatever my salary and bonus are every year—probably. I'm not going to guarantee it, but that's probably what I'm going to shoot for.

Ace just wants to give or raise funds, not to attend meetings or conventions. His long-time friend Lawrence Tisch sees him as "very generous."

Fairness is a part of his style in his financial contributions to society and even in his hobbies. I had seen pictures of him hunting big game in Africa, and I asked why he chose to shoot with a bow and arrow:

> Well, I think it improves the chances for the animal a bit—like about 1,000 percent.

Hunting is just one of his hobbies. He is a master bridge player and a magician. When asked how he can run a major securities house and still have time for his hobbies, he said he weeds out the nonessentials. "If a man doesn't play golf, watch TV, or chase girls, he has time to do a lot with his life."

When Greenberg leaves the office, he throws himself into other activities with the same intensity and the same passion that he does for his work. He gives his total attention to whatever he is doing. I was amazed that, with all of his responsibilities, he could leave the office behind so completely.

> I work very hard from eight in the morning until five or six. I walk out of here and I say, "I do the best I can from very early morning to whenever I finish." Nobody calls me on the weekend, and nobody calls me at home. About 99 percent of the calls wait for Monday morning. I work hard while I'm here and then I walk out of here. I don't work Saturdays and Sundays.

Ace works smart and then he plays smart. He is totally "where he is." I asked him if he had always been interested in magic and bridge.

"Always," he replied. "And the bow and arrow."

"Did you learn how to use the bow and arrow when you were young?" I asked.

"Yes, my father wouldn't let me buy a gun."

That dry humor of his again surfaced in his one-word response to my next question: What did you shoot? Rabbits? Squirrels? "Trees," he said.

I asked the next question expecting him to give a long-range philosophical answer about what his life and business goals were. Specifically, I asked, "What in the future are you looking forward to?"

> I'm going to two dog shows this weekend. I'm pretty excited about that.

He told me that he trains his own dogs and that he is interested only in the obedience part of the dog shows, not which dog is prettiest.

I asked, "What kind of dogs do you have?" He answered, "A big one and a little one."

I asked how he wanted his two children to remember him. He said:

> As a good father. I have a good relationship with both of them. That's all. They can do anything they want with their lives.

I wondered how he would sum up his motto or philosophy of life. He replied:

> I hope that everybody I have come in contact with feels that they received more than they gave from our relationship. That they never had the feeling of being taken advantage of.

After the interview he took me to his office which is filled with photos of his family, his trips to Africa, and some of his other recreational activities. I asked him to show me the snowshoe sandwich hand trick, which he did, to my utter amazement. I couldn't believe he could produce this magic feat right before my eyes. But part of his enjoyment in life is amazing and amusing his friends with magic.

By the end of our session, I totally agreed with his wife: He is one of the greatest allocators of time I have met. The interview was over almost before I realized it. He had given me the information I needed—while barely breaking his work rhythm—and he managed to make the experience enjoyable in the entertaining style that is the special Greenberg trademark.

Epilogue:

I called Ace after the stock market crash on October 19, 1987, to see how it had affected him. He told me his activities that day were no different than he had originally planned. He said that he had two advantages to prepare him for that kind of situation:

> First, I had the experience of 4,000 years of persecution; secondly, it wasn't as bad as Buchenwald, Auschwitz, or Vietnam. So let's keep things in perspective.

A simple philosophy but certainly the bottom line for a well organized, thorough man who seems to always keep his eye on the doughnut, not the hole.

"We live in the century of the common man, but I believe in the uncommon man . . . John the Baptist is important not because he was a radical, which he was, but because he was an unusual and great man . . . I don't mean famous people; famous people are just like everyone else."
— Charlton Heston

CHARLTON HESTON

Actor, Author: The Actor's Life

Born 1924, Evanston, Illinois. Served in the Air Force in World War II. Academy Award for Best Actor in "Ben Hur," 1959. President of the Screen Actors Guild, 1966-71. National Council on the Arts, 1967-72. Chairman, American Film Institute, 1973. Head of President's Task Force on Arts and Humanities.

I first "met" Charlton Heston in the Kennedy Airport in New York. It was to be a long overseas flight for me, so I was hustling to get a sandwich before takeoff. Running around a corner in the terminal, I bumped into not only a tall, six-foot, sun-tanned, good-looking man, but smack into the tip (fortunately corked) of his diving spear. My mind swirled and all I could think was Ben Hur! . . . No, Moses! . . . but surely, it must be Michelangelo! Obviously this bronzed man had been in a warm climate. To me, peaked from too much cold weather, he truly resembled a Greek God!

My second meeting with him was at the La Jolla Beach and Tennis Club. He was in San Diego to visit his daughter at the University of California on commencement weekend. I was jogging around a corner and again ran head-on into Charlton.

The third time was much calmer. He had come to San Diego to formally dedicate the reopening of the Old Globe Theatre. He had only a few minutes for an interview, and my TV colleagues were waiting their turn.

Looking trim and classic in his tux, he expounded on what individuals can do for their fellow man. Sharing a sense of public responsibility which most successful men seem to have, he said, "Every public person has a certain responsibility to various public work projects . . . The more you do, the more you are asked to do."

He is understandably vexed that some people have a low opinion of actors and the acting profession:

> It is widely held that actors don't need either brains or education; I don't entirely hold with that. When you play an historical role, such as Moses, your research responsibilities are obviously a prime part of your preparation. If you play a professional football player or a symphony conductor, both of which I have played, your preparation is mainly physical. A role like Andrew Jackson or John the Baptist requires a preparation in research. Some characters have more personal research materials available than others; Michelangelo's letters still exist.

Heston researched Michelangelo by reading those letters (over 600 of which exist) as well as other materials before acting the part.

In an age which denies elitism and urges the democratization of all institutions, Heston stands alone as an interesting anachronism.

> I've probably played more biographical roles than any of my colleagues, and I've found them very rewarding. We live in the century of the common man, but I believe in the uncommon man. Andrew Jackson and Thomas Jefferson and Richlieu and General Gordon and John the Baptist and Mark Antony are not like you and me. They don't need my voice to make their mark on history—they've made that. But I find them particularly rewarding to play. The uncommon men and women of the world are the most valuable role models.

> John the Baptist is important not because he was a radical, which he was, but because he was an unusual and great man. We have a short focus: We imagine that, because we see no unusual men or women in our time, that there are none. I don't mean famous people; famous people are just like everyone else. The great man, the extraordinary man, is not; and if you can't find him in your own time, you have to find him in history. You can be rewarded and educated by the examples of the great, even if you cannot follow them [i.e., accomplish their specific achievements].

Reflecting on my encounters with Charlton, I recognized that he shares many qualities with other prominent men and women. He has high self-esteem, confidence, and poise. He set his goal early, "I never remember a time when I didn't want to be an actor." He takes pride in his craft and enjoys its disciplines. It is only natural that this "uncommon man" should play the roles of so many extraordinary people.

"I think when you're serving other people, it is quality that is essential: serving and loving and caring . . . There are two kinds of people in the world: guests and hosts. As an employee of Rosewood Hotels, I am thankful that we are able to be the hosts and make the guests comfortable. One thing Rosewood Hotels stands for is Texas friendliness and lack of snobbishness."

CAROLINE HUNT

Daughter of the Legendary H.L. Hunt

Born 1923, El Dorado, Arkansas. Graduated, University of Texas. Board of Trustees, Mary Baldwin College and others. Author: *The Compleat Pumpkin Eater,* a cookbook.

With her warm, unassuming manner and open friendliness, she exhibits a sense of trust in everyone she encounters. She drives a compact Plymouth, flies economy airlines, and wears copies of designer dresses to Dallas' elite social events. I asked Caroline what success meant to her. It seemed an appropriate question to ask this member of the wealthy Hunt family. She told me:

> Success is certainly not necessarily just financial. Success to me means to live a successful life as a human being. That means being able to relate in a positive manner with other people—in a way that is affirming of them, where you're a contributor rather than a taker.

She said that success, like any state of being, is not something you achieve once and retain forever:

> You're a failure sometimes. Success is something you have to strive for. You have to strive to be a growing person and be a contributing person.

Caroline is a beneficiary of the Caroline Hunt Trust Estate set up more than 50 years ago by her father, H.L. Hunt, one of the world's most famous oil tycoons. His purchase of the Texas oil leases of C.M. "Dad" Joiner has been said to be one of the great judgment calls in the modern business world.

The trust has among its assets the Rosewood Corporation, which has as one of its best known subsidiaries Rosewood Hotels. The Rosewood Hotels' first acquisition came in 1979 when it acquired the historic Sheppard King mansion in Dallas and transformed it into a small, European-style hotel. What started as a routine investment ended up as a major project. Caroline had ideas about the hotel industry and when asked, offered her opinions. After the $21 million restoration was complete, the elegant Mansion on Turtle Creek opened. It was the first of a number of world-class luxurious hotels that Rosewood Hotels has acquired or built.

Since that time, Rosewood Hotels has purchased the Hotel Bel Air in Los Angeles, which has undergone a $12,000,000 refurbishment and enlargement. After buying the Hana Maui in Hawaii, Rosewood Hotels also renovated it. The Remington in Houston, which was built earlier at a cost of $203,000 per room, was not as financially successful and has been sold to another company. Another spectacular hotel is the Hotel Crescent Court, a part of the Crescent multi-use development, which combines a hotel with office space and commercial shopping area.

Despite the poshness which characterizes these establishments, they all carry a distinctive imprint of Texas hospitality, lack of snobbishness and care for the guests. In fact, the employees and even the valet parking attendants often remember guests' names from one visit to the next. How do the hotels do this? I asked. By careful selection and training of the staff, she told me:

> Life can be so impersonal these days because everything is so big. Rosewood Hotels has very intensive training to teach people to show that they do care. That's pretty hard to fake. You have to start out with people who really do like other people.

The training consists of giving the staff homespun pep talks, reminding them to smile, to try to remember names, and generally to show that they care about the guests.

> I think when you're serving other people, it is the quality that is essential: serving and loving and caring. I occasionally make a point of this, and what I say is there are two kinds of people in the world: guests and hosts. As an employee of Rosewood Hotels, I am thankful that we are able to be the hosts and make the guests comfortable. Two things Rosewood Hotels stands for are *Texas friendliness* and *lack of snobbishness*. I cannot stand snobbery.

The first thing looked for in picking a staff is that they be ethical. Rosewood Hotels' intention is to stand for integrity and honesty in all that it does. It is important that employees have pride in their work, and she says that most Rosewood employees have that trait. She attributes this to "the fact that we try to stand for quality, timelessness, the best, the classic . . . Rosewood Hotels always tries to do whatever it does the best it can be done, although it doesn't always make the most money. The quality almost stands above the amount of money made."

Caroline claims she gets more credit than she deserves for the hotels. If she does offer suggestions, they are usually on the practical side rather than the artistic side. Although one may be given the privilege of reviewing the interior design schemes, she says, "I learned early on that you can't design by committee." She does give her thoughts about the tone of the hotels and often the color schemes. She likes a warm, subtle, soft effect rather than a harsh one, saying, "I hate high tech."

Although she spent the majority of her years until recently raising children, she acquired some of her skills at jobs she had after college.

After getting married, she worked in her father's office and then as a sales clerk at Neiman-Marcus. She commented:

> I was taken on as temporary help, and I was proud that they offered me a permanent job in the gift department. I learned a lot in that job. I learned about dealing with the public. People can be very rude and strange.

Caroline says she is shy, something no one would suspect watching her host an event for a hotel opening or chairing a benefit or going from table to table to warmly greet several hundred guests. I asked her how she overcame that shyness and she said it is something she has to work at:

> Shyness comes from thinking of yourself and your inadequacies. To overcome that, you have to to forget yourself and think about the other person and making them comfortable. In other words to learn to be the host or the hostess. It still takes an effort for me to do that.

Unlike many of the wealthy set, Caroline prefers comfort to ostentation. In fact she says she is proud when people say her house looks "lived in." She acquired her unassuming manner and unpretentiousness early in life. "My parents were not socially ambitious," she says, "and I feel the same way. They were not snobbish. They didn't look down on any human being, nor did they particularly look up to any. People were just people." They played down their wealth so much that Caroline didn't even realize they had money until she was 15. In college she kept secret the fact that her family was wealthy. She explained why:

> I think that sets you apart. Money has its advantages and its disadvantages. Some people resent people who have money. I think it's harder for a young person. My children worry that people don't like them for themselves. What I try to tell them is that everyone is liked for multiple reasons: your character, your personality, your looks. Money is simply another facet of you. It has its positive and its negative. Even though someone may be initially attracted to you for your money, in the end they can like you for all the other facets of your being. I think it's essential that you feel that way, because otherwise you don't trust other people, and you would never make any friends.

I asked Caroline what other traits she had acquired from her parents, and she said faith in God was an important one. She went to church every Sunday as a child and is a deacon at the Highland Park Presbyterian Church, the largest Presbyterian church in the U.S.

She said she had acquired her patriotism and concern about the future of the country from her father. "He was an intense person. Whatever he did, he did intensely for 18 hours a day. At dinner we always discussed the state of the union or business. He worried that our country would go bankrupt or into debt, as we are now."

Both of her parents exemplified integrity, honesty, lack of pretense. She remembers them as kind people who rarely spanked the children and made few demands, not even about grades or about what they ate. They had a deep sense of commitment to the family, a characteristic that still prevails strongly in Caroline's family today—both with her children and with her brothers and sister. "When people ask me what is the most satisfying thing in my life, I don't hesitate to say it's the fact that my children love and respect each other and get along."

Despite the fact that she had four brothers and a sister, her parents found time for all of them. "Each of us was handled as an individual, in spite of being in a large family. Each had a lot of solo interaction with our parents."

True to her commitment to family, Caroline made a gesture to show support of her brothers during one of their difficult periods by such activities as bringing the family together to pick and preserve tomatoes.

Caroline has spent a lot of time over the years doing volunteer work. One of her challenging projects was organizing Sunday School classes for 500 children and 70 teachers for her church, which she did for seven years. "I didn't think I'd ever be able to do it," she says, calling it a "real learning experience." Currently she is on the boards of the John F. Kennedy Center for the Performing Arts, the Salvation Army, and the Presbyterian Hospital of Dallas. She frequently serves as honorary chairman at all sorts of benefits and spends a lot of time promoting the Hotel Crescent Court.

Obviously a busy woman with a variety of interests, Caroline said her formula for continuing to grow and contribute involves opening herself to new experiences and new people. I commented that not all wealthy people trust others, and she replied: "I don't know how they can take care of their material possessions if they don't trust people. One surely can't do it by oneself. All the Rosewood companies are led by talented and trusted professionals who, along with the board of directors, run the business of these companies."

Caroline went on to say she schedules opportunity into her life for experiences that encourage her growth, experiences that push her beyond her comfort zone a bit. In the last year, since becoming divorced, she has traveled frequently. She fulfilled a long-held dream of going to England to buy antiques. When she returned, she opened an antique shop in Dallas called Shopping English Countryside, which is located in the Crescent Shopping Complex. She was invited to the Aspen Institute in Colorado to attend a seminar with senior CEOs, which was another experience that helped her to reach out into a new arena for learning.

"I feel I have a very balanced life," she says. "Lots of social activity and enjoyment of the arts. I enjoy the out-of-doors and, of course, exercising and dancing. She says the exercising, which she does nearly every morning for an hour at the Crescent, is exhilarating. She has only been exercising regularly for about 10 years and wishes she had started earlier. "I don't expect to become a female jock, but I find it makes me feel energetic."

And what about the future? I asked her what she would do if she had no restrictions whatsoever. She said, "I don't really have restrictions. If I'm not happy it's my own fault, because I am free to do whatever I want to do." She says she has a cosmic view of life because of her faith in God and interest in ancient history. "When you think about the pyramids and eternity, the little day-to-day ups and downs seem sort of insignificant. I don't have a desire to have my name remembered forever."

She summarized her philosophy of life:

> I am not aggressive. I let life come to me. I try to be a positive, loving person with whomever I interact. I try to just accept life. I would say if I did anything in life it would be to live each day happily.

She said she doesn't have any great ambitions—that she can't think of anything she would want to commit to 18 hours a day as her father had. It was my observation that she is totally committed to her family and to being a positive influence to people she comes in contact with. Whether or not she considers herself ambitious, through her commitment to family and the community, she has improved the quality of life for many.

"In the happy hour of life, so to speak, having fulfilled most of my life's obligations, I finally decided that I would do what I wanted to do and explore and unlock some of the secrets of growing wildflowers."

MRS. L.B. JOHNSON

Former First Lady; Founder, National Wildflower Research Center

Born 1912, Karnack, Texas. B.A. in Journalism, University of Texas. Married Past United States President, Lyndon Baines Johnson, 1934. Author: *A White House Diary*. Founder, National Wildflower Research Center; Chairman, Beautification of America Project; Honorary Chairman, National Headstart Program, 1942-63.

"It was my way to pay my rent for the space I have taken up on the planet." Those are the words Lady Bird Johnson uses to explain her reason for launching a major project, on her seventieth birthday, the National Wildflower Research Center, outside Austin, Texas.

The "rent payment" was $125,000 and 60 acres of the LBJ ranch, which she donated to start the center. But the contribution she has made goes far beyond the financial or the material. Thoroughly dedicated to the project, which she conceived and organized, she brings to it the many friends and talents she has acquired over the years in her other ventures.

Considered by many to be one of the most effective First Ladies the country has known, Mrs. Johnson is a multi-talented woman. Using her journalistic skills, she recorded her White House years in the book, *A White House Diary*. During that period she received a number of awards for her beautification efforts throughout the country. She managed her husband's congressional office, was owner-operator of radio and TV station KTBC in Austin, Texas, and currently owns and operates cattle ranches in Texas.

Mrs. Johnson has a proven successful track record. But what are the qualities that enable her to take on such a major venture as the research center at a time in life when most people are retired? The answer seems to be that she has continued to use her mind and remain productive throughout her life.

Wildflowers are dear to her heart and she is able to bring vitality and enthusiasm to this project. She calls for support from the many contacts she acquired while doing previous beautification and charitable projects—people she knew had an interest in the environment. Laurance Rockefeller, for instance, helped her underwrite her wildflower opening in New York City, and Helen Hayes co-hosted the event with her.

Mrs. Johnson described why she had started the wildlife research center:

> This idea had lain itching in my mind for many years. Nature is a long, long love of mine. It's a source of sustenance and peace and relaxation. The happiest days I recall are ones I spent out exploring. And yet in all my years on the ranch of trying to start stands of Indian paintbrush, Indian blanket, and blue-bonnet, I was frustrated because there is so little known about them--about how and when and where to best plant.
>
> So, in the happy hour of life, so to speak, having fulfilled most of my life's obligations, I finally decided that I would do what I wanted to do and explore and unlock some of the secrets of growing wildflowers—find out how to get rid of those invading grasses and how to get consistent stands year after year.

A primary aim of the project, she said, is to encourage the use of native flowers, including native grasses and trees, in the nation's landscaping patterns. "Our population has nearly doubled in the last 50 years, and the open spaces I remember when I first came to Austin as a student are no longer there . . . The habitat of wildflowers is getting narrower and narrower."

Another emphasis of the center is education. School children make field trips to learn about wildflowers; park and maintenance employees, as well as nursery people, attend workshops there. The center's clearinghouse, or "information matrix" as Mrs. LBJ calls it, is collecting research information about wildflowers from universities, arboretums, garden clubs, and botanical gardens. The findings are shared with interested parties.

Toward that end, Lady Bird took the daring step that strikes fear in the hearts of many older people and, as she put it, "We ventured into the field of computerland. We bought a computer and we're putting all the information in it. Now we're trying to tame it," she said with a smile.

Mrs. Johnson takes an active role in promoting and fund-raising for the center. She gets support through both grants and volunteers and the center now has a national membership. She considers the Texas Highway Department her greatest ally. Through her encouragement the Department conducted a pilot project to allow wildflowers to reseed and grow more profusely along the highways. This not only made the highways more attractive but saved the state considerable money.

Americans have long benefited from her beautification efforts. While in the White House, she initiated and organized the Committee for a More Beautiful National Capitol, resulting in the planting of thousands of trees and flowers which still adorn Washington streets. Later she extended the beautification program across America, helping to eradicate unsightly billboards and junk piles along the nation's highways.

Another program sponsored by Lady Bird during her Washington days was "Headstart," a project to help disadvantaged children. She still donates her time to worthwhile efforts. She is active on several boards, including the National Geographic Society, and continues to work at the LBJ Library and the LBJ School of Public Affairs. This she does in addition to running the LBJ ranch.

What in her childhood planted the roots for this later achievement? Lady Bird, like many of the successful, was often left to herself as a child. As the interviewer, it seems to me that this isolation allowed her the opportunity to develop her creativity. She spoke of her early years:

> I spent a lot of time alone when I was young. My mother died when I was five, and my brothers were older and off to school. We lived in a very small rural community so there were no close neighbors.
>
> My father set a good example for me. I watched him at work in his little country store. He called it "T.J. Taylor, Dealer in Everything," and he did sell everything from flour to coffins. He worked hard—and he was always trying to help less fortunate people in the community.

It is her father's family that she credits with giving her "strong genes." Her grandmother, who outlived four husbands, served as a role model for her. Lady Bird recalled what her grandmother endured when her fourth husband died:

> Here was a woman with four children, eight months pregnant, no husband, and a lot of expenses. She made it. Whenever the going is rough, I always think about my grandmother.

What was most rewarding to her about her years in the White House? As she said in the preface of her book, *A White House Diary*:

> As I look back on those five years of turmoil and achievement, of triumph and pain, I feel amazement that it happened to me and gratitude that I had the opportunity to live them and, strongest of all—out of

all the trips that I made and all the people that I met—a deep, roaring faith in and love for this country. [29]

I had heard Lady Bird make frequent references to God, and I imagined that religion played a major part in her life. Betty Tilson, her long-time friend and assistant, confirmed that this was true:

> She has a really strong faith. She certainly has gratitude to that wonderful source for the kind of life she has lived and the activities she has been engaged in.

Betty said Lady Bird goes to church as often as she can and always says grace before meals. She reflected on seeing Mrs. Johnson in her office one day:

> It's a day that I will always remember. It started raining for the first time after a long dry spell. She looked out the window, clasped her hands, and said, "Thank you, Lord." It was a prayer of thanksgiving rather than just a casual remark.

Mrs. Johnson's greatest joy is her family, as demonstrated by the blessing she printed on her Christmas card one year:

> Seventy-five years of life
> Two grown children, two sons-in-law
> Four grown grandchildren and
> Four little ones later—
> Christmas is a time for counting
> Blessings of family and friends—
> Bring on the adding machines!

She enjoys spending time with her daughters Linda and Lucy, their husbands Charles Robb and Ian Turpin, and their children. She schedules a week or two every summer to take one of her seven grandchildren to federal parklands. Of her family, she said, "They are the meat and bread—the staff of my life." All other activities, she said, are secondary.

It is for her grandchildren, and those of others, that she works to keep the national heritage of America's wildflowers alive. In fact, her grandchildren provide her with her continuing zest for life. As Lady Bird phrases it, "It really gives me a sense of purpose and determination to live longer just to see their lives unfold."

"Only hire those you think are as good as you are or better. And this has nothing much to do with business techniques, which can be learned: I mean strength of character. The old cop-out is to hire only knuckleheads who make you look pretty good in comparison."

RAY KROC

Founder, McDonald's Corporation

Born 1902, Oak Park, Illinois. Died 1984. Served in Ambulance Corps in World War II. Sales Manager, Lily Tulip Cup Co., 1923-41. Owner, Chairman, and Treasurer, San Diego Padres Baseball Team. Founder of the Kroc Foundation and the Ronald McDonald Children's Fund.

Thinking of success, power, and prestige, one automatically pictures Ray Kroc, founder of the McDonald's hamburger empire. In his time, he was a piano player in a brothel, a paper cup salesman, and the owner of the San Diego Padres. Yet, until he was 61, Kroc had never attained the status of millionaire it is assumed he always had.

Kroc was particularly enjoyable to interview, due to his homespun good humor and wit. I believe he was a man who thought his way carefully into success and later enjoyed the rewards his hard work in earlier years had justly earned him.

He was philosophical about his wealth: "It's a hell of a lot more fun chasing it than getting it. Anticipation is greater than realization. The top of the mountain means there's nothing left to climb." He went on to say:

> Our world has such mercenary goals that when anybody is attentive to his work, the usual comment is, "What are you—money mad? You want to be the richest man in the cemetery?" Artists, writers, and sculptors don't hear that, because people accept that they wouldn't be doing this work if they didn't love it more than they love money. But anyone working in a business for profit is considered to be working his head off for money and working too hard for his own good. I never worked for money and I live the same now as before I had money.
>
> You're not the same person if you have a substantial trust fund and know that the money will be there every month. Expensive tastes are

> very easy to acquire: you can get used to Russian sable as easily as you can get used to gingham.

His background, which he called Bohemian German, brought him a tradition of hard work, great pride, and frugality. His greatest role model had been his maternal grandfather, who was a businessman. Kroc said he didn't really come of age until he was 52, when he found psychological and philosophical satisfaction.

In his position as sales manager for the Lily Tulip Paper Cup Company, he had observed that the store which bought the most paper cups also sold milkshakes with their hamburgers. In those days it was a novel idea to have a business that combined the two. With the store's owners, Mac and Dick McDonald of San Bernardino, Kroc decided to start a new company using the McDonald name. He went to his bank in Chicago for a loan of $1.5 million, in spite of the fact that his total net worth at the time was only $90,000. "The net worth of a business is in its future," Kroc said, "and bankers don't go for that." He was not only turned down, but laughed out of the bank. But he persisted. He went back again and again with new facts about the future prospects of his company. After eight attempts, he finally got the loan.

Thirty-six years later, McDonald's accounted for one-third of the total dollar volume of all U.S. restaurants. The chain not only made Kroc a fortune estimated at $500 million at the time of his death, but it is believed that, through his franchises, he made multimillionaires of more people in a shorter time than any other man in modern history. He is responsible for making fast food drive-ins a landmark in America.

What was the trait that made this possible? Persistence. It was Kroc's watchword. He believed so strongly in his idea that he refused to take no for an answer. He remarked:

> Intellectual work is like business. To get a musical composition published, or a book or an article, you have to spend months knocking on doors and finding out the names of all possible publishers. If they don't respond at all, send another copy in a month, but don't mention they threw the first one out. Too many young people don't have the guts to persevere.

His motto, attributed to Calvin Coolidge, exemplifies the course he followed throughout his life. It was found in his McDonald's office, in his San Diego Padres office, and on his desk at home:

> Press on. Nothing in the world can take the place of persistence. Talent will not; nothing is more common than unsuccessful men with talent. Genius will not; unrewarded genius is almost a proverb. Education alone will not; the world is full of educated derelicts. Persistence and determination alone are omnipotent.

In spite of the fact that he made so much money during his lifetime, he must have made some mistakes. How did he handle them? He told me:

> When I make a mistake I throw it off by saying, "That's why they put mats under cuspidors." You have to overcome your mistakes by making another decision. But I'd a heck of a lot rather see people make mistakes than make nothing. Mistakes are painful when they happen; but years later, a collection of mistakes is what they call experiences. When you make a mistake, you are doing something.

Ray was anti-union because he felt unions give workers no incentive: "The poor workers are averaged in with the good workers." I asked him how he chose employees. Since he could not personally select all of them, what general characteristics did he think were important in hiring new people? He paused for a moment, then said:

> I advise companies to only hire those who are good enough to take the current executives' jobs away from them. Only hire those you think are as good as you are or better. And this has nothing much to do with business techniques which can be learned: I mean strength of character. The old cop-out is to hire only knuckleheads who make you look pretty good in comparison. To hire somebody you honestly believe is good enough to take your job away takes guts.

Ray told me that as a businessman, it was "not outstandingly important to be well-liked, a personality kid, and in favor with your employees." He went on to say:

> After all, the subordinates are dispensable, the executive isn't. Besides I think there's something wrong in a person who can't adjust to his superior. I believe a man in a position of importance should make his views known; but if the majority of executive decisions counter him, he should drop his original position and agree with the company policy because his heart isn't in it.

He talked about the importance of people having a sense of pride in their work, of doing a good job, not just for the money, but for the inner satisfaction it brings:

> The difficulty most people have is associating applause with their work when they can't hear any applause per se. The applause is the faster heartbeat, the pride of accomplishment, the satisfaction. For younger people, a compliment on a job well done is the most resounding applause. If they never get one, they're missing something. If they love what they're doing enough, their natural enthusiasm will coax the applause.

Ray's wife Joan is also a strong-willed individual. I asked him about his partnership with his wife:

> I can say that we're both strong persons and neither dominates the other. It would seem logical for me to be the dominant one because I'm 26 years older, quite a difference. A man's always got to be older than his wife, even if he's lying.
>
> The old fashioned idea of the man as boss doesn't occur in our case because of the respect we have for each other's viewpoints and each other's endeavors. We are both musical. The first time I saw her, she was playing the organ in an exclusive restaurant in St. Paul and I could see she was playing it well. It's an easy instrument to fake. I said I would marry her and 15 years later, I did. Joanie doesn't care for any sports and she won't play bridge, which I love. There are many reasons why we shouldn't be compatible, but we are. I think the music is our big tie.

I asked Ray how he felt about the changing roles women were taking on today in the home and office:

> Kids these days live together or get married while they're still in college with the understanding that they'll both work. That's not normal to start with. I don't see anything wrong with the gal working as a temporary thing. But to be a successful professional, a highly-paid career woman, it seems likely she will have to relinquish old-fashioned family life and postpone having a family and maybe never have any children.

Each time I met Ray he seemed to be in good spirits, in spite of his busy, hurried schedule. He said he consciously chose to have a positive outlook on life:

> There are things to be miserable about and things to be happy about. Since you do have a choice in what you think about, why not pick the happy things? Money doesn't make for happiness, but it's easier to be happy with money than without it.

His success could not prevent his suffering from bouts of diabetes and arthritis. Like other successful men, once he made it to the top, Kroc's interests turned toward helping others. He founded the Kroc Foundation, which works with problems of arthritis, diabetes, and multiple sclerosis.

Kroc was concerned with young people and the way they view money today:

> You see these 16- and 17-year-old kids and there's nothing left for them; they've done it all. They get restless and bored and they want something new. They've got it too fast, too soon . . .
>
> If you're a graduate of Harvard Law School, the chances are you came from money to begin with, and they start you in a New York firm at $25,000 a year . . . I was married when I was 20 and I first got money when I was 61. That gives you the apprenticeship in life: coping, overcoming, doing without, sacrificing. In my case, it required even more discipline because the Bohemian time-payment plan was cash, full cash payment in advance. You waited to make big purchases until you had the money . . . you made the sacrifice before you bought it, not afterwards. To have the pleasure first, to take the vacation now and pay later, upsets the normalcy in life. You're not living where you are; you're a kind of codfish aristocrat.

With his enormous wealth, his heirs I commented, would undoubtedly not sufffer financially. I asked him what he most wanted for his grandchildren. He told me he thought that money might be more of a hindrance than a help in terms of motivating them:

> I know my grandchildren will be harnessed by the fact that they're going to be secure. And I do mean harnessed. The challenge of having to make it, to sink or swim, is hardly important or crucial for them.

> One of my colleagues says that children should not inherit any money until they're 35 years of age. Look at the free agents in baseball who are paid a lot of money. Once the money comes in, none of them has performed as well as before. I rate that figure at 100 percent. If you think you don't have to go to work, you forget how to discipline yourself. But if you pull yourself together and work, you feel a devil of a lot better. People can spoil themselves very easily.
>
> I told the Business School at USC that the first thing a businessman needs is an idea which he loves. If you don't love it, drop it. If you're going to prostitute yourself at an early age and look for a job where the money is, you'll be working for money all your life. To love your work is very important, particularly for young people; if they lose that love, then they will never be able to recapture it. Once you get married and have a couple of kids, you don't have any alternative but to look to financial considerations some of the time.

Ray Kroc was the epitome of persistence in business as well as in his other ventures. Perseverance finally paid off with his baseball team. He purchased the San Diego Padres in 1974, and 10 years later—a year after his death—they won the National League Championship.

It was persistence that got him his first loan. Being laughed out of the first loan interview only proved to be a stepping stone toward his uncanny financial success. Why was Ray Kroc, who started so poor, able to make so much? He loved his job, had the diligence to work hard at it, had confidence in his ability to achieve great results, and he took a big risk.

Ray was a happy man before his wealth, which probably explains why he could be detached enough to enjoy it when he finally made his millions.There are things to be miserable about and things to be happy about.

"We live in a time when, from what one reads in the printed media and sports or sees on film or on television, one would think there's nothing but winners. If you're not a winner, you're a loser.I think the instruction should be that all we need do is suceed at the level of doing one's best."

NORMAN LEAR

Award-Winning Television Producer, Writer, and Movie Producer

Born 1922, New Haven, Connecticut. Attended Emerson College, Boston. Served in U.S. Army Air Force. Honorary Doctor of Humanities from Emerson, 1968. Academy Award Nomination for "Divorce: American Style." Other films: "Stand by Me" and "Princess Bride." Television shows: "All in the Family" (winner of 4 Emmy Awards), "Sanford & Son," "Maude," "The Jeffersons." George Foster Peabody Award, 1977 and 1985. Television Hall of Fame.

A generous and modest man (he did not even have a business card) is Norman Lear. Agreeing that our first interview was too short, he could have held our second meeting in his office, but instead, he invited me to breakfast at his home.

Escorting me down a glass hallway lined with numerous sculptures, he revealed it was part of his growth to try to be more understanding of the modern artist's intent. We entered an enormous viewing room where, I imagined, his colleagues must gather to preview his video creations.

It has been estimated that more than 120 million Americans—over half the nation's population—watch Norman Lear's television shows. This remarkable man who, at age 30, was a successful television writer, shatters the myth that a formal college education is required to achieve success. Although he holds an honorary Doctorate of Humanities from Emerson College, he attended college for only one year. He left school to join the Army Air Force during World War II and, after his discharge, began working.

Because he is the originator of some of the most popular comedies on television, people think of Norman Lear as a very funny man. But his sense of comedy and fun are much akin to the ancient Greek concept of comedy growing out of tragedy.

Norman began his successful career at an early age. In keeping score of his parents' fights, he developed an acute sense of humor and caring. These two characteristics, which could easily have been thwarted under such violent and personally tragic circumstances, became two of Norman's most positive attributes. In his words:

> I grew up in a marriage—my mother's and father's marriage—which was, at the least, stormy. At the most, I was looking at two people who lived at the top of their lungs on the ragged ends of their nerves. In self-defense, I had to find the humor. In retrospect, this gave me an understanding of the humor in life.

He cited, as an example, the film he wrote and produced, "Divorce American Style." Recalling the scene when Dick Van Dyke and Debbie Reynolds were having a dish-throwing, shouting match, Lear said:

> The camera panned down to their kid, a boy about 12, who is sitting in the bedroom with a clip-board tallying up the score for the argument. That was me. I would sit at the kitchen table scoring my parents' arguments in full view of them. The male/female equation is something we all grow up with and it's a question of how much it touches us. I could not be untouched by it.

He continued:

> The understanding of our personal foolishness, or the understanding that in some way each of us is foolish, that we mortals are foolish, that is the essence of our sense of humor.

Lear's success in the television and movie industries was not a straight course. He tried a number of innovative ventures before finding his true calling. After his military discharge, he worked for a year at a New York publicity firm and then founded his own company to produce novelty ash trays. When that venture failed, he moved to Los Angeles, where he sold furniture door-to-door and worked as a sidewalk photographer specializing in baby pictures.

Norman began writing in his spare time with his cousin's husband, Ed Simmons. His first real success came when he began selling one-liners, comedy routines, and musical parodies to local comedians. They worked as a team, writing for such productions as the Martha Raye and Martin and Lewis comedy shows, before Lear moved on to writing and directing solo for the George Gobel show.

When the Gobel show left the air in 1959, Lear formed the partnership

Tandem Productions, Inc. to produce and package television specials. The company moved into the movie business with "Come Blow Your Horn," starring Frank Sinatra, in 1963.

Although he has won countless awards and is regarded as a winner by almost any standard, Lear said he is concerned about the emphasis society places on winning:

> We live in a time when, from what one reads in the printed media and sports or sees on film or on television, one would think there's nothing but winners. If you're not a winner, you're a loser. I think the instruction should be that all we need do is succeed at the level of doing one's best.
>
> The Emmy show gave me an opportunity to say whatever I wanted to say. There's only one brass ring, and only one person at a time can possibly grab the brass ring. The others have to be happy sitting on the carousel, reaching. So what do we want our kids to learn? It seems to me that's what we want them to understand . . . Somebody's going to get the brass ring, but for the rest of us, the joy is being on the carousel—and continuing to reach.

"Does this mean that your larger successes mean more as they come along, if you've acknowledged smaller achievements too?" I asked. Norman said that was true for him:

> Otherwise, there's no way of explaining why you read constantly about a man or a woman who seems to have everything that world deems as success—the home, the family, wealth, respectability in the community, etc.—and he jumps out of a window somewhere. You read that and think, how could that happen? It has to happen because we know about the brass rings the individual has been collecting, but we don't know about the thousands of minutes that person has not been enjoying. So where is life?

I asked Norman about his philosophy of life. What advice would he give young people? He said:

> Happiness is something you deliver to yourself; and the way you do it is exercising your vital abilities reaching for the brass ring, not necessarily achieving it, but enjoying the level at which you do achieve. That's so terribly important . . . to deliver, in my mind, a state of

> happiness to oneself. A man doesn't bring that to a woman; that is something we each do for ourselves.
>
> . . . I know so many people who spend so much time thinking about the past and saying, "Why did I miss that opportunity?" Conversely, I know people who spend so much time glorying in yesterday's success. All of that obviates the moment, which could be that moment of success.

Then, following his own advice about enjoying the moment, Lear paused to reflect on our own interaction during the interview:

> This is a good interview. I will leave here . . . and say to myself, "Terrific, Norman, you sat with Doris Lee McCoy and you got something from it and you gave something and it was good, and I will go away lifted by that. Success. I will think about it as an absolute success and it will have been at that time the first day of the rest of my life, and I will move with a sense of elevation as a result of it to the next one and try to make it another success. To be really there. That's something I learned from Jean Stapleton. More than anyone I know, that woman is always "where she is."

How did Norman Lear reach the point of being able to give himself credit just for being Norman Lear? "I don't think a lot about being," he replied, "but the essence of everything was there as a kid, I'm sure. You don't become suddenly something you never had a chance to be. You grow. You keep growing. I know it doesn't cease." He talked about how he has used art as a means to open his mind:

> I didn't know before I became involved in modern art, that I was one of those people who looked down at things I did not understand. I didn't know I was that kind of bigot.

"Like Archie Bunker?" I asked with a smile. Lear nodded and went on to say:

> If I didn't understand that man's art, I thought it was phony or fraudulent or that he was kidding the world until I got involved and learned something about it. I didn't realize that I was that narrow. I was stunned by that in my fifty-second year, and then I began to realize that man's art was very important and very serious to him. And if I listened hard

> enough and realized it was I who did not understand, there was something to learn there.

What was it that enabled Lear to broaden as a human being and opened the door as he grew older, rather than the opposite—which happens to many people as they age? His answer was, "Somebody once said, 'Each man is my superior in that I may learn from him.' And it applies to my own life."

Although a very busy man, Lear sees many people and entertains a multiplicity of tasks. How does he do it?

> The answer is in really thinking about how to collect one's thoughts. We . . . really know how to dislike ourselves. We do that so well. We do know how to be disappointed in ourselves if we're not out of the house on time and it does screw up the early part of the day; if you add one more tiny failure like that, the whole day begins to fall apart. People really are not anywhere near as good at taking bows for the little successes when they are successful. And how do you get to be where you are? You like yourself. You consciously say to yourself, "Good fellow, you said you were going to get up at eight and you did." Feel good about the contact with the newspaper boy. You made him laugh. He made you laugh. You caught a moment with a human being. You say to yourself, "That's terrific, good for you," and you collect those all the time.

To the question, "What would you say to men to help them accept women in positions of authority?" Lear replied:

> I would say how would you feel if you were standing on the beach and the radio was telling you a tidal wave was coming and then you started to see it loom on the horizon? Would you stand there and ask somebody to bring you an encyclopedia so that you could understand how tidal waves work, or would you run in the same direction as the wave so as to prevent yourself from being drowned?
>
> I think what's happened with women is happening in their hearts and in their souls. It isn't a movement so much as a ground swell and a tidal wave, and it will prevail. It will cover the world whether we choose it or not. I would not stand in its way for fear of drowning; run with it as fast as you can, *then* pick up the encyclopedia.
>
> It's going to be nice when men can drop all that macho nonsense. They

> don't have to be so strong that they can't confide weaknesses and failures, that they can't cry like women are able to cry. I know men are just as emotional as women. We've been encouraged to hurt ourselves by holding it in. It's no good being a prisoner. It's no good being the one who is holding the key. Who needs to be a saint?

Commenting on the relationship between the sexes today, Lear added:

> If there is a falling away in relations between men and women, it's temporary. By the time the ERA has passed—and I'm only using that as the tip of the iceberg—by the time both sexes accept their oneness and their equality, there will be real honesty. Men need liberation too; they are so trapped in all the macho bullshit. They are more fortunately trapped than women, but they are no less trapped.

He said that, unfortunately, men over 40 may never become aware of this unless they're "clubbed into it." Referring to Edith and Archie Bunker, TV characters Lear created, he said Archie may not have become more aware:

> . . . but Edith became more determined to proceed whether he was aware of it or not, and the audience—men and women both—cheered every time she did. You could almost follow the progress women made by looking at Edith Bunker over eight years; she no longer refused to follow her own instincts for Archie's sake. And sometimes he went along with her; and when he wouldn't, she didn't care but just marched on.

Does Lear believe the situation where the woman brings home the larger paycheck is threatening? He said it was difficult now because men still aren't used to it. But, he added:

> That's going to change and that's terrific. If the woman in the relationship just happens to be more needed in society or is in a field that pays better, the man can be relaxed and not be concerned about it . . .

I asked Norman to talk about what success meant to him. His answer indicated that his personal feeling of being successful was not always the same as the public's. "I was successful when I was 30 years old," he said, adding, "Nobody knew who I was." At that time, he was writing the Martin and Lewis television show with his partner Ed Simmons. He said that although the show was silly, whatever scene they were doing had real meaning for him:

It wasn't just a sketch. Jerry was everyman; the problems he would get into had social ramifications, as I saw them. Often they would leave the script and clown, and we had great results with the audience; but it caused me great pain because they had violated the intention of the sketch. Nobody in the world knew the intention but me, not because they weren't able to pick up on it, but because it probably had no place in a sketch for Dean Martin and Jerry Lewis—but I cared to say it.

I felt I was successful, but less successful when one of those scenes was violated, even though they were hugely successful with the audience. The next day the whole country was talking about what Dean Martin and Jerry Lewis did, and it made me a big hero on the level of writing. But in my gut, my writing, my idea had been violated.

It pained me deeply and the rest of it didn't matter. The money didn't matter. The accolades didn't matter. Good reviews didn't matter. The pain was that my work wasn't realized. Now it may not have deserved to be realized. That's not the important thing. My pleasure, my happiness, was more in the realization of my own effort. And my being pleased with it.

Lear likes the Greek definition of happiness: "Happiness is the exercise of your vital abilities along lines of excellence, in a life that affords them scope."

People today are seeking to find their identities. How does Lear think even those of middle age, who have lived along traditional lines thus far, reach out and get into the throes of life?

Success isn't one big thing. Success isn't "I just performed the such-and-such operation for the first time in the history of the world . . ." "I just got to the moon and was the first person there . . ." "I just produced the number-one television show . . ." "I just designed the award-winning car." Those things represent success for a handful. Everybody else is reaching in their own fashion in the exercise of their vital abilities.

Ninety-nine and 44/100 percent of everybody are not devising the new surgical operation, are not designing the car, are not becoming Senator or President or going to the moon. The rest of them must be involved in understanding that success is a collection of their minutes, the totality of their lives. It is no good even if one does become that doctor, devises the operation, if the minutes that preceded it were miserable. There's a candidate for a high window and a big fall. One's destiny follows one's efforts. To sit around and puzzle, "What is my destiny?" is to go slowly insane.

And what is Lear doing now? In 1985 Lear and his partner sold Tandem Productions and Embassy Communications, another joint venture they had formed, to the Coca-Cola Company. The reason Lear gave for selling the production companies was, "It was the right people with the right offer at the right time in my life. I am eager to get back to basics—to write and direct again—so I welcome the curtain going up on Act Three; Act Two was terrific."

With little hesitation Lear put his words into action. "Act III Communications, Inc." was the name he gave to the diversified communications and production companies he formed in 1986. Among other things, Act III owns theaters, a publishing company whose main publication is *Channels*, and a broadcasting company and four television stations. Norman Lear is still a busy man.

Lear's works have always carried a strong message along with plenty of laughs. He received the George Foster Peabody Award in 1977 for "establishing (with 'All in the Family') the right to express social comment in a social comedy, for devising the technique of humor as a bridge to better understanding of national issues, . . . and for providing the public with that greatest of all healers—humor." In 1982 he received the International Radio and Television Society's highest honor, the Gold Medal, for "his profound effect on a medium which has, itself, profoundly affected this nation."

His award-winning syndicated series, "The Baxters," emphasized the public's right to respond. He and Arthur Haley won a Pulitzer Prize for their television series, "Palmerstown." Many remember his two-hour television extravaganza, "I Love Liberty," which he wrote and produced to celebrate America's liberties. He created that special on behalf of People for the American Way, an organization he helped found with such community and religious leaders as the Rev. M. William Howard, the Honorable John Buchanan, the Honorable Barbara Jordan, and Dr. Martin E. Marty. He participates actively in human rights issues, serving on the boards of many civic organizations.

As an interviewer, one thing I appreciated about Lear is that when told he couldn't do something—probably because he was slightly ahead of his time—if he felt strongly about it, he had the guts to persevere and the ingenuity to take a route out of the ordinary to market it.

Norman is also bold in demonstrating his genuine concern and sensitivity toward others. Since "sensitivity" is culturally not viewed as a masculine trait, Norman exemplifies healthy androgyny. Sensitivity and a genuine positive regard for others only occurs in people who value and love themselves. Norman could be so candid about the failings and frustrations of Edith and Archie Bunker because he knows what being in their home felt like. He accepts his own human weaknesses, too, and likes himself in spite of his failures.

Norman invests himself in each moment, reaping many successes each day. He loves his job but, most important, Norman Lear loves life.

"I always spent my summers on my grandparents' cattle ranch when I was growing up. I would work for my grandfather. He had a great deal of influence on me. He had the rare ability of making a kid feel like a man."

ROBERT MAGNESS

Chairman of the Board, Tele-Communications, Inc., the Largest Cable Television Corporation in the U.S.

Born 1924, Oklahoma. Attended Oklahoma University. Graduated Southwestern State College in Oklahoma. Owner, Limousin cattle and Arabian horse ranches. Owner, real estate and cable communications businesses.

I first met Bob at the Annual Arabian Horse Sale in Scottsdale, Arizona. I had asked an Arabian horse breeder who the leaders in the field were. Among others, she pointed out cable television magnate Bob Magness and his two sons, who help him run his 3,000-head cattle ranch and horse empires. Although the number of horses varies, he averages about 350 Arabians and their fillies.

Our interview took place when we met again at the National Arabian Horse Show in Albuquerque, New Mexico. In his typical style of doing business wherever he is, he arranged for us to meet, not in a plush office, but in a small, unused storage area behind the convention booths at the State Fair grounds. I proceeded to ask him questions as we sat on two chairs, surrounded by walls of cardboard boxes.

I asked him to sum up his business philosophy. What approach did he take in creating the largest cable television corporation in the nation? "If you don't have a deal that is good for both parties when you start, then you're dealing with the wrong people," he replied. "I make lots of deals and I make them so they come out good for both sides. That's the only kind of deal I make."

He credits Anderson/Clayson, where he worked for nine years after college, with instilling in him some of his business principles. In fact, he says, "I learned more working for them in nine years than I did in college." As the world's largest cotton company, they trained him extensively for his job of buying cottonseed. Through what he was taught and what he observed there, he picked up much of the technique that enabled him to acquire over 800 television stations when he later started his own company.

But it is from his parents and grandparents that Magness feels he acquired the basic traits that have made him successful in so many areas today. He said:

> I think there are always people that have an influence on our beliefs and our conduct. I had a very fine mother and father. My mother is still living and she is a wonderful lady. She's 83 and still has a horse and saddle.

His father worked as a warehouse foreman in the wholesale grocery business. Bob didn't see him much during the week because of his long work hours, but his father was a role model in terms of hard work and his belief in treating people fairly and honestly.

From his grandparents, he acquired not only his love of horses, but a number of attitudes toward life. Bob reflected:

> I always spent my summers on my grandparents' cattle ranch when I was growing up. I would work for my grandfather. He had a great deal of influence on me. He had the rare ability of making a kid feel like a man . . . He had me qualified to ride with the cowboys when I was probably 10 or 11 years old . . .
>
> That was a real nice time in my life and it had a big bearing on me. Since then, I've influenced a lot of people that I've trained. I think we have certain experiences in life that formulate our attitudes and our principles. I got a little publicity a few years ago about being a hard trader. But I tell our people when they make deals to be *firm but fair*. Let's be fair and let's leave enough on the table for both sides. I think that's been the big principle in our company.

I asked Bob if the church had any influence on his life. He replied:

> I'm very religious. I believe in God. I don't attend church today, but when I get in trouble, I'm not too proud to call for help, and I usually get it. I also don't ask for things that I shouldn't really have. I think church is important, but I believe God is more important.

Bob told me how he got started in the cable television business. It was at a time when technology was causing the cotton company where he was working to close down mills and lay off people. He felt that it was time to make some kind of a change.

> My wife and I went shopping one day and I saw a sports coat that I fell in love with, but it had an unheard of price. It was about half a month's wages. I bought another coat instead, but I can still remember that other coat I liked so much. It became apparent that working for that corporation wasn't going to give me the standard of living I wanted. And so I started looking for things I wanted to dabble in elsewhere where I could make money.
>
> Television was around at that time. It started in the late forties . . . This was a new field, which most people didn't understand. I didn't even have a television set because there wasn't any reception in the little town where I lived.

Television intrigued him—not just the financial opportunity, but the idea that people were building new systems, making new deals. In order to find out more about it, he had lunch with two men involved with television and asked a lot of questions. He decided he could put the deals together himself in his own home town:

> I put up a tall tower and did what I think was the first helicopter survey signal to see what reception we might be able to get. I shared the idea with a few other people and we decided we were going to build it. So we took everything we had—I had some cows which I sold. And we got in business with very little money.

He laid the first system in the Texas Panhandle in 1956, and thus began a cable television empire. Bob looks back on those first few years fondly, saying they were a lot of work, but a lot of fun. "Most of it is still fun," he added. "It's always fun when you win."

Bob's positive attitude and high energy kept surfacing during our interview. I asked him: "What do you do when the going gets tough—when you're afraid things aren't going to work out?" He replied:

> I never worry that I'm not going to make it because I know I'm going to figure out how. I never fear, because if you're willing to put the time in it, you can make it work somehow. I'm up very early in the morning. I sleep less than most people. I sleep a little more now but for 20 years I slept 4½ or 5 hours.

I asked what he thought made his company so successful. What made it different from other companies? He said:

> I think the big difference is I can delegate. We've got good people, and I let them develop. I don't mess around making changes unless it's a deal I'm personally working on. I've had to bite my tongue several times to keep from saying, "Look guys, I already did that and it didn't work." I let them go through some of their own mistakes.

I was surprised that he knowingly allowed mistakes to occur and asked him about it. He answered:

> Just the small ones. You have to find a diplomatic way to not let the big ones occur. Our team is out doing three big deals at a time sometimes. You can't be everywhere. Besides, I'm getting older and I don't want to do all those things.

Bob's confidence in his company was put to the test at about the time of our interview. It was in October of 1987—just days after the stock market's greatest crash since the Great Depression. Rather than taking a negative, fear-driven approach to the fact that his company's stock prices were down, he took advantage of the situation and expressed confidence in his company by buying large quantities of the stock.

> I was able to buy back a very substantial portion of our company out of the market at what I considered a very good price. We have a good company. There is a great team of people running it. We have a cash flow that is extremely predictable and assets—value underneath it. I couldn't find any place to expand better than buying our own stock back. So I sat there and bought stock all week and spent many millions. And I'll be there Monday morning, and if they still have stock for sale at these prices, I'll be buying some more.

I asked him if he made his decisions quickly, intuitively. He replied:

> I make decisions as soon as they need to be made. I don't always announce the decision until it needs to be announced. I think any time there are decisions to be made you should keep gathering information as long as you can before the decision needs to be made. I can make a multi-million dollar decision in 30 seconds, but I don't make it unless I know the facts. If I have the facts, it takes no time to make the decision.

Bob is very close to his two sons, both of whom work with him on his ranches. His son Kim sums up his father's success formula succinctly:

He uses the same system in his real estate and cattle dealings as he does with the TV business. He feels that people are his greatest asset. He surrounds himself with supportive, bright people, and he loves to delegate.

The mutual respect that he and his sons share was evident in Bob's answer to my last question: "You're in your early 60s, Bob, and you've done so much. What do you think your next big challenge will be?"

> I still enjoy working. And I enjoy working with the people I meet in the Arabian horse business. I enjoy going to the office. If I didn't, I probably wouldn't go as often.
>
> But my big challenge right now is helping both of my sons get into what they want to do for the rest of their lives. One of them works in cattle. The other is helping with the horses and he likes it but it may not be what he wants to do all his life.
>
> I want to allow them not to just follow me, but help them get on their own path. I'm more happy about being able to help them have the financial structure to do that than I would be to leave them all the money they can spend—because this will make them men, and I'm very proud of them.

And so he passes on the heritage that he received from his parents and grandparents, not just financially, but as a role model, an inspirer, a builder of men. With his philosophy of delegating, and his energetic, positive style, he encourages the growth and advancement of all those around him—and in the process, multiplies his own success.

Three weeks before her death, at age 101, Maria was autographing books at a bookstore in Albuquerque, New Mexico.

MARIA MARTINEZ

Internationally known Native American Indian Potter

Born 1881. Died 1983. Aroused interest in traditional methods of pueblo pottery-making among Indians. Successful entrepreneur; brought prosperity to Indian villages. For 60 years head of San Ildefonso Pueblo Women's Council. A spiritual leader for her community.

At one hundred years of age Maria Martinez sat like a queen in her buckskin shoes, red print calico dress with the traditional overdress, and squash blossom turquoise around her neck. I met her while she was demonstrating an ancient Indian pottery technique at a summer art class sponsored by the University of Southern California in Idylwild, California. Her shiny black-on-black pots are found in major museums throughout the world.

Maria's permanent home was the San Ildefonso Pueblo, which is located 20 miles northwest of Santa Fe, New Mexico. She was first taught, around the age of eight, to make pots by her Aunt Nicolassa.

When she was just a young woman, an archaeologist sought out the best Indian potter to see if she could discover the ancient method used by the early Pueblo potters. Maria was chosen. The archaeologist gave Maria a shard taken from a digging on the site of an ancient Pueblo village on the Pajarito Plateau. Maria, with her husband Julian, experimented with various ways of making the pottery.

Finally, they settled on a method that seemed to reproduce the ancient style. The pots were not fired in a brick oven, as is the customary manner, but in an open fire kiln on the ground. Maria formed the pots using the coil method. As was usual for the Indian men, Julian then painted the design. The pots were then stacked on a screen grate and covered with cedar chips and cow dung and the fire was lit. The firing process took a couple of hours, followed by a period of waiting for the pots to cool. The finished pots were then removed.

Later, Maria's son, Popove Da, took on the responsibility, and a grandson, Tony, continued the tradition.

Although Maria held tightly to the ancient ways, she broke customary patterns occasionally, when it seemed most beneficial to all. She was ostracized at times for her deviations, but the criticism and resulting isolation did not stop her.

One tradition she deviated from came after she and her husband discovered the method for producing black-on-black pottery. A number of pueblo women asked Maria to share the Martinez secret. It was against custom to do so, since only the family was to receive the benefits of such a successful discovery. But Maria shared their techniques with other pueblo tribal women because she wanted everyone to gain from her good fortune.

Maria's commitment to passing on her Pueblo heritage is demonstrated by her 60 year headship of the San Ildefonso Indian Women's Council. The Council is an organization responsible for regulating everyday conduct in the San Ildefonso tradition.

Maria was invited to the White House on four occasions, and held honorary degrees from several colleges. She won the American Ceramic Society award and the Charles Binns Award. Upon receiving this acclaim, she spoke in her Pueblo dialect and her son translated to the audience. Maria could not accept the award for herself, but would do so only in honor of the large group of Indian women potters who also practice this craft.

Maria knew some of the unique difficulties and hardships which many of her Indian contemporaries shared. She lost several of her babies to disease. There were seasons of little rain to nourish the crops when many went hungry, day after day. And perhaps most devastating was Julian's slow death, due to alcoholism.

In each of these hardships, Maria found a deeper compassion for others and a greater strength within herself. She offered her earnings or pottery techniques to pueblo families hit hard by the lack of rain. Many would not accept her help, which was a painful rejection to her. To those that would, she became a consultant in business matters and craft techniques, as well.

As far as alcohol was concerned, she aided authorities in their attempt to eradicate liquor sales to Indians and, at one point, spent all her earnings buying the house of a Spanish pueblo dweller who was illegally selling liquor to Indian men.

Maria loved her pueblo home, but since the excitement and stimulation of travel helped Julian abstain from alcohol, she lived many months away from her extended family and friends. They demonstrated their black-on-black pottery techniques at World Fairs and toured other cities throughout the United States as well. Maria's separations from her spiritual and physical homeland were of benefit to her husband, brought greater prosperity to her village, and aroused national interest in southwestern Indian art.

Maria's outward expression of caring and service complemented a very deep spirituality. Maria participated in the dances and rituals of her pueblo and strongly encouraged others to do the same. She also respected the rites of Catholicism and made a pilgrimage when she was very young, after recovering from a life-threatening illness.

Devotion and discipline were one and the same for Maria, not only in a religious sense, but in her business as well. Maria loved her work, but it also cost her a lot. The pottery could be made only after the household duties and the children were taken care of. Julian and Maria worked all day and then practiced their craft in the evenings. This regimen was necessary for their business to prosper and expand.

Maria enjoyed the business, though. From an early age she had learned to be a discriminating trader and she liked the challenge of making a good deal. She was the financial planner and investor for her family. She saved her money and spent it carefully. Maria was the stable element in her partnership with her husband, artistically as well as financially. She formed the pots; Julian was the designer and innovator. Together they made a powerful team.

Maria mentioned in our conversation that she had always truly liked people. It was very evident by her friendly give-and-take conversations with the participants at the summer arts camp in Idylwild. Some of the women seemed to feel a close kinship with Maria and approached her as though they were receiving her blessing.

Maria, at age 100, was a most lively woman whose sparkling eyes reflected her enthusiasm for life, in spite of her need to use a cane as she completed her daily tasks. Maria was one of the greatest ladies I have ever met. In her presence, I had an immediate, intuitive awareness of this quality. She emanated a sense of deep spiritual harmony with the earth and its people. She was extremely wise and one could sense it by her animated, alive eyes. She was an understanding woman who truly cared about her fellow human beings.

In my interview, I asked Susan Peterson, author of Maria's biography, "Why did Maria live so long?" "Probably because she was not finished with her task," she replied.

Maria Martinez accomplished much in her long and full life. She brought increased prosperity and interest to her pueblo, which was losing rather than gaining membership. She helped her village appreciate its traditions and pass them on to future generations. Maria's inner strength enabled her to weather hardships and respond lovingly in the midst of them.

Maria worked very hard at her craft. Her love for her art and her desire to produce high quality pueblo pottery can best be seen in the finished products themselves. Her pieces are classics, skillfully made by an ancient method, simple yet elegant. Her pieces are found in the major museums of the world representative of Native American pottery.

The crafts express the craftswoman quite well: simplicity and elegance. Maria led a full, productive life. Three weeks before her death, at age 101, she was autographing books at a book store in Albuquerque, New Mexico.

"If I have a project that I have to complete or a goal related to my career, there is nothing in my social life that comes first. I think that is most natural to men. They're programmed that way. I'm not saying one is better than the other; they're just different. But it certainly creates much less conflict for individuals who are clear about their priorities."

JEWELL JACKSON MC CABE

Founder and President, National Coalition of 100 Black Women.
President, Jewell Jackson McCabe Associates consulting firm.

Born 1945, Washington, D.C. Graduate, Bard College, New York, School of Dance. Former Director of Government and Community Affairs Department for WNET/Channel 13 in New York. Gubernatorial appointee to New York State Council on Fiscal and Economic Priorities. Chair, New York State's Job Training Partnership Council. Serves on 12 boards, including National Urban Coalition and Planned Parenthood of New York, National Alliance of Business, and Economic Club of New York. Advises accounts such as Seagram's, American Express, and Pepsi Cola.

Jewell Jackson McCabe has so many different job descriptions that it is difficult to put a label on her. As *Fortune* magazine put it, "Once an avid dancer, McCabe now gets her exercise holding down three jobs." [30] Any one of the three jobs would seem more than full-time to most. But Jewell is a quick-thinking, energetic, decisive woman whose far-reaching ideas roll off her tongue, and suddenly things start happening—big things. She is often called a publicist and a lobbyist, but "People Broker" is the title this articulate woman gives herself.

Jewell is president of the National Coalition of 100 Black Women (with a current membership of some 6,000), an advocacy group she founded in 1981 to help black women gain political and economic power. She was appointed by Governor Mario Cuomo to chair New York's Job Training Partnership Council, a $208 million project which trains approximately 50,000 disadvantaged employees. In her latest venture, Jewell Jackson McCabe Associates, she gives advice to such companies as American Express, Pepsi Cola, and Phillip Morris on employee relations activities, government relations, and selling to minorities and women.

Jewell explained how she uses her skills as a "people broker" in all of these roles:

> I have this unbelievable address book with which I can identify and call men and women at every level of society. I can broker and resolve problems. I can broker relationships. I make deals happen. I can organize around important issues those people who can make a difference. That skill is very much needed today.

Jewell said she acquired her ambition early in life:

> I have always had a drive and determination. I came from a very loving family that gave me a sense of self-confidence. I have an exceedingly high energy level and have been ambitious since I was three years old. At that time the ambition was driven by wanting to be a dancer. I was in dance class at three years old—by my own choice.

That determination took her to the High School of Performing Arts in New York, where she practiced dance a total of six hours a day, and then on to Bard College, where she majored in dance. She compared the training required of a dancer to that of a football player:

> You can aspire to be the quarterback or to be the lead dancer; but you may be the lead dancer in one piece and the next piece you're part of the corps. So you have to learn team work or corps work and then when the time calls for it, you have to become a leader. The uniform or costume has nothing to do, necessarily, with one's character, but it certainly has to do with what image one is projecting.

After college, she traded in her dance costumes for business suits, but she believes the drive and discipline required of a dancer are what enable her to take on the myriad responsibilities she has today:

> If I have a project that I have to complete or a goal related to my career, there is nothing in my social life that comes first. I think that is natural to men. They're programmed that way. I'm not saying one is better than the other; they're just different. But it certainly creates much less conflict for individuals who are clear about their priorities. Prioritize your career if that's what is most important to you.

Jewell's father, "Hal" Jackson, was the first black radio broadcaster in the country. In the early 50s, he hosted a Sunday morning television program called "Frontiers of Faith," which spotlighted the humanitarian and spiritual activities of individuals from wide-ranging backgrounds. Jewell said both her father and mother were models for her in exhibiting a sense of responsibility to give something back to the community. Of her religious faith she said:

> I think that every black American who is southern-rooted, as I am, has basic Protestant beliefs that were probably stronger than those of our white counterparts, because religion was such an important part of our spiritual upbringing to give us a sense of self and a sense of determination.

I asked what other characteristics were helpful to her today that she acquired early in life:

> There is a trait I was keenly aware of from the time I was a teenager which I think is just as apropos today. I have an insatiable desire to be a part of the game or a part of what is really happening, in any form. It can be very taxing, because it is hard to "dance on every set." Yet I tend to be driven to at least understand how different sectors operate, how decisions are made, and how institutions function. I'm obsessed with a hunger for that kind of information.

Jewell said she thrives on tackling new projects which challenge and expand her skills. "I reject being pigeonholed or boxed into any category," she told an interviewer for *Ebony* magazine. "If you reject that, then you've got to be able to move in different sets . . . That means you've got to work hard because you've got to know a lot about a lot of things . . . I believe you have to shoot for the moon to get halfway there." [31]

Her life has been a rich tapestry, woven together by several common threads. Although her previous positions have been varied, they were all service-oriented. She has been Director of the Government and Community Affairs Department for radio station WNET in New York, Director of Public Affairs for the New York Urban Coalition, and Director of Public Information in the Office of the Governor. As a consultant to the Commonwealth Fund, she worked with issues related to women, children, and family, focusing especially on youth unemployment. In her personal life, she has been marrried twice, for a total of 18 years, and has no children.

Another thread that connects many of Jewell's endeavors is her deep drive to provide more opportunity for minorities and blacks. In her position as chair of the Job Training Partnership Council, she works with disadvantaged, displaced employees. The emphasis of her Coalition of 100 Black Women, however, is on leaders, women who are ambitious and high achievers. Acknowledging that there has been an unbelievable burst of access for blacks in the various professions, and for black women in particular, she said the focus of the Coalition is developing leaders by finding, showcasing, and networking talented women:

> We provide a linkage of leadership that brings together role models and makes a public statement by the bonding of achieved women. When the average person talks about blacks in American society, they don't think about the best or highest of our achievements. They tend to get an image of the downtrodden and the under-class. It is important for black women to continue to carry a positive image and achieve in every aspect, whether it be science and medicine, arts and culture, the entertainment community, academia, whatever.

She said that although there are many more leadership opportunities for minorities and women today, the individuals filling them feel very isolated. One of her aims is to remove that sense of isolation. She talked about the need to involve blacks more fully in decision-making at national and international levels:

> We are clearly and keenly aware of the need for a revised trade policy, for example, including small business and connecting with third world countries. We certainly have an ability to communicate with the two-thirds of this world that are black, brown, and yellow. Increasingly, Americans are going to have to look to us as part of their team of ambassadors to ensure America's sense of world peace.

Jewell also serves on the board of the National Alliance of Business. I asked her what she believed her unique contribution to that organization was. She said it was the skills she had acquired as a careerist, publicist, and lobbyist through the experience of having been a black woman for the past 42 years, many of which were spent in community service. She added:

> If you could break leadership into three categories: 1) resource leader, 2) institution leader, and 3) mass leader, I have moved within those three categories. I think that I bring a sensitivity about

> minorities and women and a global ability to communicate and to organize, which is so often lacking in many groups.

Jewell told me that she is very energetic and requires little sleep. In fact, she says, "If I sleep eight hours I can hardly function the next day. I'm a four-hour to six-hour sleeper. And," she added with a laugh, "I wake up speaking paragraphs."

She rises between 5:30 and 6:00 every morning, and the first thing she does is her exercise regimen. When she found herself getting out of shape (by no one's standards but those of a disciplined dancer accustomed to having a trim, taut body), she began looking for an exercise program. She tried attending a regular dance class and going to a health club but found that working out in her own home every morning with videotapes is most effective for her. She alternates among three: Jane Fonda's basic workout, a low impact aerobics tape, and a new one, which she likes best, "Callanetics." She said:

> After I turned 40, the only way I can stay in charge of my physical self is relating to my own vanity. So I live in one of those all-in-one leotards. Whenever I pass a mirror, I'm conscious of the way I look. It's my way of putting a picture on the refrigerator.

When I asked Jewell what she does for relaxation, she replied:

> This is always a hard question. When I was a little girl, my mother told me that she wanted me to have hobbies because she thought I was too obsessed with dancing. And so I would learn how to knit and make a coat in a month and then put that aside. And then she'd say six months later, "Don't you think you need to have a hobby?" So I learned how to play tennis and I beat everybody. Then I stopped that. I've stopped trying to learn how to relax.

Jewell doesn't move at anything less than full speed. She said she doesn't take long vacations but will take a few days off if she is really exhausted. I asked how she managed to keep her "batteries charged" while going at such a pace. She thought for awhile and then said:

> I guess I am a person who relaxes with diversification of projects. So right now I'm working on a Michael Jackson concert, for example, to raise money for the United Negro College Fund. I'll design the room. We're going to do it at the Rainbow Room in New York City. I'll do

> the flowers and the invitations and the negotiations. I get my relaxation or enjoyment, I guess, through diversification—going from one major different project to another.

Another program she works on is helping her father produce a television talent competition with teenage minority girls. "So I go and change my business clothes into stretch pants and Reeboks and hit the production trail." Jewell said she also finds diversification in the types of people with whom she works:

> I am entrenched in political involvement and government people. On the other hand, I'm entrenched in a world of high rollers in the private sector with a totally different style, a totally different mission. And of course, I work with the minority community and women.

And what is next for Jewell? She says she won't be satisfied until she sees further progress in educating people to the full scope minorities and black women posess. "Right now I am still organizing the National Coalition of 100 Black Women, and I'm not going to be happy until I'm in 100 cities."

Jewell said she wants people to be aware of the achievements of black women, women such as Suzanne DePass, who headed up Motown Productions, or Shirley Ann Jackson, the first black woman to receive her Ph.D. in Physics from MIT. But she still sees the great challenge of improving the situation for the one-third of the black population who are in poverty, 70 percent of which are female heads of household. She is especially concerned with minority children who are increasingly poor and illiterate.

Who knows what project will be next?

"We had a house filled with books. My father and mother were avid readers. If you weren't working out on the ranch you were reading, and that was the kind of existence I had as a child."

SANDRA DAY O'CONNOR

First Woman Supreme Court Justice in United States History

Born 1930, El Paso, Texas. B.A. and L.L.B. Stanford University. Admitted to the California bar, 1952; Arizona bar, 1957; Arizona Senate, 1969-74; Judge Superior Court, Maricopa County, Arizona, 1974-79; United States Supreme Court Justice, 1981.

It was 7:45 on a bright hot Monday morning in Phoenix, Arizona at an exercise class at the Arizona Biltmore Hotel. The petite gym instructor was directing the women. "Pull to the right and stretch . . ." One of their "regulars" was Judge Sandra O'Connor, shortly after her nomination as the first Woman Supreme Court Justice in the history of the U.S. Supreme Court. "Sandy," as she is known by her friends, started her workday off five days a week with this class.

She was given many kind wishes of support and praise by her admiring class members. The instructor, not interrupting her instructions to the class, pointed out a bulge in the back of Sandra's leotards. Without missing a beat, Judge Sandra pulled out the black bulging object, looked at it, and said, "I wondered what happened to John's other sock when I took the clothes out of the dryer." She laid the sock on her exercise mat and continued working her muscles. Judge Sandra O'Connor will take whatever comes her way—in stride.

Sandra O'Connor had granted me an interview after I reached her at her legal chambers in the Phoenix Court House. "I've turned down all other interviews," she said, and went on to list ". . . TIME, LIFE, etc. I have a tight schedule." I offered to pick her up at her house and drive her to work. "Yes," she said, "that might be the only time I have free."

A few days later, I called from the airport. Judge O'Connor asked, "Why don't you meet me at 7:45 Monday morning at the Arizona Biltmore Hotel women's gym class?"

Judge O'Connor is very efficient in organizing her schedule, and she asked if I minded stopping afterwards at a gasoline station with her as she had to get the oil changed in her car. Would it be possible to continue the interview in the waiting room of the station while the car was being serviced? she inquired.

This was the first time I had gone to an exercise class and waited at a gasoline station to get an interview. But it's her style to make each moment count. Where did this pattern start? What was in her childhood that helped her be so efficient now?

Sandra's mother, Ada Mae Wilkey Day, who lived on a remote ranch in Duncan, in eastern Arizona, went to her mother's home in El Paso, Texas to wait for the birth of her first child. She did this to gain the convenience of a modern hospital. The Texans may claim her birth on March 26, 1930, but Arizonans claim her early days of growing up on a very inaccessible ranch, the 162,000 acre "Lazy B." As the oldest of three children in the pioneer ranching family of Harry A. and Ada Mae Wilkey Day, Sandra learned self-reliance early.

Self-reliance is a keystone of the O'Connor family. Asked about what she gleaned from that early period of her childhood, she answered:

> Obviously, the heritage that you get from living out on a ranch in a remote area is a sense of self-reliance, because to operate the ranch in an area like that you have to solve all the problems yourself. You can't call in an electrician or an auto mechanic or a windmill mechanic or a ditch digger or a veterinarian—so you do those things yourself. My father has had to be all those things all his life, and as a result, he knows more about more things than most people ever do.

She went on to comment about her daily schedule:

> We had a house filled with books. My father and mother were avid readers. If you weren't working out on the ranch, you were reading, and that was the kind of existence I had as a child. I think it's not a bad existence.

In her own family experience of raising three boys, she added:

> My own children have not experienced self-reliance to the same degree. I hope that they learned a little of that when they were on the ranch. I think what our boys have learned, though, because I've been working,

> as has my husband, John, during most of their growing up period, is to be pretty good managers.

She spoke of being alone in those early days on the ranch. Most women have not had to experience so much separation from society. She seemed to have appreciated it or to have grown emotionally from that period. "I'm sure that I did. I had a lot of time alone as a child that I certainly haven't had as an adult," O'Connor said.

In thinking about today's women and the necessity for more of them to work outside the home to maintain a certain standard of living, the conversation focused on Sandra's having both a career and a family life. I asked how she was able to manage that. "I've been blessed with a high energy level," was her answer. She elaborated:

> It isn't easy—you can't have any quiet periods or rest periods. It's a constant activity of one form or another and you have to have a lot of energy to do that. I can never recall just sitting down with my feet up and relaxing—that's not been part of my life. No, I don't eat chocolates on the couch.

She went on to say that she had to be quite efficient in scheduling her time in both her professional life and her home life. "You have to do things quickly in as little time as possible. If you're cooking, you have to learn techniques of preparing foods that don't take very long." Since she has always worked outside the home, Sandra said she has relied on domestic help over the years:

> I had outside help, particularly before the children started to school. I was desperately in need of help—whether it was babysitters or other help. It was simply required. As they have gotten older, I've been able to manage without that.

Sandra's nickname, Sandy, is very appropriate because of her gray wavy hair set in a soft pageboy style and outlining her pleasant, assured face. She wore a plain navy blouse and beige skirt. When she was first made judge, her husband of 29 years, John Jay O'Connor III, humorously commented to the press, "Being on the bench will cut down on her clothing bill."

Sandra stands straight and is relatively lean. In her 50s, she has kept in shape and looks healthy. Her somewhat slow and deliberate way of talking leads one to believe that she weighs her words well and with thought. This is a trait that is valuable in her position on the Supreme Court. Sandra talked about how she was able to keep in touch with her family as a mother, while maintaining her demanding professional schedule:

> Children normally get up early, so you have time with them before you go to work and then you pick up where you left off as soon as you get home. In the summertime, when the children were small, was the most difficult period because they weren't in school. Since I was working, that meant they had a lot of time on their hands. In order to make that time more productive for them, I specifically tried to hire some attractive teenagers—more often male than female because we had three little boys—and I would get some teenage boy who would take them out to engage in a lot of sports activities.
>
> The boys spent some time on my family's ranch during vacation periods. My brother, who now manages the Lazy B, has given each of the boys jobs when they wanted them. That's been a real lifesaver through the years to have them get to know their grandparents and to be part of the ranch.

The conversation led to activities the family did as a group. She said they particularly enjoy doing things outdoors together:

> We've taken a lot of camping trips, hiking with them for several days at a time. We like to ski together, play tennis, and golf. We've all enjoyed pretty much the same activities and it's been fun.

Sandra had used "we" so often, obviously she was referring to her husband. It seemed as though they both were responsible for raising their children. "Yes, we both have been involved to the same degree in spending time with them," she said when asked.

"It sounds like he's been very supportive of your career," I commented:

> He's been fabulous—I just can't imagine anyone who would have been more supportive and better able to handle what has to have been a burden to him at times in view of my career. We just continue to have a wonderful time together. He has enjoyed the things that I have done as I have enjoyed what he has done.

The next question was: When you did choose your husband, was it because you believed he would be a cooperative person? Sandra replied:

> I don't recall if we ever put it into concrete terms. We met in law school as students. We were assigned to do a problem together for the law review, so we first became acquainted in a working setting. It never occurred to either of us that I wouldn't be working for a large part of my life. I think we have always assumed that would be the case. If you marry with the expectation that both spouses are going to be in the work force, then it's probably easier all the way around when that occurs.

I asked what she thought were the most important values she had stressed with her children:

> Obviously, it's crucial that they develop a strong set of sound moral values. That is what is really important, that they develop into decent, honorable citizens who know right from wrong and who want to be of service to others.

A significant factor, in her opinion, was the education her children had. Her three boys attended a Jesuit Prep School in Phoenix. The priests and teachers, she said, "had such a keen interest in each boy—in the individual. They got wonderful training in service and in moral precepts and values there. You hope that that is greatly reinforced by what you do and are at home."

I asked if religion was an important part of her life, and she replied, "I see service to God as being very much a part of service to one's fellow man and woman. My own personal experience has been largely one of trying to give service to others."

Sandra has held offices in a variety of civic groups. She's been president of the Phoenix Junior League, Vice President of the Community Council, and President of the Heard Museum. She also served on the Board of Trustees of Stanford University, the Salvation Army Advisory Board, and was a founder of Charter 100, a professional women's club.

"Judge O'Connor, your car is ready," said the mechanic, and off we went again down the freeway toward town. The interview continued on the road.

"What are your hopes for your family in the future?" I asked her. She said she hoped that they could have enough time to continue to share together and to enjoy each other. "That's a real concern because the work of the court is tremendously time-consuming," she continued.

She was parking the car now in the underground garage of the courthouse and we took the elevator up to her office. Her secretary,

Bernadine, greeted her at the door of her somewhat dark, book-filled office. Her interest in native American Art was reflected by a handsome Indian pot.

Standing in her office, we continued our conversation. I asked how she had adjusted to being in a male-dominated profession and now being the only woman on the Supreme Court. Surprisingly, she said she really didn't think that being a woman had made much of a difference:

> I have found that people have been very helpful and cordial to me throughout my career. I just have not found barriers. I have discovered that if I worked hard and did a job well, that I have been respected, whether it was by men or women. It's a source of tremendous delight to me to see the legal profession open in recent years to women as we see now. The law schools are running between 30 percent and 40 percent women. We are seeing more and more women lawyers in practice and in the courts as judges, and it's marvelous.

I asked her how she responds to the pressure she must feel at times. "By working harder," she said. "Solve the problem, whatever it is."

Those in political life are subject to public opinion and approval. I asked how she dealt with negative responses:

> Obviously, it's a concern to you if you're subject to criticism or there are substantial numbers of people who disagree, but I think the response is to re-examine whatever the issue is. Make sure that your own response is the appropriate one and simply become a little thick-skinned about it. Frankly, I have typically put out of my mind the things that seemed to me troublesome at the time. Make the decision that you have to make as best as you are able and don't look back. Certainly a judge has to do that a lot.

I asked what was most meaningful to her about being nominated to the Supreme Court, and she answered:

> The most moving part of the whole event has been the outpouring of joy and support that I have received from people from all over the country. I am so touched and so honored by their reaction. I truly believe that many have seen it as being, personally, very important to them.

She became philosophical at this point:

> We don't accomplish anything in this world alone—and whatever

> happens is the result of the whole tapestry of one's life and all of the weavings of individual threads from one to another that creates something. I've been so very much aware of the enormous tapestry that came together in making it possible for me to be nominated for this particular position. It's something that I can only pray that I can respond to by providing the kind of service to the court and the nation that will continue to cause people to have that kind of outpouring of pride and affection.

Later, in the Senate Judicial Committee hearings in July of 1981, O'Connor acknowledged this support. "As the first woman to be nominated as a Supreme Court Justice, I am particularly honored," she told the committee in her opening statement. "But I happily share the honor with millions of American women of yesterday and today whose abilities and conduct have given me this opportunity for service."

I took a few pictures of her at her desk and then she suggested her secretary call a cab. In her usual manner of finishing one task and moving on to the next, she said goodbye and turned her attention to the papers piled high on the desk.

"I push myself hard because I believe whatever talents you have been given, you have a responsibility. You're only a trustee for those talents, and you ought to use them as vigorously as you can to the betterment of society."

ANTHONY J.F. O'REILLY, Ph.D.

Chairman, President, and Chief Executive Officer, H.J. Heinz Company

Born 1936 in Dublin, Ireland. Graduated Belvedere College, at University College Dublin, and Incorporated Law Society of Ireland. Ph.D. in Agricultural Marketing, University of Bradford, Yorkshire, England. Rugby player for British and Irish teams. Formerly Managing Director of Irish Sugar Company and of Erin Foods Ltd. Currently: President and Chairman of the Board, H.J. Heinz Company, World Headquarters, Pittsburgh, PA. Board of Directors: Bankers Trust, Washington Post Company, and Harvard School of Business Administration.

Forbes magazine dubbed him "The King of Ketchup." [32] But ketchup is only one of the many food products he markets. Besides running the Heinz Company, he also owns one-third of Ireland's largest newspaper group, has an oil and gas exploration company, and has founded a "confederation" of organizations in countries around the world to help his Irish homeland.

As a child growing up in Pittsburgh, home of Heinz International, I saw the Heinz pickle everywhere—even wore a Heinz pickle pin to school on my cheerleader sweater. The Heinz 57 variety sign (because of the 57 varieties of food the company produced) was seen constantly. Today we have to refer to it as "Heinz 1,500 varieties" because that's the number of food items the company now produces in 15 countries and markets in 150 countries around the world.

As I approached the Heinz headquarters, I wondered what kind of a man Dr. Anthony O'Reilly would be. On meeting him I got an immediate feeling of his warm outgoing, positive personality. He asked me to call him "Tony," as he is called by everyone.

The first question I asked Tony was: What would you say came from your childhood that helps you function so well now? He replied without hesitation, "The unquestioning love from Mother and Father—and it was very focused because I was the only child."

Commenting on the fact that he and his wife have six children, I asked if he thought being an only child put him in a special position. He said yes, but it had its pluses and its minuses:

> Its pluses are the sort of invincible cocoon that you're in. Its minuses are that you do not learn as much about the arbitrage of life as in the normal course of a relationship between brothers and sisters. As a result you tend to be a lot more self-centered and I think a little more selfish—a little more expectant that the world will go your way. Also on Christmas day it's quite lonely.

It was Tony's athletic ability that helped him overcome any tendency toward self-centeredness. An international rugby star at the age of 18, he learned on the field to be a team man. "That was my salvation," he said, "that I was good at sports." He described that period of his life:

> By the time I was 15, I was sort of marked out as one of the people who were going to be lucky enough to have the gifts to become an international star. By the time I was 18 and probably 5 years ahead of my time, I was already the Irish equivalent of the All-American Heisman Trophy man. All of that happened in my 18th year. So there I was, just in my freshman year in college, on the national football team; I was on the Great Britain team, which was bigger than the Ireland, Scotland, and Wales teams; and I was touring South Africa, Rhodesia, and Kenya for seven months, playing with the best in the world before the largest crowds and getting all that applause—which is a real test, by the way. It's a litmus test because the crowds can easily turn against you, as they did with me.

He broke the world record in rugby on that trip, and on the next trip 5 years later to New Zealand and Australia, established a world record for touchdowns. Amazingly, those records still stand 30 years later. He called this period of his life a time of learning:

> Learning, first of all, about yourself and how to handle the good days and the bad days. The second thing was realizing, despite all these touchdowns and the adulation that went with them, that a hell of a lot of other guys—14 in all—had helped to get the ball to you. Without them you weren't going to get one touchdown. So I think it taught me a great deal about the frailty of fame and the interdependencies of life. I think football has been the great template of my life—a lot

> better than the Harvard Business School. If you don't train, you can't perform. You have to meet with triumph and disaster. In 80 minutes of rugby you mimic so many of life's situations.

I asked Tony why he gave up the fame of being an internationally known athlete to go into business. His response was:

> If you are a top sportsman in a game as violent as rugby, there are a number of cautionary ways in which the size of your head gets deflated. It's a game of great physical activity. You get broken up. I had a lot of physical injuries, a tremendous amount. I had shoulder trouble, broken noses, broken cheek bones, broken teeth. It's a very tough game.

Tony started his business career in Ireland where, as the youngest chief executive of a state company, he earned a reputation as the "whiz kid" of Irish dairy marketing. Later he took charge of a joint sugar venture with Heinz. From there he began running the firm's British operations and 10 years later was made Chief Executive of the entire company.

His Irish heritage is everywhere apparent: in the Irish accent of his articulate speech; in the photographs on his desk of his wife, three sons, and three daughters; in his charming, soft-spoken Irish secretary of over 30 years. I asked Tony if it was difficult for him to leave Ireland and move to America. He replied:

> Well I don't think I've ever left, that's the point. I mean I've come over to work in America, but I actually still live in Ireland. If you asked me where I live, I'd say I live in Ireland. My home, my principal home, is in Dublin. I work in the United States. And of course I own the largest newspaper group in Ireland. It's a group that's worth probably $170 million U.S. And I own over one third of it, so it's a very big piece of change—a big estate to have in Ireland. I also have a very large industrial holding company and an oil and gas exploration company. So I have three major corporate activities there, and I'm a partner in a law firm there, so 50 percent of my corporate life is still focused on Ireland.

With all of his business activities on both sides of the Atlantic and the various boards he serves on, such as Bankers Trust, Mobil Oil, Notre Dame, and the Washington Post Company, I asked him if he has time to relax. He admitted that he wasn't able to devote as much time as he would like to relaxation. An avid reader, he said most of his reading these days is confined to material that contributes to his "fiscal education." He said he is "trying to read" *The Decline and Fall of the Roman Empire,* along with *Tenants of Time* by Thomas Flanagan, but, he says, "I limp through these books instead of sprinting through them. It annoys me." He went on to say that his business involvement was at the sacrifice of other areas of his life:

> I think there's no debate that the corporate life that I lead imposes an enormous toll on my domestic life. It makes domestic living very much more difficult. I am essentially a "commercial itinerant."

Fortune magazine called his business style "stingy," a term that usually carries a negative connotation. In this case, however, it translates into a compliment. Although the company pays its employees a base salary that is lower than its peer companies, Heinz pays a very large long-term incentive package. The company is known for its efficiency in cost-cutting through consolidating its plants wherever possible and working with a surprisingly small, centralized management team. Tony commented on this style:

> I'm proud of the fact that we manage to combine a very frugal management style and fearless dedication, total dedication, to being the low-cost operator. I like to believe that we control that sort of frugality with quite an innovative, radical, sort of new product development program that produces in Weight Watchers dramatic new opportunities for our business.[33]

When Tony says he is "stingy about what we buy," he really means smart—such as paying $371 million *cash* for companies over a 10-year period that are now worth $1 billion. I asked Tony about his business approach which is sometimes called conservative: "Is this your conservative Irish background coming out?"

> I wouldn't say it's conservative. I suppose it's as much peasant cunning as anything else. I don't think it's conservatism, because in buying Weight Watchers, I took an enormous risk that it would somehow turn out to be ephemeral or a fad, and it's now a billion dollar business, making $100 million a year—and we bought it for $100 million. There are not many companies that actually earn in a year what you paid for them eight years earlier. So that was a home run for us.

I asked what his basis was for making decisions, such as acquiring Weight Watchers. Was it based on extensive research, analysis and advice from his vice presidents, or did he make the decisions intuitively, from his gut-level?

> I think in that particular case, it was intuitive. Looking at the demographics of the United States and at the trend, the human interspection, I decided that body watching and calorie counting were going to be the essential change element in the feeding industry, as well as in the wellness and health care industries in the late 80s and 90s. And so it has proved to be. Health care is a major, major business and growing fast, and of course all the other things to do with nutrition and calorie-counting and nutrition labeling have shown that this is a firm focus. The change that is coming about was hard to discern 10 years ago. We were lucky to discern it and lucky to get the vehicle. I suppose I should say we were lucky/clever.

Tony went on to talk about the success of their "fats and cats" strategy, referring to the company's acquisition of Weight Watchers and its expansion into the cat food industry.

> It's now really our "fats and pets" strategy. We're beginning to unveil a strategy in regard to pet feedings. Not just cats, but dogs as well that will catapult—and I guess dogapult—us into the number two position in the United States in pet food. We're going to be right up there. We're not going to be as big as Ralston Purina because they're very big in dry food. But we'll be the number one company in canned feedings in America. We'll be a $750 million business in pet feedings, which was only a by-product for us 10 years ago.

Heinz' expansion into the tuna market has also been a prosperous one. They acquired Star-Kist some years ago and recently bought Bumblebee, the third largest tuna business.

As part of their "Asian Rim Strategy," which previously involved marketing in Japan, Korea, and Thailand, they recently expanded to People's Republic of China selling—of all things—baby food! This could be considered something of a marketing coup in a country with an annual birthrate of 16 million! According to analyst John McMillin of Prudential-Bache Securities, Heinz has boosted its gross margins from 27 percent to 40 percent in the last 10 years. He credits the company's management for this, calling it the best in the industry. "It is no exaggeration to call it brilliant," he said in *Dun's Business Monthly*. [34]

The idea of selling baby food to the Chinese struck me as very innovative. I asked Tony where he got his creative ideas. He said:

> I sit in my bath. I think creative ideas are ideas that occur to you in the most improbable places: on the tennis court, at your desk, watching a television show. None of us fully understand . . . creativity is not a logical process. It's visceral; it's lateral; it's logical; it's illogical. It's a combination of all you've read, sensed, thought about, encountered, talked about. It's curious. The catalysts of creativity are hard to identify.

He said he does have a vivid imagination and that he is constantly challenging the status quo, constantly looking ahead for trends, constantly looking at the demographics and what their implications might be for his business. Referring to the higher population of older people in the United States, he said:

> What does the "graying of America" mean for us? Well, it means more pets. It also means probably more soft drinks. Does it mean more hard liquor or less hard liquor? What are the trends in some of the products that we have? What about the phenomenon of take-home? Is that going to enhance restaurant feedings? The answer is it will probably diminish them a little. Burger King's problems are partly because Domino's is taking part of the share that they previously got, and so on.

Tony said the microwave has had a tremendous impact on their product line, as have a number of other new trends, such as the popularity of the video recorder. "What's the implication of the VCR?" he asked. "More people will stay home and eat." And therefore, his logic ran, they'll be bringing home more bottles of ketchup, making it worth Heinz' effort to repackage the ketchup bottles and corner an even larger portion of the market for this 118-year old Heinz best-seller. Tony said he takes pride in the fact that Heinz never accepts such a thing as a "mature market," but is constantly looking for ways to further improve even their best-selling products, which are already successful: "We admire companies like Smucker's and Kellogg who stick to their knitting. We find them what we describe as hero companies, and we try to emulate them."

I asked Tony what other qualities about his company he was most proud of. He said:

> I'm most proud of the spirit of collegiality of the people. There is a

> very low threshold of politics. Secondly, I'm very pleased that all of the senior management, and a great deal of the mid-management and work force, believe they're owners of the Heinz Company. That's very important.

Important, yes. Easy to achieve? No. I asked Tony how he managed to do that. He told me they have a share ownership plan which encourages employees to buy shares by subsidizing their purchases:

> We put 50-cents for every dollar they put into the company share ownership plan, to the point where 14 percent of the company is now owned by the executives and the work force. And *Forbes* has it that my particular stake is worth $78 million. Whether it is or isn't, it's somewhere around there. We're not managers, we're owners of the company.

Knowing that Tony is on the board of directors for Notre Dame, I asked him about his religious beliefs. He said:

> I'm a believer, obviously, in the Judeo-Christian ethic. I'm strongly against authoritarianism in religion. I grew up in a Catholic church in Ireland which was authoritarian. The thing I like about the American Catholic church is that it is a participatory church. I like the sentiment of the American Catholic church, which I differentiate sharply from other churches around the world . . . So far as my basic beliefs spiritually are concerned, I am dedicated to the Judeo-Christian ethic at work and in terms of public morality in dealings with people and with our customers.
>
> Also in relation to Ireland, I am dedicated to healing the wounds, and I have founded the Ireland Fund of America, the Ireland Fund of Australia, the Ireland Fund of Canada, and last week the Ireland Fund of Great Britain, so now I have a confederation of concern all around the world for the Ireland fund.

"You're talking about newspapers in Ireland and ketchup in Pittsburgh and the Ireland Fund all around the world," I said. "How do you manage it all?" Tony replied:

> Probably expensively in the sense on the first of September last I decided

> that I'd look after myself a little better, I've probably taken lots of risks with myself by pushing myself too hard. But that's, I suppose, the way I'm built. So I decided to lose weight. I've lost 35 pounds.

"Through eating the Weight Watchers International dinners?" I asked. "Yes, all through the help of Weight Watchers," he replied. "And now, six months and 4,000 Chicken Imperial dinners later, I'm at the weight I was when I played football. But," he added with a smile, "the quality is not that good."

I asked Tony what gave him the motivation and the energy to fill his life so full with so many different activities. He said:

> I push myself hard because I believe whatever talents you have been given, you have a responsibility. You're only a trustee for those talents, and you ought to use them as vigorously as you can to the betterment of society.

"I have never looked back on an age and said I wanted to be back there. Every age—including the present—seems to be the best. I've had it all!"

RONALD REAGAN

Fortieth President of the United States

Born February 6, 1911, Tampico, Illinois. Captain, U.S. Air Force 1942-45. Sports announcer. TV and movie actor. President, Screen Actors Guild. Breeder and trainer of thoroughbred horses. Rancher. Governor of California 1967-74.

"I don't know what it would be like to wake up in the morning bored," said Ronald Reagan.

When I interviewed Ronald Reagan, he was Governor of California, and we were unaware that he was on his way to becoming President of the United States. He had just finished making a speech and took a short break to talk to me.

"What shall I call you?" I asked him, as we sat down together, "Governor or . . ."

"Most people call me Ron," he replied. And Ron it was for the duration of our talk. As we spoke together, I noticed that his voice was not the polished one used in public, but quiet, deep, and warm.

For Ronald Reagan, life has always been exciting. From the time he was just a boy, he said, "there were adventures to be found. I never saw a key to our front door. We'd take off to the river that ran through our town, down the river, out into the woods, out into the countryside."

I asked him to tell me about his childhood, and he replied:

> Well, we were poor. We lived in a small town in Illinois. I think the difference between then and today is that the government didn't keep coming around telling us we were poor, so we didn't know it. Also, my mother was always finding people who were poorer than we were and helping them.

"That must have helped you to develop a concern for others," I probed.

"Yes," Reagan said. "My mother would even go visit the jail and talk to the inmates. And, come Christmastime, she'd see that they had—"

"A hot dinner?" I added.

"Uh-huh."

"From your family?"

"Yes. And candy—and things like that."

Reagan talked quite a bit about his mother and the values he'd learned from her.

> My mother had a great faith. My father was Catholic; my mother was Protestant and, as so often happens in that situation, if we were to gather for religion, it was by way of our mother. She took us to Sunday school and to church. I know now that she imparted to me a faith that is very sustaining. It has been increasingly so throughout my life . . . I have a very deep-seated belief that if you ask for help, it will be given. I don't want to paint any picture here of fanaticism or anything of that kind. It was just that my mother was deeply faithful and a kind and generous person.

Reagan added that he did not know whether he had succeeded in implanting the same kind of faith in his own children, but that he wanted them to "have the knowledge that when all else fails and it seems like you're at the end of the line, there's Somebody you can turn to—put it in His hands."

As a teenager, Ron already took it for granted that he would have to use his own efforts to succeed:

> My parents had never gone to college, had never gone to high school for that matter. When time for college came along for my brother and me, my father explained to us that he'd try to help if he could, but that we'd have to work our way for most of it. I chose my own school, worked, had a job, played football, and so forth.
>
> Life was down to one simple predicament during those depression years. You wanted—I don't want to call it materialism—you wanted to earn money because you knew what it was like to be without it. And yet, at the same time I have to say that, from the very first, I knew what I wanted to do: enjoy what I was doing. And I think the bug that really took me to where I was to go was that when I got out of school I became a sports announcer. I found that exciting; I loved every part of it. Then,

when I found myself in Hollywood in a motion picture studio, well, that was my fairyland.

"During those Hollywood years, did you ever think about going into politics?" I queried. Reagan laughed and said:

When they came to me and talked to me about running for Governor, I thought they were out of their minds. I had no desire to leave the life that I had. I didn't see any way to do it. I said, "I'll help you elect someone else. I'll campaign for someone else you choose." It was never really planned. And a couple of years after it happened, Nancy and I looked at each other one night and said, "You know, this makes everything else we've done as dull as dishwater."

"You didn't anticipate that?" I asked.

No. It was so fulfilling. I mean when we agreed to run, once in there, coping with the problems instead of just making speeches about them—being able to do something about them was, I think, the most fulfilling thing of all. And I say "we" because it was Nancy and myself. It's always been *we* ran for Governor.

"You and Mrs. Reagan have a happy marriage, a happy home?" I asked, already knowing the answer from the look on the man's face. He said:

Approaching my front door, I start walking faster. I don't know whether I can put it into words or not. When I'm away, and no matter what happens, my mind translates whatever experiences I have into how I'm going to tell her about them. I once attempted an autobiography and I used a line that was not mine. I quoted it. Clark Gable had said it, as a matter of fact. Not in a picture. It was his own—and I think it describes it. "The greatest thing a man can have is to approach his own front door knowing that someone on the other side of the door is listening, waiting for the sound of his footsteps."

"It certainly sounds as if there is deep feeling between you two," I said. "Tell me, do you express this to each other?" Ron replied:

Nancy and I do it without planning. Not like saying to yourself, "I must say I love you." It's spontaneous. Once in a while, even just riding along in the car, one or the other or both of us will say "I love you."

> Nancy and I have often said that we're very fortunate that most of our circle of friends seem to be very happy, also. I think marriage is something you should work at, but it's pleasant work. It's wanting to please someone else. And I guess it's a sense of giving, not getting.

"You sound like a man who appreciates women," I said.

> Yes. I like women. I marvel at you women. The capacity, the capabilities you have. I think most men know down inside that if it weren't for women, men would still be carrying clubs.

I pointed to his public opposition to the ERA, and he explained:

> I don't think there's anything wrong with putting women on a pedestal and recognizing that they are the civilizing force to mankind . . . There are two sexes. They were made differently . . . You know, if you look at some of the most primitive tribes, the most ignorant, reduced down to almost caveman standards of living, we still find that somehow, instinctively, the men are the warriors and the hunters. They do not ask the women to go out and march side by side and fight with them. Which must mean there is some recognition very basically and instinctively involved in the need to be progenitors of the race.
>
> I don't want discrimination. I don't want anyone, certainly not women, not being paid equally for the work they do. If there are such things going on, I think they should be corrected by statute.

"But not by the ERA?" I persisted. "I think it's going to open a can of worms," said Reagan. He went on to discuss some of the problems he saw arising from women serving in the military:

> Maybe what I fear most about what's going on is that from just asking for the elimination of some discriminatory practices, we've moved to a point where it almost seems as if the women's movement appears to be trying to destroy the stereotype: that there is something wrong with being a housewife.

"What about equal educational opportunities for women?" I asked. In answer, he quoted a man who had been a noted educator that fought very hard to get a girls' educational institution added to a men's school: "Educate a man and you just educate one person; educate a woman and you educate a family."

From there we went on to talk about education in general. I asked him, "What are your thoughts on today's young people, those kids who will someday lead our country?" Reagan had evidently given this matter a good deal of thought and he spoke at length:

> I worry that this younger generation is not getting as much out of life as they think they are. I think part of it may be because they have decided there are so many traditional values that are no longer important. Of course, every generation examines the mores and customs of the generation before. I've looked at this younger generation and I've wondered, first of all, about their belief that marriage isn't necessary. No, I don't care how much they say that a marriage certificate is just a piece of paper, and a few words aren't really important. What they're saying is they're copping out. They don't want to make a commitment. Unless you make the commitment, you can't get all the joy there is to be had.
>
> I worry about them sometimes, too, if another great depression should come along, would they take it as our generation did? Would they cope with it? I realize myself, my goodness, I bought my son a car when he got out of high school. Then I stopped and thought. I never had a car until I'd been out of college about two years. And then it took two years to pay for it. I almost put talcum powder between the rear wheels . . . Would they keep their self-respect? Remember, when government relief started, people fought against going on it. They didn't want to. Now we have had 40 years of telling people that government has a responsibility to take care of them . . . Would we see food riots and demonstrations of people demanding that the government do something? Have they forgotten *we're* the government?
>
> . . . And with this I also wonder—do they get the same feeling that we get when the flag goes up the pole and the band is playing the National Anthem? Would they have the same feeling if the necessity came to defend our country? Now I know a lot of young people . . . would say, "Well, that's your generation where war was wonderful." I once had it out with my children, when they were college age. They were talking—it was at the height of the Vietnam war . . . finally one of them said something that made me say, "Wait a minute! Do you

> have an image of us as marching off to war, couldn't wait to get to the enemy and fight?" And my daughter said, "Well, you know. The bands played." And I said, "Wait a minute! No generation ever went to war more seriously or regretfully than ours."
>
> I remember standing there on the dock in San Francisco. I was on the coordination crew that was sending troops out . . . helping load the convoys . . . and these kids were walking up the gangplank, wind blowing. They'd turn around to take a look at that sky and you just knew they were thinking, "Will I see it again?" One kid was waiting his turn to go by and I started talking to him. I said, "How do you feel about this?" And he said, "Well, I don't want to go. No one wants to go, but" he said, "the quickest way home is through Tokyo."

"All those things you mention," I said, "sounds like you're talking about respect for the basic values in life?"

"Yes," he said, nodding. "You know, I saw a movie the other night called "The Magic of Lassie." It was beautifully done and wonderfully believable and it didn't bother me at all that when the picture was ending, Nancy was wiping her eyes; and I said, 'When you get through with yours, wipe mine.' "

"Are you saying that you were crying?" I asked.

"Oh heavens, yes. I think that men who can't cry—that isn't macho."

"May I print that?"

"You sure can!"

The time allotted for my interview was running out fast, but I wanted to know what this busy man did to relax. I asked him, "You certainly must have had a lot of stress or, at least, certain stressful periods in your life. How do you counteract that?" He answered quickly:

> I have a love of the outdoors to the point that I can get a real feeling of claustrophobia in a city and, well, I think I could sum it up with a line from the scriptures: "I look to the hills from whence cometh my strength." Every once in a while I just have to get out there. We have a ranch. We renamed it Rancho del Cielo, which means Ranch in the Sky. It's up at the top of a pass in the mountains. You can sit on horseback and see the Channel Islands and the other way you can see the San Inez valley . . . Some of it is rock formations, and then there are meadows and there are deep oak forests . . . It's a total getaway from the world.

> And you know, the other thing we were talking about—I think one of the things I'm also happy about is that I know I cannot do the things I did when I was playing football. I know I can't go out and run a quarter mile again, but I have never looked back on an age and said I wanted to go back or be back there. Every age—including the present—seems to be the best. I've had it all!

"But we're in a youth-oriented culture today," I reminded him. "While I can appreciate your view of aging as enjoying each moment and not looking back, I wonder how the young people would look at it."

"Maybe the kids ought to read Browning," said Ronald Reagan. " 'The last of life for which the first was made.' Yes, the best is yet to come!"

"I'm a compassionate guy. I believe in helping people. I believe that if a kid needs help and I can help him financially or any other way, I will, because when a person suffers, I suffer."

JUAN "CHI CHI" RODRIGUEZ

Professional Golfer; Outstanding Senior Tour Winner; Senior Player of the Year, 1987

Born 1935 in Puerto Rico. World Series of Golf's First Ambassador of Golf Award, 1981. Byron Nelson Award for Lowest Stroke Average of Year, 1986. Senior Arnold Palmer Award, 1987. Winner of 1988 Skins Golf Tournament, Turtle Bay, Hawaii. Father of the Year Award, 1982. Salvation Army's Gold Crest Award, 1986. Horatio Alger Award, 1986. Founder of Chi Chi Rodriquez Youth Foundation for abused children, Clearwater, Florida. Heads annual fundraising tournament for disadvantaged at Children's Hospital in Puerto Rico.

He is often referred to as pro golf's international ambassador of goodwill, a title that he earns on or off the course. On the circuit, Chi Chi Rodriguez entertains the fans with his quips and antics, his congeniality and wit. When he puts down his clubs, his Puerto Rican good nature and compassion motivate him to a number of philanthropic projects, most of which involve helping children.

His wonderful warmth and depth of character were immediately apparent when I met Chi Chi for a dinner interview. The surroundings were a second-rate fast food restaurant that was not full during this busy golf week, but his story and words of wisdom turned the place into a palace filled with many gold gems. Chi Chi is small in stature, standing 5'7" and weighing in at 135 pounds. His eyes are penetrating and perceptive, sky blue in tone. I liked him immediately, and it was easy for both of us to share our stories.

I wondered about the learning experiences of this man who was raised in a poor family of six children in Puerto Rico. What did his lessons in life have in common with those of the successful who grew up in the more affluent American society? What motivated Chi Chi to develop his ability and to persist at his golf career to become, at age 52, the leading golfer on the Senior Tour?

These were all questions that ran through my mind as I asked Chi Chi the first question: Who in your childhood gave you your philosophy of life? Chi Chi replied:

> I believe, my Father. Most Puerto Rican people by birth are philanthropists; they have a good heart. When they love you, they love you. They don't just like you.

Chi Chi's deep admiration for his father continually crept into the interview. His father was a laborer who never made more than $18 a week, although he worked six or seven days each week and, according to Chi Chi, never missed a day of work in 30 years.

> We were very lucky. My dad was a very smart man. My dad was the smartest man I've ever known. He was an uncut diamond. He knew more astronomy than anybody in Puerto Rico. He was a genius that never fully developed, and fortunately, all my sisters and brother have a tremendous I.Q.

It was from his father that Chi Chi learned his compassion. In fact, asked who his idols were in life, Chi Chi named his father and Mother Theresa.

He related a story about his father that he remembered from childhood. His father awakened him in the middle of the night because he heard someone trying to steal bananas from the tree in their yard. He went outside and asked the man for the machete he was using. Chi Chi recalled:

> The guy could have killed him. But he didn't. He handed over the machete. My father went over and cut the banana bunch in half. He gave the man half and said, "Now, whenever you want bananas and I got 'em, if you want half, you can have half."

> Although we were very poor, if a kid would go by the house with no shirt or shoes on, anytime we were eating, my dad would call the kid in and give him his food. How he survived, I don't know—by the will of God. He would give the child his whole plate. I'd say, Dad, you're hungry. He'd say but that child is more hungry than I am. And that was after working 12 to 16 hours a day.

> So I learned from his example. I'm a compassionate guy. I believe in helping people. I believe that if a kid needs help and I can help him financially or any other way, I will, because when a person suffers, I

> suffer. Why, I don't know. That's why I don't watch football. We believe in all these beautiful things about how life is, and then a football player gets hit on television, they break his knee, and they all say "Did you see that hit?" Now, here the man just got his leg broken or they hit him in the head and knock his helmet off and knock him out, and they say "Did you see that hit, ha, ha, ha, ha." Where is the compassion?

Chi Chi also spoke with respect for his mother. When she was 70, Chi Chi asked her why she never seemed to age. She said "Son, I have never in my life been mad." She said, "I've been disappointed but I have never been mad." She had strong religious beliefs and went to church three days a week.

When he was 19, Chi Chi joined the Army, where he served for two years. He made $72 a month, of which he sent $50 home to his family. After his discharge, he returned to Puerto Rico and worked as an orderly in a psychiatric clinic feeding and showering the mentally ill. Chi Chi's gentle quality, which was so apparent to me on meeting him, made him a favorite with the patients. He was often called on when one of them became violent. "I would calm them down just by looking at them," he said, adding:

> That's the best year I ever had in my life because I was doing something for somebody. It gave me more satisfaction than winning golf tournaments. Of course, I wanted to do better in life, so I went into golf after that.

He worked the night shift at the clinic, which enabled him to practice golf during the day. His love for golf began at an early age. At seven, told he was too small to be a regular caddy, he took a job as a fore-caddy. His job, watching to see where the balls fell, paid him 35 cents for 18 holes. One day he surprised himself and others by picking up a club and finding that he could handle it. Not having money to buy his own equipment, Chi Chi got his early practice by hitting a tightly rolled can with a guava stick.

Although his golf career began early, his real success in tournament play has been relatively recent. He joined the PGA Tour in 1960 and won his first tournament in Denver in 1963. In the following 25 years, he won only seven tournaments and a little more than $1 million. After joining the Senior Tour at age 50, however, he matched that sum in just two years. At the 1988 Skins Tournament in Turtle Bay in Hawaii, he walked away with $300,000 in winnings.

Chi Chi takes the game seriously, but he sees no reason it can't also be fun. He has long been known for his antics on the golf course. One ritual that captures his style is the matador act, in which he pretends the golf hole is a bull and the putter a sword. After wiping imaginary blood from the "sword," he replaces it in an invisible scabbard at his side. This "act" often replaces an earlier one, The Mexican Hat Dance. After sinking a putt, Chi Chi would throw his hat on the hole and do the hat dance. This ritual, Chi Chi explains, had its origins when he was a child in Puerto Rico playing golf with another boy, with a five cent wager on the game. Chi Chi made a 40-foot putt, but they were both surprised when a toad jumped out of the hole, bringing the ball out with it. The boy wouldn't let him count the shot, and to prevent a re-occurrence, Chi Chi began the practice of trapping the ball in the hole with his hat.

After a number of other pro golfers complained that his antics distracted them, Chi Chi has discontinued that routine. Now he makes sure that any colorful performances are done only after everyone else has putted. Chi Chi explained why he continues his light-hearted entertainment on the course:

> People don't have enough fun in this life. Most people work very hard. They work five days a week, maybe they work 50 years and then finally retire. They go to a tournament and, you know, golf is a dull sport, very dull. Golf was a sport that was originally created with neckties and tuxedos. It wasn't a game that was meant to be . . .
>
> He hesitated, and I asked, "Like sandlot football?"
>
> Yes. Golf is a kind of a stuck-up sport. So a lot of people follow the original game the way it was created. Therefore, it's tough to be a golf fan, because a golf fan has to go there and be like a deaf mute. He can't speak, he can't even cough when a guy is hitting a shot. They have to be quiet all the time, but they pay their money and they work hard to get there, and when they come to watch, I'm going to make sure that I do something to make them laugh or make them enjoy themselves. What is life without a laugh?

Chi Chi's generous nature is apparent on the golf course in his attitude toward his competitors, although, he said that hasn't always been the case:

> Golf is not a team sport. If the other guys shoot a better score than you do, you're out of luck. When I first came on tour, if a guy made a 6 and I made a 3, I wouldn't feel sorry for him. I'd say, "I got him by 3 strokes. Better for me." But now if a guy makes 6, I feel sorry for him even though we are not competitors . . . I'm not jealous of

> anybody. I see guys like Tom Watson do real well and I'm happy for them. They're people with destiny; they do good for our tour.

Chi Chi takes that concern for others to a more serious level off the course through a number of worthy causes, with primary interest in helping disadvantaged youth. A foundation he supports for abused children in Clearwater, Florida is named for him. The proceeds from an annual tournament he puts on in Puerto Rico go to a children's hospital there. Chi Chi's goal is to make sure that any child needing surgery is able to get it—regardless of whether he is rich or poor. Among his other acts of service, he conducts golf clinics for underprivileged children. In 1986 he was awarded the Horatio Alger Award for his humanitarianism, a first for an athlete. Of his philanthropic ventures, Chi Chi says:

> Sure, I like to help every charity I can. I have all kinds of charities. But the ones I help, I do make sure everybody knows that I have no profits at all from them. When I make a personal appearance at those places, I pay my own way. That's very important. In some charities, only 20 percent of the money they collect goes to an actual thing and the other goes to administration; I don't believe in that.

Chi Chi's attitude towards money is certainly different from what one might expect of a big tournament winner. I talked to him shortly after he won the 1988 Skins Tournament in Hawaii and asked how it felt to win $300,000 there. He said:

> It's good for your ego and for your bank account. But it doesn't mean anything. Money is a big thing to have if you don't use it as a weapon. Use it as a weapon and you're in bad shape.

He summed up his philosophy, which brings him inner peace by saying, "I'm a man who lives with my needs, not my wants."

Surprisingly, Chi Chi said his proudest moments were not his golf victories. Of his recent golf successes, he said:

> Well, that's nothing that makes me proud. Being a golfer is great for my livelihood, but the biggest thing that ever happened to me was when I met Mother Theresa in the Philippines. I spoke to her for about 45 minutes. When I shook her hand every hair on my body stood up. I think that was one of the greatest moments of my life.

Again, his atypical view of success surfaced. He admires Mother Theresa for having worked almost 50 years in Calcutta with the lepers. "She never worked for money," he said. "All the money she gets she gives to those people, trying to get cures for them. That is what I call an angel."

I knew that religion played an important part in his life, and so I was surprised when he told me he never attended church and doesn't have a formal religion:

> I'm everything and I'm nothing. I have funny beliefs about religion. Most of the wars have been caused by religion. Man becomes a fanatic when it comes to religion. I believe in people and I believe in Christ.
>
> Anytime I see a priest, I have him bless the cross that I wear around my neck, and I also have the Hawaiian ministers bless it, and I love little town ministers who work in the ghetto—real people. I just don't like the ones with the big airplane fleets and the big business.

He went on to say that he didn't like the television evangelists who are after people's money for their own use. As he put it, "I cut the middleman out. I go straight to the Man. It's cheaper and it's safer." He went on to say:

> I have God always with me. If psychiatrists had to rely on people like me, they would go broke. I don't even understand what the word depression means. I never have any guilt. I never have a guilty conscience. I feel like everything I get, I deserve. I'm never lonely because I enjoy my own company and I enjoy being with God. So when my wife is away, I miss her, yes, but that's not being lonely.

Given his spiritual beliefs, I asked if he felt it was his destiny to spread compassion. He replied:

> Yes, absolutely, to share my things. You know it's amazing, the more I share the more I get, too, because I never expect anything in return.

What is Chi Chi's definition of success?

> Success to me is having peace of mind. Not being jealous of anybody, being content. I think the most successful human being I've ever known was my Dad and he never had any money. See, money doesn't always bring success. Peace of mind does.

> You know, man lives with a lot of egos. Everybody asks me if I want to be the greatest golfer in the world. When I first started, I was a good player and I had a lot of ego. I wanted to be the greatest golfer in the world so I would own a beautiful home and beautiful cars. But I outgrew that. If I became the greatest golfer in the world, what I would do is I would help Mother Theresa build that leper colony that she wants to build.

I asked Chi Chi what he thought makes the difference between those who succeed and those who don't. He told me he thought it was in the genes:

> The genes make a person . . . I'd say Nicklaus' genes made him the greatest golfer of all times but my genes have made me one of the most compassionate guys. So each one of us has come to this earth for something.

Chi Chi and his wife, Iwalani, have been happily married for 25 years. Amazingly, he told me, they have never had a fight. I asked what advice he would give to married couples. He stressed the importance of patience. He said it was especially important to be patient around their children to encourage them to grow up to be good husbands and wives and good citizens. "Instead of just giving them hope," he said, "give them a chance."

He and Iwalani have a daughter in her mid-twenties. I asked him what he would want her to remember about him. His reply was, "That I was a compassionate, good man who tried his very best at everything he did and did it with honor." I asked him if he was teaching her that trait, and he said, "She is learning." But he cautioned:

> You don't teach people that. You just show it and they decide to use it or not. They live and learn. My daughter never knew me much until she took a year off from school and traveled with my wife and me. We really know each other now. I am really proud of her because she is very compassionate. That's the biggest word of my life, compassion. That's what I hope people will learn.

"Inch by inch, life's a cinch."

ANN RUTH

President, Ann Ruth Company; Quadriplegic Artist; President, Greeting Card Company

Born 1964, Palos Verdes, California. B.A., Sports Communications, University of Southern California. Post-graduate work, Cambridge University and University of Madrid. Computer programming student.

Annie Ruth is a fun-loving twenty-four year old who enjoys challenge, likes being with her friends, and keeps on the go. She has a true zest for life. Isn't this average behavior for a young woman? Yes, but Annie has a few obstacles (she calls them inconveniences) that many her age do not.

When she was five, Annie tried a stunt on the balance beam which she had seen "the big kids doing." Since she was well-coordinated in other sports, this did not seem difficult to her. However, it resulted in an accident that left Annie with an injured spinal cord, paralyzing her permanently from the neck down. She was taken immediatley to a hospital. Her parents, Marion and Craig Ruth, were told that if she lived, she would have to stay in an iron lung for the rest of her life.

But Annie comes from a family of positive people with a highly competitive style of living. They all excel in sports, and one brother holds national championships in water skiing. They encouraged Annie to adopt that positive attitude early in life. Despite what the doctors had said, her family looked at other alternatives for her future. After nine months in the Rancho Los Amigos Hospital in Downey, California, Annie's parents decided it was time to take her home.

Several of her doctors were strongly against the move from the safety of the elaborate equipment at the hospital. As a matter of fact, they were horrified with the breaking of a formerly-held standard medical procedure. But Annie's parents thought the hospital environment was apt to keep her a patient rather than encourage her to become a functioning human being—not because the personnel were unkind or incompetent, but because the usual hospital procedures and attitudes were not conducive to patients developing their independence after this kind of accident.

"I thought it was about time," she said. She smiled and added, "I got tired of all those Kentucky fried chicken dinners Dad used to bring me and I wanted a change!"

Annie's father told of how she arrived home in the iron lung. The doctors and nurses stayed about three hours to set up the equipment, instructed them in its use, and tried to make her as comfortable as possible in her home environment.

When they left, Mr. Ruth asked Annie what she wanted to do. Annie gave a surprising response, "Go to Jack-in-the-Box!" So her father and brothers packed up all of her equipment (which meant a respirator, suction device, and emergency breathing apparatus), made sure Annie was getting proper air through her tracheal tube, and loaded everything in the van. In addition to visiting the Jack-in-the-Box, they went to Toys R Us.

It was while Annie was looking at toys that her father began an experiment that would finally lead to a major medical breakthrough. He reasoned that if Annie were enjoying herself, she might make more of an effort to do new things. He wanted her to try to breathe without the use of her equipment, even if, at first, for only a few seconds. So the practice began of taking Annie to interesting environments, where she was encouraged to make every effort to breathe on her own. This experiment has been so successful that Annie has moved from breathing on her own for only a few seconds to currently using the iron lung only for sleeping. For Annie, breathing is a voluntary action; she uses her neck muscles to help gather air, since her lungs and diaphragm are paralyzed. According to some doctors, it is impossible for her to breathe on her own. But she does it!

I wondered what helped her when she was going through her major operations. Her answer surprised me, "Feeling lucky that I was in a body cast for only three weeks, rather than the two months the doctors originally told me it would be. Also having someone to talk to every day helped, mainly my mother."

Her father related a story about a ten-hour operation Annie underwent. Back in the intensive care unit after her surgery, her father winced at all the I.V. equipment and hoses attached to her and wondered what her reaction might be. Picking up on his feelings, Annie smiled at him and said, "Inch by inch, life's a cinch." He said the amazing thing about Annie was she has never lost that spirit. She even said she doesn't feel bad very often, although "bad" may be different for her than for most of us.

When she first came out of the hospital, Annie attended a school for the handicapped, but since they did not have grades and expected little from the students, there was not much challenge for competitive Annie. Her parents fought for her right to go to the "regular" school. Amazingly, the main complaint came from the school psychologist who feared that Annie's presence might have a negative effect on the other children.

In response, the neighbors wrote letters to the school board, and Annie was permitted to go to summer school on a trial basis. When that proved successful, she moved on to the regular school. An adult aide was with her at all times and raised her hand for Annie when she wanted to answer a question.

Despite missing nearly two years of school, Annie managed to keep up with her fellow students. She attended class with her peers and got excellent grades. She was even elected class representative.

Annie said her friends have been very important to her, "They helped me do a lot of things and made me be with them and participate with them."

Her father said he believes her friends have made a point to be with Annie and include her in their lives because she has remained vitally involved in life, has many interests, and is not negative about her situation. Rather, she is very positive. Because Annie is so active, her friends often call and ask what she is doing and if they can come along.

What about Annie's relationship to her brothers and sister? Surprisingly, it is quite normal. Although she is the "baby," she doesn't get special treatment from them; in fact, they tease her a lot, but she can hold her own and returns the teasing. One incident that is typical of sibling playfulness occurred when she was in high school. Annie maneuvers her wheelchair with a rubber device, which she pushes with her chin. One day, when she noticed her brother standing in the garbage enclosure at their home, she used the wheels of her chair to close the door, trapping him inside. It was only after his repeated pleas that she let him escape.

I asked Annie about her interests. She told me:

> I'm a real Los Angeles Dodger fan and a really big fan of San Diego Padres, Steve Garvey. When he was with the Dodgers, an interesting thing happened. We were at a game and were sitting right behind the other team's dugout. He came over and said "Hi" and promised he'd get a hit for me in that game. At that time, he was in a bad slump. He went back to the Dodger dugout feeling uneasy because he had promised me a hit when actually he hadn't had one for some time. Then he started to pray. He went up to bat and hit a double and thought to himself when he came back to the dugout that that was good, but not good enough. He prayed again. So, the next time he got up he hit a home run, then a grand slam home run, and two more doubles.

> That game he got five hits and drove in five runs. It was the greatest day in his career. About ten days later, I got a note from him saying that *he was my fan!*

Several months later, Annie and her father were at a multiple sclerosis dinner and Steve Garvey was there. Annie's father introduced himself and thanked Garvey for writing that note. Then Garvey told Annie and her dad his side of the story about the slump and his prayers that he make a hit for Annie. He believed it was the greatest day of his batting career, and Annie had been the great inspiration for it!

Once Annie left home in her wheel chair at 9:00 a.m. for a "walk for a charitable organization." Her parents were concerned, but knew that Annie needed to do this on her own. Two times her wheel chair broke down, but Annie took care of the matter and went on. At 9:10 p.m., in the dark, she finally was ready for their help. She had someone dial home from a pay phone and asked to get a ride back home. But not until then was she ready to accept their help.

I asked her about some of the things she would like to do in the future:

> I don't know—I haven't thought about it very much. I enjoy each day without worrying about the future, because I might not be here tomorrow. So if you asked what I would want to do tonight, I would open up the paper and see what's going on.

Then Annie thought a while longer and said:

> I want to get my greeting card business going. When I was nine a friend of my mother's, Mrs. Thelma Steinberg, got me interested in painting. She is a talented artist. She began teaching me how to paint during my recovery, and she is still my teacher. [Annie paints with a brush clenched between her teeth.] I am doing oil paintings and have the illustrations put on greeting cards. I'm doing it to earn money but I also have a good time.

When asked if she thought she would be a good business woman, she said yes. Her father agreed, saying, "She has a great sixth sense. She can spot the phonies right away. Her sensitivity is uncanny."

Annie's father has always put particular emphasis on making life fun, and it is obvious his philosophy has imbued Annie with a deep joy of living. That attitude has been of primary importance in helping her overcome her handicap. Encouraged by her positive-thinking parents, Annie describes what most people might consider a major handicap as "a slight difficulty" and continues to live an active, adventuresome life.

As a Sports Communications major at the University of Southern California, Annie interviewed sports figures and graduated with a 4.0 record. She went on to study a year in Spain and do graduate work at Cambridge in England. She was one of a few chosen by IBM and other top companies for a nine-month training program on computers. Before even finishing the term, she was offered a job.

And what about adventure? Annie's most recent activity was jumping out of an airplane at 12,500 feet with a 2 ½-minute free-fall. She was strapped in front of her instructor, who pulled the rip cord, enabling their slow descent to the ground. The instructor was first to land and caught Annie as she touched ground.

Ann contributes her unique expression to the list of successful people who use crises or difficulties to push them into discovering more of their potential. The confidence and encouragement instilled in her by family and friends strongly influenced her ability to transcend "impossible" physical obstacles. Their confidence in her became her own.

Demonstrated by her position as class representative and participation in the walk for a charitable cause, Ann places a premium on service to others. She exudes self-discipline in overcoming her physical hindrance, in her studies and in her artistic career.

Whether facing possible rejection during trial enrollment in a public school, coping with wheel chair breakdowns during a walk for charity, or free-falling from a plane, Ann Ruth perseveres until her goal is realized. She adds one success to another as she lives moment to moment, inch by inch.

"... integrity makes enthusiasm possible. Only honest people are subconsciously liberated to be totally spontaneous. Without that quality, enthusiasm is contrived and not an authentic motivating factor in life."

ROBERT H. SCHULLER, Ph.D.

Founding Pastor, Crystal Cathedral and "Hour of Power" television ministry, Author

Born 1926, Alton, Iowa. B.A., Hope College, Holland, Michigan, 1947. Attended Western Theological Seminary. Ordained in Reformed Church of America, 1950. Author of more than 22 books, including best-sellers *Tough Times Never Last, But Tough People Do, Tough Minded Faith for Tender Hearted People,* and *The Be Happy Attitudes.*

A revolutionary new era of spreading the spiritual message began in 1955 when Dr. Robert Schuller and his wife Arvella, with a total of $500.00 rented the Orange drive-in theater in Southern California and launched their ministry from the snack-bar roof. From that unlikely pulpit, he conducted his weekly services, with his wife as organist, to a congregation listening from their cars and trucks. The growth of his congregation led to the first "walk-in/drive-in church."

In 1970, he expanded his ministry with the production of his "Hour of Power" television program, with Arvella serving as Program Director. As his highly successful ministry grew, he realized the need for a larger structure. He commissioned the design of the Crystal Cathedral, a 415-foot, all glass structure which he dedicated on September 14, 1980, "To the Glory of Man for the Greater Glory of God."

The size of the structure, 207 feet wide and 128 feet high, is enhanced by the all glass covering that encloses the entire building. More than 10,000 windows of tempered silver colored glass are held in place by a lace-like frame of 16,000 white steel trusses specifically fabricated for this engineering feat.

The sanctuary alone seats 2,890 persons, and more than 1,000 singers and instrumentalists can perform in the 185-foot chancel area. Two doors 90 feet high open electronically behind the pulpit to allow worshipers in the drive-in part of the sanctuary to participate in the service. The service can be viewed on a giant indoor 11 ½ x 15-foot Sony "Jumbotron" television screen, the first of its kind to be used for worship purposes.

I went to the Crystal Cathedral to interview Dr. Schuller in his offices on the 12th floor of the building overlooking the architectural phenomenon, which is the home base for his international ministries, including a congregation of 10,000-plus members and his internationally televised program. I was intrigued to hear the story of this innovative man who has led such a successful ministry for over thirty years.

Dr. Schuller reaches a broad range in his ministries. He is known for appealing to a congregation that includes many who are "unchurched," but he is also sought out by a large number of ministers and missionaries. I asked how he accounted for this and he told me:

> This church became one of the first fast-growing churches in the United States beginning at a time in 1955 when there were predictions that the church was going to die out and fade away. There were many, many ministers who wanted to know why we were growing when all other churches were dying out . . . . So we set up a time once or twice a year when I would speak on the basic principles of self-esteem, theology, and possibility thinking which under-girds everything we do here.

Reflecting on all that had happened since he started his unique ministry, I said, "It must seem like a long time from when you started here in 1955." Dr. Schuller responded:

> Well, it doesn't seem like a long time because I'm looking to the future. If you look to the future, you don't have time to add up the past. And I have so many exciting things tomorrow that I don't take time to relish the achievements of yesterday.

Dr. Schuller grew up on a farm near the small town of Alton, Iowa. I asked him what experiences he had there that have been helpful to him, and he said:

> Iowa farmers are not tenant farmers. They own the land and they expect that the family farm will continue for generation after generation. That means there isn't a single Iowa farmer who lacks integrity. Acting with integrity is the only way they can operate if they plan to spend their whole life there. All the surrounding towns are so small that every

> merchant would get a guy's number in a hurry if he was dishonest, and he would be driven out of the state.
>
> So integrity is into the marrow of the bones of the people who come from this territory. I think that's the greatest thing I got, because integrity makes enthusiasm possible. Only honest people are subconsciously liberated to be totally spontaneous. Without that quality, enthusiasm is contrived and not an authentic motivating factor in life.

I asked Dr. Schuller what other values he acquired in his childhood and he replied, without hesitation, "Hard work." He elaborated:

> If you were given an assignment, quitting was never an option. Problems were expected. There could be a tornado, there could be a blizzard, 30-degree below zero weather. But if you were a farmer and you had milking cows, the cows had to be milked every day, come hell or high water—and they were.
>
> We never had a day off. We had a tornado that wiped our farm out, and there was nothing that stopped you from milking the cows, because if a milk cow is not milked one day, the milk collects in the bladder and disease sets in and you lose a milking producer. So what I learned from that is the problems are never allowed to be excuses for lack of achievement. You add that on top of a layer of integrity and you're on your way toward the quality of character where success is almost inevitable.

Dr. Schuller was inspired at an early age toward his ministerial work. In fact, he told me, "It was my uncle, who was a Princeton graduate and a missionary in China who inspired me. He came home and gave me that challenge at the age of 4 years and 11 months." When I asked where he had acquired the dramatic, creative method of presentation which characterizes his writings and his speaking, he replied:

> From my mother's grandfather. It is an inherited genetic quality. My uncle died recently at 91 years of age. He knew my great grandfather and said that I have the same gestures, the same personality. I am a genetic freak.

Dr. Schuller received his Bachelor of Arts in 1947 from Hope College in Michigan, concentrating in psychology and history, and winning awards in debate and oratory. After attending the Western Theology Seminary, he was ordained in 1950 and served for five years at the Ivanhoe Reformed Church in Chicago before moving to California in 1955 to begin his unique ministry.

His ministry blends psychology and theology to formulate an inspiring, positive faith which he calls "The Theology of Self-Esteem." I asked him to explain this philosophy, and he told me:

> We deal with three things. First of all self-esteem theology. We have to believe in people and we have to get them to believe in themselves. They won't even believe in God if they don't believe in themselves. I don't know of a single atheist who doesn't have a problem at a deep level in his life with his own self-worth or self-dignity. He may not even be aware of it, but it's there. So self-belief is important.
>
> Secondly, we deal with possibility thinking: If I am somebody, then I can do something. Then we move to the third level which are ways of marketing your ideas, your products, or your services that you intend to distribute.

Dr. Schuller is also well known for his inspirational books. More than 22 books have been printed in hard cover, including *Tough Times Never Last, But Tough People Do!*, *Be Happy You Are Loved*, and *Self-Esteem: The New Reformation*, with a profound effect on innumerable individuals. I wondered particularly about the emphasis he places on the need to develop self-esteem. He told me where this emphasis came from:

> Classical Protestantism, like classical Roman Catholicism, has defined the doctrine of sin and evil in a negative way and I think it has to be defined in a more constructive way. Anyone who denies the reality of sin and evil is stupid. You can't do that and deal with a guy like Adolph Hitler or Jim Jones. You can't deny sin and evil and explain some of the bad things that happen around us all the time.
>
> I've defined sin and evil as lack of self-respect, lack of self-esteem, which is nothing more than to say a lack of faith in myself which is tied into a lack of faith in God. So I've taken a classical theological position and without being heretical, have re-defined it in positive terms.

The subject of love is a commonly recurring theme in his books. I asked how that fit into his message at the Crystal Cathedral. He said:

> This is a Christian church. At the bottom line, a Christian church is defined as a group of persons who love each other even if we don't approve of each other. That's the essence of Christianity. It's called grace. Grace is accepting with authentic love, people whose lives you probably cannot approve. That's the hallmark of Christ and therefore of this church.

I asked Dr. Schuller about another of the innovative concepts he originated at the Crystal Cathedral, his telephone crisis intervention service. He said:

> It's one of the things I'm very proud of. Come fall of 1988 it will be 20 years. We are the first church in the United States of America to organize and launch a 24-hour suicide prevention telephone counseling program. It has saved untold thousands of lives.

Dr. Schuller's resume contains an impressive list of awards, including many for his creative communications style. He has honorary doctorates from five universities and is the only non-architect on the Board of Directors of the American Institute of Architects. In 1973 he received the Freedoms Foundation of Valley Forge's Principal Award, the highest national award for a sermon. I asked which of the awards meant the most to him, and he said:

> I can answer that very quickly: The Wishbone Award. It is made by Make a Wish Foundation of America. They look at a child who is dying and ask that child what they want, and then they provide it. There was a young child who was dying in Colorado and of all the persons he wanted to meet, he wanted to meet Robert Schuller. He was up in this office in his wheel chair, and I met him. He's dead now, but to be honored by wanting to be met as the last wish of a dying child is the greatest honor I've ever had.

When I asked Dr. Schuller how he would define success, he referred to his latest book, *Success Is Never Ending—Failure Is Never Final*:

> Success is never ending—because success is a process! You will never

> be able to measure all the good you do! It will trickle down and ripple on and on!

I asked how his philosophy applied specifically to his own life, and he said:

> I think all the principles that have made my marriage and my family so super successful are the same positive principles that I articulate in my book.

He told me the greatest joys in his life were his marriage, his children, and his grandchildren. He has been married more than 35 years and has five children. His only son, Robert, is also an ordained minister of the Reformed Church in America. I asked Dr. Schuller what advice he would give to parents. He said:

> Give your children great moral integrity. Moral integrity means assignments, obligations. Demand that they be fulfilled—whether it's chores in the house or whatever. Young people need to be taught that they have to learn to make promises and fulfill those promises.

Given the revolutionary ideas and institutions this man has initiated and the hundreds of thousands of lives he has touched worldwide, I asked him how would he like to be remembered. He answered in his unhesitating, succinct style: "He encouraged people."

From all accounts, he has done just that. Armand Hammer, Chairman of Occidental Petroleum Group's comment on him was, "I am honored to be an example of a super possibility thinker. Your encouragement, support, and friendship mean a great deal to me." The late John Wayne said of him, "I like the Reverend Dr. Schuller because he is ever thoughtful of other human beings and stands proud in his love of God." California Angels pitcher Don Sutton remarked, "I had almost decided to quit baseball, then I read Dr. Schuller's book, *Self Love,* and began believing in myself again." And, says actress Lucille Ball, "I go to church every Sunday—no matter where I am I find you."

"Pick a good man for the job. Then leave him alone."

FORREST N. SHUMWAY

Vice Chairman, Allied-Signal Companies (Retired November 1987)

Born 1927, Skowhegan, Maine. Former President and Chief Executive Officer, The Signal Companies, Inc. An avid hunter and fisherman.

Forrest N. Shumway is a trim man in his 60s, standing six feet tall. He grew up in Maine and felt as much at ease in the outdoors as he did in his role as a top executive at the Signal Companies. He is casual, down to earth, and to the point.

Forrest's decisiveness and determination may have roots in his Maine upbringing or may be inherited from his iron-nerved uncle, Sam Mosher, founder of the original Signal Oil and Gas Company. Years in the Marines and in the rough oil fields served to strengthen Shumway's character even further, readying him for law school, several challenging legal posts as Deputy County Counsel, and, at age thirty, Signal's legal department. Within seven years, he moved up to assume the Presidency. He became Chief Executive Officer in 1968.

Through Shumway's forceful negotiations and calculated risks, Signal developed from a regional $400 million gas and oil company in 1964 to a $4 billion conglomerate. He is philosophical about risks, "In 75 percent of the cases, over the course of a lifetime, I will be intuitively correct and that is a fair enough percentage."

Our interview took place while he was Chief Executive Officer of the Signal Companies. He told me he had looked at the 50-year involvement Signal had with oil production and, with an eye on the future, made the tough decision to get out of that business. "It is all different now; it takes huge amounts of capital—literally billions—to sit in the oil game. Oh, there are a few companies, but the major ones are all giants—there is no sense in selling out and putting our chips in technology, which is what we did when we bought Universal Oil Products in 1975."

He told me UOP has a unique technology, backed up by thousands of patents in the petroleum and petrochemical fields. Signal's two other major companies were Mack Trucks, Inc., which renders $1.5 billion in sales, and the Garrett Corporation, with $1 billion in sales.

In addition, Signal had about $100 million in sales from its Dunham-Bush Subsidiary (heating, air conditioning, and refrigeration equipment), and from Precision Rubber Products, Corp.

Shumway said his personality was formed by several important factors. One of them was growing up in Maine where, he says "There is a strong sense of the worth of the individual. Life in that part of the country is hard enough that people learn to make strong decisions early in life."

His Maine boyhood also gave him a deep love for the outdoors. He is an avid hunter and fisherman. In 1971 he set a world's record for catching a 163-pound Pacific big-eyed tuna on a 30-pound test line. He is a devoted supporter of the Boy Scouts and has been on its National Executive Board. His feelings about that organization reflect his belief in traditional training and values:

> The Boy Scouts had their greatest value for millions of men, now grown, who learned about woods and streams and weather on the trail and camping. We used to take city boys up into the wilderness areas and they loved it. They are going to find out more about our country and how to keep it clean and beautiful by going and finding out what makes nature tick.

Shumway told me the second major influence on his life was the Marine Corps. He joined when he was seventeen and believes that being a part of that organization taught him to work in a spirit of cooperation. It also exposed him to many forceful, decisive men, who served him as role models.

Attending law school was the third major impetus in developing Shumway's character:

> I don't care if you never use the law degree; it's the nature of what you learn that's valuable—a sense of negotiating. Issues you see in law are not black and white, such as those a chemist or engineer deals with. In law, issues are shades of gray—you are not dealing with absolutes. You have to work things out. In the process you learn flexibility.

The effectiveness of this background was put to the test on Shumway's first day at his first job after graduating from law school. He was working as Deputy County Counsel, advising the administration of the county hospital. He would tolerate anything but indecision. He was told that there was an unconscious patient who would die unless his gangrenous leg was amputated at once. However, the patient's wife and daughter belonged to a religious sect that forbids surgery, and they refused to grant the necessary permission to operate. In fact, they threatened to sue Shumway and the hospital if the surgery was performed. For Shumway, it was an easy decision. He said, "Take it off." Not only did the law suit not materialize, the grateful patient actually located Shumway five years later and thanked him for his decisiveness.

Forrest Shumway's traditional background also influenced his strong support of the family unit. He is the father of two and has always spent a lot of time with them. He believes that it is unnecessary for even a major executive to work both day and night. Seldom did he bring work home with him at night, nor has he been away from home more than four or five weekends in the last ten years.

But does he bring his *problems* home by talking about them with his family? He answered, "No, somehow I am able to turn it off and really be home when I am there."

He believes relaxation is a necessity for a successful lifestyle. This conviction often impelled him to try to convince his other executives to slow down. "If they are staying late or taking home a lot of work, I encourage them to spend that free time with their families."

"Pick a good man for the job. Then leave him alone," is one of Shumway's mottos. Although he was the head of a major conglomerate, Shumway didn't feel a need to be personally involved with each subsidiary in detailed management directions. With a man of high caliber at its head, "each unit runs its own operations. We watched the bottom line and only stepped in on the allocation of resources, or if a problem developed." Shumway believes so strongly in the talent of his managers that he thought most would be qualified to run any company.

Shumway stated his general view of business, "I think people have some terrible misconceptions about business, namely, that it has to have more and more restrictions and regulations by government. And the government is always eager to oblige." He continued:

> No one seems to understand that the only organization generating money—and that means jobs—in this country is business. Government gets its money from business, and private individuals get their money from business. The fact that business is financing the whole country is never mentioned anywhere, not in the classrooms, not in the newspapers, not on TV. In the last analysis, business is paying everyone's salary.

What are Shumway's other interests? He believes in a good plan for physical fitness, and often rode a bicycle three miles from home to his office.

A strong supporter of laws to reduce air and water pollution, he says:

> We've been very wasteful. We've wasted our clean air and water, wasted our natural resources, built great gas-guzzling behemoths getting six miles to the gallon, and despoiled our outdoors and wilderness areas. It's time we faced up to reality and stopped it.

How can this be done? Shumway believes in money incentives to solve the problem:

> When I grew up in Maine, every few years we were overrun with black bears. They put a $25 bounty on bear skins and that got rid of the extra bears immediately.

Following that model, he asserts that government tax incentives or a different tax structure might be helpful in solving the energy shortage.

In summary, how has a country man been so successful in city life? Forrest Shumway has translated the values and skills he learned from the outdoors to the rigors of the corporate world. From the woods he learned rugged discipline and applied this in the decision making which was the key to his law school success. The woods also taught him the importance of keeping fit. Finally, Shumway experienced refreshment and gratitude for the simple pleasures in life from his rural environment. This remarkable ability to distance himself from business pressures may be one of the reasons for his success in handling them.

He went on to be Vice Chairman of Allied-Signal Companies, and, having completed a successful career, retired in November of 1987.

"I don't think success is very difficult to achieve. I think that when the good Lord puts you on this earth, you are gifted with some type of talent. The biggest problem is that people are not willing to sacrifice what it takes to achieve their potential . . ."

LEE TREVINO

International Golfing Champion

Born 1939 in Dallas, Texas. Chairman of the Board, Lee Trevino Enterprises. 1971 Associated Press Pro Athlete of Year, *Gold* Magazine Player of the Year, and *Sports Illustrated* Sportsman of the Year. Member of Texas Hall of Fame.

With a single swing of his six iron in November of 1987, Lee Trevino earned himself $175,000. It was at the three-par 17th hole of the PGA West Skins Game, La Quinta, California that he hit the 161-yard hole-in-one! The reason the winnings were so high for that particular hole was that it was a "double carry-over." The golfers had tied on the two previous holes, resulting in the prize money accumulating for three holes. His total winnings for the tournament amounted to $310,000, with two Toyotas thrown in for good measure.

That was only the second time Lee had hit a hole-in-one in his 35-year golfing career, but his record—both of tournaments won and of financial earnings—clearly showed him to be a winner. He has won tournaments world-wide, received countless awards, broken numerous records—and all without the benefit of a coach or a college education. Lee is a self-taught golfer, a self-made man.

As I approached him, I wondered what, to him, was the secret of good golf. That was the first question I asked. He promised to tell me before the interview was over. Between my other questions, I kept trying to find out his secret, but he kept prolonging the answer. It wasn't, in fact, until the end of the interview that he finally told me. In the course of answering my questions, he gave me a number of other insights into the qualities he thought had helped him do so well. One surprising observation Lee made was that he actually considered being self-taught an advantage. The reason, he said, is it enables him to continue the learning process, to constantly upgrade his game. He explained how he uses feedback to improve his strokes:

> I probably have as much knowledge of my golf swing as anyone who has ever played golf. The reason is because I'm self-taught. When I hit a bad shot I know exactly what I did wrong. If I miss a shot I can give myself an instant lesson. I watch the flight of the ball. The greatest thing in the world is feedback. If I want the ball to turn to the right and it turns to the left, I know exactly what I did wrong and I won't do it again. It's not difficult to teach someone how to play. The most difficult thing in the world is to get that person to teach himself after you get through with him.

We talked about the fact that often, after hitting a bad shot, golfers will admonish themselves for the next two or three holes. Lee said it takes self-discipline to avoid letting a bad shot spoil the rest of the game:

> Discipline means not to get upset and let it bother you for the next three shots. That's something some people have never taught themselves. When you hit one bad shot, you don't want to follow it up with another one. I don't believe in past history. When a shot is over, I don't give a damn if you threaten to shoot somebody or if you cry. The rules of the game declare that they are not going to let you take the shot over. Once you strike that golf ball and it goes in the air, it's gone. Nothing is going to bring it back.

Some athletes use hypnosis to improve their mental discipline, but Lee said he does not believe in using hypnosis or even golf psychology:

> I learned a long time ago that the best psychology in golf is to watch your hands bleed. You hit so many golf balls that your hands get blistered and crack and start bleeding. That's the best psychology I could ever tell anybody. I am self-disciplined. I don't need golf psychology. Basically, psychology is trying to get someone to believe in himself.

Lee said he believes sacrifice is an important element in success and is usually the difference between someone who reaches the top and someone who doesn't:

> I don't think success is very difficult to achieve. I think that when the good Lord puts you on this earth, you are gifted with some type of talent. The biggest problem is that people are not willing to sacrifice what it takes to achieve their potential in the field they are talented in.

> I didn't have a coach. I had to do it on my own. Every time I meet a superstar or a very successful individual in any field, I know he's not only done it on his own, but he did a tremendous amount of sacrificing to get there. It didn't come naturally. He had the basic fundamentals and the roots of the game and maybe he was quicker to learn. But the main reason he was more successful than the other is because he was willing to sacrifice.

Golf has been number one in Lee's life for a long time. When he got out of the Marine Corps at age 21, he started practicing to become a professional golfer, and everything else took a back seat. His motto was: "If there's sunlight, there are golf balls to be hit." While acknowledging that he was born with a natural talent for the sport, he said that even more important was his willingness to sacrifice everything else for golf:

> Someone said to me, "You're the luckiest guy in the world. I wish I could do what you do." Little do they know that they probably could. But you have to sacrifice if you pick one field, regardless of whether it's computer operator or sportsman. You have to devote every spare moment to that particular field. To do that, there are lots of things that you are not able to do—like going away on weekends and spending time at a lake camping or water skiing or horseback riding. There are a lot of golfers with potential, but they won't sacrifice for what they are striving for. They would rather quit practicing at 2:00 in the afternoon and go have a beer with the guys.

I asked Lee if the time he spent on his golfing career had been to the detriment of his family life, and he said, "Yes. Probably the only drawback to the whole thing is not spending enough time with the family."

Trevino admitted in a TV interview that he wasn't as close to his children as some fathers, because he had put golf first for so many years. He is now married for the third time and has four children by previous marriages.

He said several "close calls with my Maker" had caused him to believe in a hereafter and to recognize that he has a purpose in life. He won a bout with pneumonia and with back operations, but the event that really made a believer of him was surviving a lightning strike:

> It was in 1975 at Butler National in Chicago. There was a ringing in my ears and I couldn't breathe. My left side went numb and I blacked out. In those few moments, maybe seconds, my whole life passed in

front of me. I was very, very warm. There was no pain and I was very comfortable.

So I have come to think we are going to a better place. Not that I dislike this place. Don't get me wrong. I enjoy doing what I'm doing. I'm probably one of the only people in the world that has no worries, no problems. The event made a tremendous difference in my life. I appreciate more of the things that I have, including my spouse, my children, my fame. I think sometimes that even as well disciplined as I am, I took things for granted. Since I got hit, I've worked extremely hard, but I have learned to relax and enjoy other things.

He talked about his more relaxed style of living and golf:

A few years ago I couldn't have stayed a day away from the game. It was such a love affair with the game and myself that I hit balls and practiced almost every day. Not that the game and I have gotten a divorce. It's just that we have learned to compromise a little more.

I was surprised to learn that Lee doesn't set goals for himself. I asked him why he didn't use a goal-setting method so commonly recommended for achieving success:

I don't like setting goals because if you don't achieve them, I think it's depressing. You get down on yourself and say, "I'm not ever going to amount to anything." I've got a strong will. I've got guts. I've got a heart. I try the best I possibly can, and I know I can achieve it if I work on it. Again, it all comes down to sacrifice. There are many athletes that have been exceptional in a team sport, but they didn't give 110 percent of their energy simply because they knew someone else was going to help them down the line.

As serious as Lee is about golf, he also has a reputation for his quick wit and repartee, often joking with members of the crowd while he golfs. He said he developed his sense of humor and ability to relate to others while working in a pro shop where he dealt with a variety of people:

Most of the tournament players who come out today have never had a job, much less worked with the public. You learn to be humorous and to talk and to listen simply because of being around different types of people, different religions. My spontaneous wit, I guess you would call it, comes because I feed off of people. I'll hear someone say something and it reminds me of a joke. Then while I'm telling the joke, it reminds me of another one. Someone will say something else and it will remind me of another one. I really need a straight man and the crowd provides it. They enjoy it because they get to participate.

Calling his humor on the golf course "a little gift I try to give back to the people," he thinks it is important to reward the fans who have supported him. I asked him if there was anything else he gave to his fans. He said:

I just give them good golf. I think the reason the majority of people like me to meet them is because I was an underdog. I was a minority when I came on the circuit. You know as well as I do that 75 percent of the people in the world are underdogs. So the audience can identify with that quality and they like that.

It was time for our interview to end, but Lee still hadn't given me a direct answer to my first question. I wasn't going to let him off the hook, and so I asked him one last time, "Now come on, Lee, give me the Trevino secret to good golfing." I'm not sure what complicated formula I expected to hear, but when he finally told me, it seemed all too obvious:

"Practice, practice, practice," he said.

I should have known. After all, this was a man who would practice until his hands bled.

"It's not pleasing to write a book. It takes many hours and it's great agony, but I'm looking for the rewarding results. I persist because one of these days I will enjoy attaining the goal. It's a postponement of gratification."

VENITA VAN CASPEL

Author; Financial Corporation Executive;
First Woman Member Pacific Stock Exchange

Born 1922, Sweetwater, Oklahoma. B.A., University of Colorado. Phi Beta Kappa. Founder, Owner, President. Van Caspel & Co., Houston 1968. Owner/Manager Van Caspel Planning Service. Author: *Money Dynamics, Dear Investor, Money Dynamics for the 80's, Money Dynamics for the 1990's,* and video cassette tapes: "The Power of Money Dynamics." Moderator, national PBS television show, "Venita Van Caspel Money Makers."

Venita was one of the speakers in the Successful Women Seminar. She was attractively dressed in a light blue suede dress. She was tall and thin and looked more like a high fashion model than a member of the stock exchange. The first question I asked her was, "What circumstances in your childhood enabled you to become so successful?" She answered:

> I was the oldest child. It was not the kind of family where we had books and were encouraged to read. I don't know any of the children's stories for instance, which I think is too bad. But I had a loving family. My mother and father were happily married and I think I was sort of like Topsy—I just grew. I don't know where I got the desire to excel. That's hard to tell. We did not have a lot of financial means . . .
>
> Perhaps most important was the realization that if I wanted to have a different life I must get prepared for it, and if I prepared for it, it would come. It never occurred to me that it wouldn't. At that time we were in the dustbowl of Oklahoma. My father was an automobile salesman and we moved to a farm. We were very poor. I started working very, very young in a dime store and various other places—just anything to earn extra money.

> Actually, the desire to excel probably came in school. That was one way that I could win—making good grades. I basically have a fairly competitive nature.

Lacking money for college, Venita worked for two years after high school. She went to Duke University and when her money ran out, got a scholarship and took two jobs to stay in school. She transferred to the University of Colorado, where she majored in economics. She commented on why she chose her major: "Maybe because I'd never had any dollars, I had always been interested in how the economy worked." She continued to support herself through college:

> It gives you a great deal of appreciation to work for your education. It gives you the feeling you can do whatever is necessary to succeed. I do have a great deal of discipline, and I am looking for pleasing results rather than pleasing experiences.

After college, Venita married a fellow student. His death sent her on a soul-searching journey to find her mission in life. She was very devoted to the church, and the pastor suggested she become Director of Christian Education. She declined, partly because she didn't want to be paid for an activity she had been doing voluntarily. She continued exploring possibilities:

> In searching for what I was supposed to do, I actually went to England to a Billy Graham Crusade. It was a wonderful program, but it wasn't what I thought I was supposed to do either.

She returned to the United States and started looking for ways to invest the insurance money her husband had left her. Although she had majored in economics, she realized she needed to go back to college because:

> My college background was not sufficient for me to even know what to do with my own money. Our educational system is not geared the way it should be. It teaches you a few academics. Brigham Young University is one of the few that offers a course on the practical application of financial planning and a degree in it.

With the intention of boning up on her economics education, she attended the University of Houston, where she discovered her life's calling:

> I became interested in helping other people with their money. I decided

> I wanted to be a stockbroker. It was, in a sense, a Christian dedication, because I felt people needed help with their money, and I felt the only way I could help them was to become a stockbroker. I felt that people shouldn't have to retire in desperation. They should be able to retire in financial dignity. And that's going to be my goal.

Becoming a stockbroker in the early 60s, however, was not an easy task for a woman. "I had to come in through the back door," she said, referring to the only position available to her in that field, a clerk. "I worked for the firm for six months while studying the material. Then I took the exam and passed it."

She became philosophical about her work with others and said:

> I get joy out of seeing people learn what to do with their money and how to put it to work. Money gives you options in life that you don't have without it. It won't make you happy but neither will poverty.

"Did you start working with older people at first?" I asked. She replied:

> No, just anyone who wanted to come. I started doing seminars and anyone who came was entitled to a personal consultation.

I asked Venita how she has been able to maintain her femininity while functioning in a male-dominated field. She said she hadn't found it difficult:

> I have a fairly logical mind, and men respect that on the whole. I never wear masculine-looking clothes. I feel that's a mistake. I try to wear soft colors and speak in a soft voice. When I open my mouth I have something to say. Consequently it's never been a problem. I think if I were to march in with a pin-striped suit and a loud voice, it might be a problem.

She went on to express her gratitude for those in the women's liberation movement who opened the door for her own achievements. She said, "I realize that the pendulum had to swing very far in order to get to the middle, and I am benefiting greatly from it." Although she claims that it is not her style to take an active role in the movement, she did make a contribution in another way. By becoming the first woman member of the Pacific Stock Exchange, Venita has been a role model and a trailblazer for others to follow.

I asked what advice she would give a person trying to find financial independence. "The first thing they must do," she said, "is to seek out a financial planner who is interested in them." She added:

> There's no magic way to do this. You just have to talk to a few to see if you can communicate with them. If you talk to them for awhile and they ask you a lot of questions and aren't just anxious to invest your money immediately, then you've probably found a caring person and, presumably, a knowledgeable one. Once you've found that, you're probably much better spending your time doing what you do best and letting them do the investing for you. If you want banking advice, go to a banker. If you want tax advice, go to a CPA. But don't go to any of those for financial planning.

She recommends that women who have never really handled money go to seminars or read books on the subject, although, she reflects, there aren't many good ones. "I think that's one of the reasons my books are being so well received," she said. "They fill a void."

Venita has always been a hard worker, a characteristic she believes is sadly lacking in people today. She says many people are only looking for the immediate gratification and give up before reaching their goal if it isn't easily attained. For instance, she said:

> It's not pleasing to write a book. It takes many hours and it's great agony, but I'm looking for the rewarding results. I persist because one of these days I will enjoy attaining the goal. It's a postponement of gratification.

Venita admitted that she sometimes gets so involved in the future she has to remind herself to stop and appreciate the present:

> Every time I hear an inspirational speaker, I begin to analyze my priorities. I have a very imaginative and creative mind—I can always think of things faster than anyone can ever accomplish them. I've got a staff which just can't do things as fast as I can think them up. In the coming year I want to slow down and enjoy the "now." I put too much in each day, and after a while, the body will just not absorb the stress.

I asked Venita to describe her philosophy of life. She said:

> I think the greatest thing you can do in this world is to make a

> contribution to other people's lives. Of course, you mustn't forget your own, too, because God loves you and wants you to love yourself. One of the things you have to realize is that you are self-determined and that you must allow others the same right. That's especially important if you have a career and are married. You have to realize that you can only take responsibility for your own life. You can pray about the others, but you cannot determine anybody else's life. You can try to give them an example, but that's all you can do, and don't feel frustrated about that. What someone else chooses to do with their life is their own affair.

Venita married a rancher four years after her husband's death. She is divorced from her second husband and is now happily remarried. Although she has no children, I wondered what advice she would give a daughter, if she had one. She said:

> I would say make the most of your God-given talents. Keep moving and keep taking the next step. Do the most with what you've got and the rest will take care of itself.

It is because Venita has followed this advice all throughout her life that she made such remarkable strides in a field previously dominated by men.

Recently she joined a large New York firm as senior vice president of Raymond James and Associates. Her five books have sold over a million copies. Her sixth book, *Money Dynamics for the 1990s,* has been chosen as the feature book by the Fortune Book Club and as an alternate for the Book of the Month Club. Her sense of purpose in life, her ability to set far-ranging goals and put the needed energy into meeting them have not only led her to great personal achievement, but have enabled her to enrich the lives of countless others, as well.

STUMBLING BLOCKS TO ACHIEVING SUCCESS

There are many barriers that we, or life, seem to put in our way to keep us from success. A few seem especially important to mention: a career not suited to your talents, over-competitiveness, stress, unrealistic goals, an overly inflated ego, inappropriate life partners/companions, excuses, fear—even of our own success—and excesses in other parts of our lives outside of our jobs.

This section is intended to point out the pitfalls to avoid. See if any of them apply to you.

A CAREER NOT SUITED TO YOUR TALENTS

This point was overwhelmingly named as the number one problem. Many people choose a "convenient" career, one in which they merely "put in their eight hours" and then go home to pursue what they really enjoy. The successful choose three routes: 1) They find out what career is most rewarding to pursue in order to use their full potential; 2) they sometimes find it necessary to go from job to job and in the process test and discover new talents; and 3) they use their jobs to develop their talents and potential. This often means looking to the areas in your life that are most enjoyable. Usually the areas in which you are most talented and, consequently, in which you will do your best.

OVER-COMPETITIVENESS

From my observations, a competitive nature may be of great help in pushing one toward doing an outstanding job, but it can also hold him back from enjoying the success he does attain. This characteristic seems to pertain particularly to men who have been brought up with a strong emphasis on competition. In conversations on success with executives, I have often found them belittling their efforts by comparing their accomplishments to the giants in the field who have done "better" than they. These comments, although perhaps true, detract from the appreciation and sense of accomplishment one has a right to expect upon achieving his own goal.

On the other hand, there are those who try to build themselves up by downplaying the worth of the successful. They take a sour grapes approach by making statements such as, "It was easy for him because he was born rich," "He had all the breaks," "His father-in-law helped him." If you catch yourself putting others down, consider what you're trying to say to yourself about your own talent.

STRESS

How do you deal with life's problems, whether they be major anxieties or even boredom? Handling stress is a key factor in success. Fighting the clock is one contributor to stress. Trying to do too much in too little time creates anxiety. Letting yourself get overly tired is another contributor. Excesses often cause stress: too much time; not enough time, too much structure, not enough structure.

Stress can be a useful tool, indicating that a change is in order. It is important to learn to recognize the first signs of stress and deal with it immediately. Remember too, that what may be stress for one person may be sheer delight and relaxation for another.

Depending on the intensity of the stressful situation, the remedies may vary. Exercise is one of the best stress relievers. Taking a few minutes to walk or exercise while breathing deeply can refresh you physically while giving your mind a rest, too. Sometimes it may be advisable to completely remove yourself from the situation for a longer period of time to totally relax and recover. It may be necessary to change either your attitude or the conditions so they are more realistic and conducive to good mental and physical health.

UNREALISTIC GOALS

Another deterrent to success is setting goals so high they are impossible to attain. The popular philosophy suggesting that simply looking into the mirror and telling yourself you are great, you will make a fortune today —all without any effort on your part—does a great disservice. Even the successful, although they enjoy their jobs, say it takes work but they enjoy the challenge.

An example of this is Robert, a bright, attractive, likable, eager young man. He had been told that all he needed to be a great success in his job was to have the desire to make it happen. When "it" didn't happen—the Rolls Royce, new house, lots of money—he felt further dejected. His educational background was not good, and he hadn't done the remedial work he needed to become a success in his job with the demanding, critical public that he dealt with.

The desire may start your internal engines going but doing your part is essential—whether it is getting more education, studying longer and playing less, or even realizing that the particular goal you are striving for is not appropriate for your talents.

AN OVERLY INFLATED EGO

The overly inflated personality requires a lot time and energy to maintain. It comes down to choosing between how you would like to see yourself and the reality of who you really are. Can you "own" all the parts of you, even those you really hate? Or do you want to continue to expend energy feeding this insatiable monster? Chi Chi Rodriguez says he is able to avoid letting all of the "hype" of the golf wins sway him because he has internal peace of mind.

AN INAPPROPRIATE SPOUSE/COMPANION

Choosing a companion or friend who helps rather than hinders your growth is an important factor. The right kind of person can help you organize and prioritize your life while encouraging you to stay on track by giving honest feedback. This is such an important choice because it may determine whether your way through life will be bumpy, rough, or even fun.

> *You might ask yourself some of the following questions: Do you need to be in control in a relationship? If so, you will obviously only be attracted to the kind of person who can be controlled. Do you find yourself spending time helping the other person find his potential to the exclusion of your own? Do you expect another person to do the emotional growing while you concentrate on growing financially or intellectually? Do you surround yourself with "yes people" who just say what you want to hear? Who don't make ripples on the water but neither do they encourage you to move forward?*

EXCUSES

Are you stopped by such "self-talk" as, "I can't do that because I am too old, too young, haven't enough money, have children, have to think about my next payment, don't have anyone to support me, if I go back to school I may fail, am not pretty enough, too fat, too thin, can't, can't, can't?"

FEAR

Fear is a great saboteur of progress and potential opportunities. If you listed all of the difficulties you had anticipated that never materialized, you might stop giving this monster the right to hold you back. Has the fear of your own success tripped you up when you were just ready for a victory?

You may be helped to discover this point by asking yourself:

Do you feel guilty about the success you do have? Do you belittle your talents by devaluing the worth of your job, while seeing certain other professions as more worthwhile?

EXCESSES

Another way you may miss out on success is to deal with stress by indulging in excesses:

- Too much food
- Too much alcohol
- Drugs
- Too much work, so that we don't take time to enjoy the successes we do have.

OTHER STUMBLING BLOCKS TO SUCCESS:

- Berating yourself for past failures.
- Failing to recognize the joy and fulfillment of what you are doing now. Crowding your schedule so that you can not appreciate the achievements you have accomplished.
- Resting on your past laurels, forgetting that success is an ongoing process.
- Limiting yourself to only those areas you know and with which you feel comfortable.
- Taking "No" as the final answer.
- Going for the quick sale, the instant success, to the detriment of the integrity of a business or a relationship.

- Letting others (parents, colleagues, teachers, counselors, spouse) make your career decisions for you.
- Being unwilling to break traditional sexually stereotyped barriers.
- Assuming the role of victim by pretending to be powerless over circumstances and individuals.
- Letting pride motivate you. Putting ego, status, image ahead of good judgment.
- Procrastination. If you're avoiding doing something you say you want, find out why you are doing this.
- Letting greed get in the way by pursuing more than your fair share.

"I don't know what it would be like to wake up in the morning bored."

— President Ronald Reagan

HOW YOU CAN USE THE SECRETS OF THE SUCCESSFUL

MEGATRAITS! You've seen how they have worked in the lives of the prominent people in these pages. How do they apply to you? How can you use these traits as catalysts to fuel and ignite more of your own potential? This chapter will give you an opportunity to acknowledge those traits you already have and to further develop others.

The twelve MEGATRAITS are summarized below. Note the italicized suggestions, which you may find helpful to stop and consider. Do they pertain to you? What action can you take to incorporate these traits into your life to make it more fulfilling? Will these points help you be a more successful parent in directing the growth of your children? How can you use them in your own job and with other employees?

1. WORK AT A JOB YOU ENJOY

To say that the successful enjoy their work is an understatement. They are absorbed by it, consumed by it. They totally immerse themselves in it! This is not to say they are all workaholics. As we have seen, most of them work hard, often long hours, and then, with that same intensity, turn their energy to other activities. They are enthusiastic about whatever they are doing.

If at times they found themselves in jobs that were less than satisfying, they immediately began working to change their situation. Money may have been the primary motivation at some point in their lives, but their main focus now is the fulfillment, the satisfaction, and the fun of their work. As Malcolm Forbes of *Forbes* magazine said in a recent interview:

> Probably more important than money or even your determination is that ability to be totally consumed by something. You eat, drink, and sleep it, because you love it and you want it so much. When you're goal-oriented, the hours of the day don't matter. All you regret is that there aren't enough of them. [35]

The late Ray Kroc, who earned his millions from the McDonald's chain, also made this clear:

> To love your work is very important. If you are going to prostitute yourself at an early age for dollars, you'll be working for dollars all your life.

Multi-millionaire Neil Bergt, former Chief Executive Officer of Western Airlines, has been, for many years, Chairman of Alaskan International Industries, a large business which owns companies in such diversified fields as drilling, real estate, and the airline industry. His thoughts on money are:

> If you put the money before the goal, then it will never come true. You have to be goal-oriented. You have to get the goal first and then the money not only follows but it follows in amounts you never even dreamed of. I know that money follows success.

"Success is enjoying what you do," said Don Koll of the Koll Company, a land development firm he started and operates. He continued:

> It would be terrible to come to work and not like it. No matter how much money you were making, that wouldn't be successful. I'm really lucky to do exactly what I want to do. A lot of people don't know what they want to do. People at any level of work can do what they want to do if they would just figure it out . . . I think you're successful when you're happy at doing whatever you're doing. If you're not happy, I don't really see a very successful person.

He went on to say:

> I've been really lucky because everything I do I really enjoy. Some people like to put puzzles together. I think the development business is really that way. I would rather put puzzles together than make money. It's fun assembling. Even when it was tough it was fun. It's too bad that most of the people in the country don't have fun at what they do or they would be successful.

Sometimes putting together the "puzzles," or whatever project these individuals are working on, requires odd—and long—hours. The successful are not nine-to-fivers. They may get caught up with a project and focus on it non-stop. Although for the most part they lead balanced lives, each *day* is not necessarily balanced. They may forgo leisure and other interests for long periods of time to accomplish a compelling goal. During this period, family, meals, or appointments are often put far in the background, sometimes to the chagrin of those around them and to the detriment of relationships.

Bill Daniels, owner of sports TV channel Prime Ticket and part-owner of the Los Angeles Lakers, said he has always put his business life first:

> Putting deals together is my life, and my business comes first. I've been married and divorced four times, and the reason is because my business always came first. I get my kicks out of going someplace and putting some kind of deal together. But that's my joy in life and I love it.

The successful are enthusiastic about whatever project they're involved with. Dr. Morton Copenhaver, a retired dentist with real estate holdings, exemplifies this enthusiasm. It took him 10 years to construct his home, an 8,000 square foot Medieval-style castle, 300-plus feet across, which he built on the side of Camelback Mountain in Phoenix. He was told it was impossible to build on this rocky location but his excitement propelled him to do it. The castle features a waterfall/fireplace, sliding ceiling, and dungeon. At times it has been open to the public with proceeds benefiting the Castle Foundation to pay partial costs of orthodontal care for less privileged children. Of this venture, he said:

> It was fun building the Copenhaver Castle or whatever professional project I undertake. If there is a way to think of a job as fun, then the task is easy. It becomes like play. It is a pattern I started in my childhood.

Mort's first creative construction project was at age six, when he put a washing machine engine on a soap box and built his first set of wheels. Not satisfied with this effort, he went on to improve on the design by adding a Model-T frame and rear end, then a Salsbury motor and, eventually, a motorcycle engine. Many of the successful were early achievers who took pride in—and had fun at—their creative endeavors.

The need to enjoy your work is really so obvious. We spend the majority of our waking hours involved with our work. And yet so many Americans work at jobs they don't enjoy! Why would we do this to ourselves? Many of us feel locked into our jobs. We don't recognize our options or don't have the courage or the energy to make a change.

Florence Chadwick, record-breaking channel swimmer, became a stockbroker late in life and, at 60, had the mettle and the initiative to change firms when she became dissatisfied with where she was working.

Before his success in creating "The Wizard of Oz," Lyman Frank Baum couldn't hold a job, failed at managing a hardware store, and had little respect shown to him in his own home. He was middle-aged when the Oz story came to him. His thoughts poured out after an electrical storm, and he wrote most of the tale in 40 minutes. He went on, after this first major success, to produce over 250 successful entertainment programs in Hollywood. He had failed to enjoy his other jobs until this childlike creativity emerged, and he found a gratifying profession.

Sam Huff was in the National Football League Hall of Fame for 13 years and made the cover of *Time* magazine as one of football's greatest linebackers before switching careers to become a vice president of Marriott Corporation. He believes success is a matter of hard work, and he credits Vince Lombardi with instilling that quality in him. In a newspaper interview he said, "Lombardi could make you better than you could make yourself. He worked hard and he dedicated himself harder and he made you do that." [36]

Even though they enjoy what they're doing, none of the people in this book denied achieving success involves hard work. Dr. Charles Edwards, a neurosurgeon who is head of the renowned Scripps Research Foundation in La Jolla, California, credits his father with giving him the desire and ability to work hard at a rewarding profession:

> I grew up during the depression at the worst Midwest drought in history. My father was a small-town physician. He was extremely successful but extremely hard-working. From an early age I would go on his rounds with him and watch operations and see babies being delivered. I saw things most kids never see. I saw that nothing comes free in this world; you have to work for it. I think the dedication he had to his work inevitably wore off on me.

David B., one executive interviewed, told me he and several friends, all financially successful men in their late thirties and early forties, sat talking one day and realized that, although they loved their wives and children, they were bored. A prominent opthomologist said he admired David's courage in changing his career and choosing where he wanted to live rather than accepting the presidency of a company in a remote, uninteresting town. David's response was, "It wasn't courage; I was merely trying to survive. When I am unhappy, I do something about it."

Although his friends admire David's lifestyle, they have been unable to make such drastic changes in their own professional and personal lives. They believe they are locked into a lifestyle of expensive homes and cars, country club dues, and special privileges for their children, which each year complicates their lives even more. David admitted:

> Going to another job, leaving this style of comfort, is hard to do. The change usually requires simplifying the whole family's lifestyle. But there may be great rewards for everyone from allowing the breadwinner to follow his or her deepest wishes.

Ridding himself of his Mercedes and second car, David biked two blocks to the university where he worked toward a law degree. The spin-off was that his wife and three boys began to develop in new ways. They learned to economize. The boys took on paper routes and odd jobs, becoming more responsible and self-reliant and were granted more freedom by their parents.

David changed careers three times in his life. Each time he revitalized himself with new skills and a new lifestyle. But most of all, he enjoyed his job. Making major changes takes a great deal of courage, but I think it is well worth the risks involved if you succeed in maintaining enthusiasm for your life's work.

At Ford Motor Company, Philip Caldwell said one of his key executives complained that, although he had just been given a bonus, he would rather have more responsibility. Their managers were motivated by the desire to do a job well. Caldwell agreed with the Harvard executive who said "you must *love* your product."

Oil and gas businessman Tim Mantzel, who started a wildlife park out of his love and concern for endangered species, defines success as, "Enjoying what you're doing and being good at what you enjoy doing." He advises people to change jobs if they don't love their work, even if it means earning less money. "Life's too short," he says. "We're all going to be in a pine box pushing up daisies some day."

STEPS YOU CAN TAKE TODAY:

- *Do you feel locked into your job? Recognize that other options exist. See a career counselor; start talking to people; look in the Yellow Pages for ideas. An excellent book to help you with this process is* What Color is Your Parachute?, *which has helped many people come up with innovative ideas to earn their livelihood.*

- *Take the time to analyze your interests and talents. Totally forget, during this process, any thoughts about making money or whether the job is available. Think only about what gives you the most satisfaction. What activities excite you? What do you get the most praise for? Make a list of these things and then brainstorm ways to turn them into money-making opportunities.*
- *Learn from previous jobs that you didn't like. What tasks seemed difficult and unfulfilling? What was it that made you dread going to work?*
- *Take risks! Jump into a job you think you might like. Try learning the skills on the job, even if it means taking an initial cut in pay. If you want to take a safer avenue to get experience in a new line of work, find a way to volunteer. This gives you an opportunity to get on-the-job experience while receiving praise or personal satisfaction, without being judged as a paid employee might be.*
- *Get rid of the idea that work should not be enjoyable. The more you like a job, the more productive you will be; and, chances are, the more money you will eventually make as a result.*

2. DEVELOP YOUR SELF-ESTEEM. ACQUIRE A POSITIVE ATTITUDE

"No one can make you feel inferior without your consent."
— Eleanor Roosevelt

When I asked Xernona Clayton what trait she considered was most critical to her career successes—the latest being named Corporate Vice President of Turner Broadcasting Corporation—she answered without hesitation that it was her high self-esteem. She said even when she encountered bigoted people who were rude to her because she was black, "I had the strength inwardly not to feel inferior." She credits her father with instilling that quality in her at a young age:

> I remember I never had to worry about that feeling of black pride when the country was saying "Feel proud. Be proud of your blackness." I've been black all my life. He taught me to feel good about myself because that's something I can control.

Connie Engel's high self-esteem was one of the factors that enabled her to become America's first female Air Force flight instructor, despite discouragement and "unmerciful teasing" from the men. She described how she overcame the situation:

> It was the fact that no matter what these guys said to me, it did not affect my worth. My worth comes from God, and that's all that counts. If a guy cuts me down or says "I don't want women in pilot training," it doesn't affect my worth. People are going to criticize you no matter what you do, no matter what you say, no matter what you are.

Tim Hansel, author of *When I Relax I Feel Guilty,* has designed a survival school which encourages people to draw on resources they didn't know they had, thus building their self-esteem. A former college teacher, Tim now uses the world as his classroom to conduct his unusual and highly effective workshops. In four different environments—the ocean, the desert, the mountains, and the city—Tim's students confront situations which are unfamiliar and challenging. The activities test their strengths, flexibility, and resourcefulness, providing learning opportunities which develop their self-confidence. Accepting the challenge and attending programs like Summit Expeditions can be helpful. It is one of the most effective ways to simulate new difficult experiences while building trust and team spirit. Self-confidence can be built in a short time when one takes on new or hard tasks and completes them.

You must confront your real self before finding a healthy position from which to relate to others. Ed began to realize that, because he was always extremely demanding of himself, this carried over into expecting perfectionism in others. Once he became more tolerant of his own shortcomings and took positive steps to overcome them instead of beating himself over the head, he began to empathize with other people.

"You turkey!" How many times have we heard a tennis player say that on missing a shot? W. Timothy Gallwey, author of *Inner Tennis; Playing the Game,* understood well the principle of self-acceptance and attempted to teach it to tennis enthusiasts. He advised, instead of yelling "you idiot!" at yourself when you miss a shot, that you realize you are only human and instead praise yourself when you hit the ball *correctly*. Then, physically retrace the path of the racquet to "groove" the correct pattern in your memory. [37] In the words of Norman Lear, tell yourself "good fellow!" It is well established that athletes play significantly better when they visually imagine themselves performing correctly before competing.

Constantly maintaining a high self-esteem is not always easy, but if our inner person is needy and feeling unsatisfied, we will view other people as objects to fill the void. We will doom our relationships to fail, getting angry or manipulative or setting traps to entangle others instead of working to build our own inner strength. We need to honor the "unacceptable" parts we hide, as well as the pleasant, appealing parts we are quick to acknowledge.

We may need some support to improve our self-image. How seriously a person concentrates on being positive about himself often makes the difference. In my practice, I work with people who say they want to change a pattern, but a year later they may not have altered their behavior in any way. Apparently their desire to change is not yet strong enough. The psychological payoffs they receive for retaining the habit outweigh the drawbacks. So changing negative behavior can help build your view of yourself. Feeling good about yourself is important to high self-esteem.

A patient announced to me that he was "giving up smoking," as he looked me in the eye and lit up another cigarette. I asked him how, with that attitude, he expected me to help him. He continued smoking.

Three years later, he became disgusted with himself because he didn't have enough lung capacity to swim laps or even climb stairs without huffing and puffing. He called me to say he had finally quit and would never again touch a cigarette. When I asked him what made him change his behavior, he said, "Simple. Please tell everyone that in making such a decision the most important thing is to have self-respect." He had lowered his self-esteem to a dangerous level. Finally, he chose respect for himself instead of continuing the smoking habit. Although is was not easy to quit, the need for personal respect finally outweighed the pleasures of smoking.

Changing a behavior is often hard, but once we discover the payoff that prevents us from giving up an undesirable habit, most of the battle is won. Sometimes there are underlying beliefs about ourselves (our worth or self-respect as in the above example with the smoker) which will be altered if a "bad" habit is discarded. We often feel so comfortable with the habit that we would feel vulnerable and threatened if we gave it up. Since self-respect was an underlying issue for the smoker, as he stopped smoking he felt better about himself. Perhaps as a result he took on other hobbies, sports, or challenges which had always intrigued him, but which he avoided due to a fear of failure or lack of self-confidence or self-respect. As he let go of his bad habit, he freed himself to try other new things. Sometimes the thought of these resultant new ventures is so threatening that people choose to hold on to the old but comfortable bad habits.

In changing a bad habit, first ask yourself "What payoff am I receiving from this habit?" and, "Do I really want to embrace the possibilities that freedom from it will allow me?" If your answer to the last question is yes, then make a list of step-by-step goals which are practical and attainable.

Have a positive, healthy reward for succeeding as you complete each goal until you finally have overcome the bad habit.

A few other tips are:

- *Make a list of every talent you have, however small, every goal you set that you accomplished, what you did in your younger years and on that made you feel good about yourself. Recite them to yourself from time to time.*
- *Consciously give yourself affirmations when you succeed and say "Good for you! You did that well!"*
- *Surround yourself with positive, supportive, nurturing people, remembering that one of the ways to feel good about yourself is to help and be supportive of others. In the last analysis, of course, you have to support yourself, rather than going on an insatiable quest for approval.*
- *Life is fleeting. Honor yourself by taking your life goals seriously and taking time for yourself. Make a list of ten things you have always wanted to do during your lifetime, no matter how small, and start doing them.*
- *Tackle projects that you can handle and then enjoy your success. Accumulating successful projects is a good way of building self-confidence and can lead to more challenging tasks, pursuits, and accomplishments.*
- *Listen to your inner voice; you usually know what you want. Follow it in constructive ways. Recognize that you are unique and you are bound to need something different from your friends, spouse, or co-workers.*
- *Talk over your feelings and aspirations with friends. Most people love to give advice. And you may just find that others have the same doubts and fears you have.*

It is axiomatic that if we are out of alignment with our inner selves, we will deal with others in a less than healthy and fair way. Forgiving and accepting our mistakes helps us move on to a higher level of emotional health and productivity. High self-esteem enables us to accept our best efforts at success when there's only one possible "winner" in a crowd. As Norman Lear believes, self-esteem will give us strength to face the fact that:

> . . . there's only one brass ring and the others have to be happy sitting on the carousel, reaching, never stopping their reaching . . .

Keep your goals simple. Many of the successful accomplished their goals because they had a *very clear* idea in mind of what they wanted to achieve. They believed they could attain them, and they put 100 percent of their energy into their pursuits. Often people feel defeated because they reach for too many goals at once, or they reach for goals in areas which they are not as well suited for as others. Identify and appreciate what you do well and *perfect it!*

A quality that goes hand-in-hand with high self-esteem is a positive attitude. If you're feeling good about yourself, chances are everything will look brighter to you. Some people seem to have a positive attitude no matter what life delivers. These people are not blind to the negative forces or negative people around them. They acknowledge them. They simply don't focus on the negative.

Robert Magness' positive attitude keeps him going even when the going gets tough, "I never worry that I'm not going to make it because I know I'm going to figure out how." He put this philosophy into action during the stock market crash in October of 1987, when others were seeing only the worst, by buying large quantities of his telecommunications company's stock which were being dumped by fearful stockholders.

If you tend to be a student of Murphy's law, who believes whatever can go wrong will go wrong, you're probably going to be right. Prophesies tend to be self-fulfilling, and we find pretty much what we look for.

We all get a chance to choose our attitudes. A positive outlook, as well as a negative one, is infectious and is spread to those working around you. A positive attitude can set up an environment for others to grow, to see more of their possibilities.

As Dr. Hap Brahams of La Jolla Presbyterian Church put it, "There are only 18 inches from a pat on the back to a swift kick on the behind." Raise your sight 18 inches. It's only a few inches but it makes a whole world of difference to the receiver.

- *Start becoming aware of your negative thinking. Notice how often you complain. When you hear yourself criticize something or someone, see if you can't find a way to change it. Give and accept compliments.*

- *Identify the areas in which you feel insecure. Become aware of the situations that make you feel uncomfortable.*

- *Whatever it is you feel weak in, fix it!*

- *Get help! Read up on the subject. Take a class. Go to a counselor.*
- *Visualize yourself as you want to be. Pretend you are already there! You may convince others of it and, in the process, start believing it yourself.*

3. USE NEGATIVE EXPERIENCES TO DISCOVER YOUR STRENGTHS

"Do not grieve. Misfortunes will happen to the wisest and best of men . . . Misfortunes do not flourish particularly in our path. They grow everywhere." These words, spoken by Omaha Indian Chief Big Elk in 1815, are worth repeating today. When adversity appears in our lives, we often feel victimized, alone, helpless. A look at the lives of the successful shows that misfortune does not just strike selected individuals. It is inevitable in all our lives. The big challenge is how do we choose to handle the situation and what can we learn from it?

The ability to learn and grow from adverse situations is a trait that surfaced consistently during these interviews. The events are powerful enough to command their attention, forcing them to consciously take charge of their lives. They do not get caught up in a wave of decision-making beyond their *choices*, but play an active part in it.

Significantly, the egos of these individuals were already sufficiently developed at the time of the crisis so that they had the strength to surmount defeat. This might not have been the case if their egos were weak at the time of the events. Additionally, as it turned out, the experiences often gave them an opportunity to develop new strengths and etch their personal statements on life with deep conviction.

Philip Caldwell was thrown into a difficult situation when he first came into the truck division of Ford Motor Company. No one was interested in the truck business, which was faltering, so he and two fellow workers undertook a "failure analysis." Within a few years, the division was "on the way to market leadership," and Caldwell had become tougher for the experience. As a result of these efforts, in 1987 the Ford Ranger was #1 in sales in the small truck category.

Norman Lear grew up in a family where his "parents lived with constant bickering and 'one-up-man-ship.' " Out of that situation, he chose to make a positive statement about a negative view of life in the form of comedy. As a result, he wrote "Divorce American Style," "Maude," "All in the Family," and other television shows. This probably helped to heal some of his internal childhood wounds. Perhaps one reason these shows have been so popular is that they touch a familiar chord in many of our hearts.

San Diego Police Chief William Kolender attributes his success today to his willingness to overcome obstacles and learn from his mistakes. He was not a high achiever in the early part of his life. In fact, he flunked out of high school and had to go to summer school to get his diploma. "I even found myself in jail for being drunk, which is no big deal as a kid." He went into the Navy after high school because, as he said, "I was kind of kicking around . . . I never shined at anything."

But this man did go on to "shine." How did he break the pattern of failure? He credits a religious upbringing which inculcated in him inner values, along with a willingness to overcome transient obstacles and to learn from his mistakes. In his words, "A man who has failed does a little better."

Today he is not only successful, but he is also a leader. He is Chairman of the Major City Police Chiefs Association, a national organization with members in more than 47 major cities in the United States and Canada. He also serves as President of the California Community Colleges Board of Governors.

J.B. Fuqua is head of Fuqua Industries which, at one time owned over 200 movie theaters. He was motivated at an early age to overcome the poverty he experienced on a tobacco farm in Virginia. Observing in his teens that the townspeople who were influential and had the most money and possessions were the bankers, he decided to learn about finances:

> I discovered that the Duke University library would send me any book they had through the mail. I was raised about 75 miles north of Durham. And I just read dozens of books about financial things. Some books I would read, I wouldn't understand more than a couple of paragraphs, but I got a grasp of what I was looking for.

Fuqua's actions showed that one of the ways successful people learn is by taking the initiative in their education: The library is available to everyone.

Philip Caldwell, of Ford Motor Company summed up a similar philosophy:

> Every job in my life wasn't a tragedy — but those are the ones you remember more — where the going was a little tougher. Learning totally new things all the time, that's when . . . you were building something.

Mary Tyler Moore believes the difficulties she has encountered in her life have made her stronger. A diabetic and recovering alcoholic, she suffered the tragedy of having her son fatally shoot himself. She said, philosophically: "Pain nourishes my courage. You can't be brave if you've had only wonderful things happen to you." [38]

Tom Mantzel, a Texas oil and gas businessman and wildlife rancher, said he acquired the ability to achieve from the necessity of having to work as a child. Because his father was an alcoholic, his mother supported the family, and the children took jobs at an early age to help. "I think the best thing that happened to me was growing up, as they say, on the other side of the tracks, without having the benefit of a wealthy set of parents," he said. "Anything we wanted we had to go out and hustle and scrap for, and I think that was a definite advantage to me."

General Jimmy Doolittle, World War II Ace, spent eight years of his childhood in the tiny town of Nome, Alaska. He had to endure the hardships of living in that part of the world, where simply surviving is a struggle. He said that he had two handicaps to overcome in order to be successful:

> One was that I was very small, and being small, I had to work harder to do whatever a larger boy could do.
>
> By the same token, I wasn't too smart and so I had to study a little harder in order to get through school.

These limitations, as he viewed them, forced him to work for greater physical and mental heights. He believes that adversity brings out the strengths not only of an individual, but of a nation as well. He agreed with a friend of his who said our country could benefit from some difficult times: "We are suffering from the ravages of prosperity. We've had it too good for too long. We'll have to have adversity in order to sharpen our skills, to straighten out our destiny."

Charles Woods, a highly successful businessman, said, "Adversity tempers the soul." He was orphaned as a young child, and at age 23 he had most of his body burned when his military plane exploded. He spent the next several years in hospitals, undergoing 60 operations. Although they were considered "successful," his reconstructed face shows no emotion and his fingers remain fused together.

> I was five years in the hospital, so it gave me a lot of time to think. I discovered there was more to life than flying a plane or chasing a good-looking girl . . .

> Everybody's got some sort of disability. Being female is a disability, being black or a member of a minority group or being tremendously shy is a disability. It is just that I have one that is visible and attracts more attention.

How did he manage to start a new life? Not by taking the advice of a "friend" who suggested that, because of the physical scarring, Charles buy a remote chicken farm. (Reflecting with humor on that suggestion, Charles said, "I don't even *like* chickens!") Instead, he went on more determinedly than ever. After purchasing a corner lot, he used his truck as collateral to get a bank loan to purchase building materials to construct a house. Today he owns six television stations and considerable real estate holdings. His net worth is estimated at $100 million-plus.

How can you profit from these experiences of others? By learning how they pushed themselves past tragedies or difficult times that could have provided a haven for self-pity. Charles admits that if this accident had not occurred, he would have been just an ordinary pilot. He "took the bull by the horns," refusing to let himself wallow in the mental state I call "being on a button that is stuck."

By being flexible, he created a new life, one based on his assets rather than on his earlier goals. We can learn to work through a situation and find ways to succeed, given who we *are,* not who we might have been.

Some of these successful people have had childhood hardships. Author Eugenia Novello's mother died when she was an infant, necessitating a move to Mexico City to be cared for by her grandmother. They grew to love each other; then abruptly, Eugenia's father moved her to Ensenada to live with him and a new mother, a traumatic change. She says:

> It was a hard childhood that made me look into myself and from there, to know people. I built up that strength to sustain myself, because I had so many shocks delivered to me from infancy on. I had to pull myself together to survive. I found that the negativity happening around me could be surmounted by something better.
>
> . . . I think most of us have qualities which enable us to overcome crises, pain, or even the boredom of routine.

As we have seen in a previous chapter, artist and business woman Ann Ruth has known a life as a quadriplegic, which most people would call hardship and suffering but which she calls an "inconvenience."

Norman Cousins' story of childhood hardship may be one of the most amazing contained in this book and has undoubtedly influenced his later life:

> In my ninth year, I was sent to a public sanitarium in New Jersey. Kids can be pretty rough. The second or third night I was there I was dumped far out in the woods . . . and warned not to follow them back. After I made it through that, I knew that death would never scare me.

He also learned about youth gangs and how they operate. Taking an unusual view of this experience, he said:

> I learned how to "tame the beast." I just figured out a way to deal with these kids that gave them the satisfaction of being decent.

It is probably because of this experience and what he learned from it that Norman is often chosen for the U.S. advanced guard in treaties and negotiating groups working to establish peace with the Soviets.

What are the components of a tragic situation? In "A Gift of Hope: How We Survive Our Tragedies," Robert L. Veninga summarizes five stages one goes through during a crisis: *The Bombshell,* (a period of numbness), *Illusion of Normalcy, Hitting Rock Bottom, The Awakening,* (a restructuring of our view of ourselves and the world — an awareness that there might be hope . . .), and the final stage, *Acceptance*. He is quick to add that "acceptance does not mean forgetting." [39]

During these stages, I have noticed that those who have been brought up to think of life as tough and tragedy as just one part of life seem to recover faster from a crisis.

> *If you have experienced a tragedy or painful experience, you might try to discover what positive lessons the circumstances may hold for you.*

Some tragedies occur in which it seems impossible to find a blessing. Among these are accidents in which young children are killed long before they have begun to live, accidents such as those occurring on the highways and in war, and natural disasters such as earthquakes.

As difficult as these occurrences are to accept, we still must deal with them, and we can *choose* how to respond! The quality of the rest of our lives depends on our choices. Will we survive with our egos intact and without holding on to the bitterness for the rest of our lives? And can we survive with dignity?

Ask yourself: Does this event speak to the general condition of my life? Could it be God or life itself is trying to shock me into paying attention to something I need to hear—a warning of a need to change a certain behavior—perhaps to create a new way of responding to events or of being more responsible?

Elisabeth Kubler-Ross is well known for her views on death and dying and the meaning of suffering in our lives. In a world where pleasure seekers and advertisers seek to convince us that physical gratification and happiness are one and the same, we can be reminded that even in suffering we can learn. In the words of Ben Franklin, "Those things that hurt, instruct."

This is not to suggest that we become masochists; however, we need to learn how to deal with difficult situations. Kubler-Ross asks her audiences to think of the most painful experiences in their lives and reminds them:

> Were it not for the painful moments, the individual would not grow. That fact affects the way you look at the tragedy . . . and the question of how you will endure suffering during our lifetime. [40]

On the other hand, we have a warning from Dr. Francis MacNutt, author of *The Power to Heal*. He is a charismatic leader and healer, who often deals with this issue. Dr. MacNutt spoke on the subject of pain in our interview:

> Like most things in life, pain can be helpful or harmful; its purpose is to call our attention to the afflicted part so we can remove what is hurting us. A headache is not in itself naturally helpful; it is helpful in that it indicates to me that I am harming myself in some way [like worrying too much] and that I should change my lifestyle. [41]

When faced with an adverse situation, consider the broad implications of the event. Analyze the situation in detail. This gives you a chance to be objective. What actually happened? What was your part in it? Did you compulsively push through something that did not really "fit?" Was the timing wrong?

In retrospect, Mary Cunningham could see the role she played in her own victimization at Bendix. She *chose* to isolate herself from others in the company, revering her sole mentor (William Agee, then chief executive officer), thus inviting estrangement and resentment. As one of her colleagues put it, she "should have been seen at lunch with *anyone* except the CEO." This is one of the things Harvard didn't teach her in its MBA program.

> *During the difficult period, were you sensitive to other people who were involved and did you have their cooperation? Did you expect a miracle that did not happen? Was it just a matter of the external situation of the world? Were other people involved who were not acting responsibly? Did some of those people "use" this situation to further their own cause without concern about the specific project? Did you not have a supportive backup team?*

In my clinical practice, I see many people who are not willing to subject themselves to this intense scrutinization. Peter found himself after 20 years of marriage, getting a divorce. Six months later he met Pam, 21 years younger than he and thrilled to bask in his accomplishments. He, in turn, enjoyed having this pretty young woman on his arm, to serve as his hostess. She was the anesthesia that prevented him from analyzing, however painfully, the reasons for the breakup of his marriage. They married the day his divorce became final. Seven years and one child later, Peter found himself again filing for divorce, realizing that, this time, he must analyze the causes of his broken marriages and his contribution to them.

Virginia, another client, found herself in her 40s ending an 18-year marriage. She went through a grieving period, followed by an analytical phase in which she realized that in many ways her personality did not really fit with her former spouse. When she started to date, she was shocked to realize that she was attracting the same kind of man as her husband. These were men who had been emotionally scarred at an early age but were often unconscious of this fact and had stopped growing emotionally. They realized she would go to great lengths to keep the relationship together. Finally, listing the traits that did not "fit," she was able to do some critical thinking. Her husband had seemed to fall in love with her for her brains but he was not very sensitive to feelings. Next, she proceeded to develop her masculine side or left-brain thinking and dropped such dead-end relationships at their inception. She grew emotionally healthier and started to attract a more sensitive man who also was quite bright.

Psychologists have taught us that if a person has not altered a faulty pattern of dealing with others, he will indeed attract the same kind of person in the next relationship.

Can you identify recurring patterns that cause you pain in your job or your relationships?

Life pushes us to grow, and even though we holler, drag and stamp our feet, we will be confronted over and over with the choice of fighting this growth or moving ahead. We can remain complacent, or we can ask some questions about ourselves and the direction our lives are taking. The people in this book are successful because they are not complacent.

4. *BECOME MORE DECISIVE AND DISCIPLINED. SET GOALS AND REACH THEM!*

The successful know what they want and go after it with gusto. They set a goal and then stick with it until it is achieved—no matter how many people tell them they can't. If we don't make a conscious choice about what we want, we will end up with whatever life hands us and wonder why.

Decision-Making

Former First Lady Eleanor Roosevelt remains a model to many Americans long after her death. She was active and vital into her late eighties, leading a full schedule that would have exhausted many younger people. She is quoted as saying:

> When I was a young woman at the age of 26, I did a long, thoughtful analysis of my life—and I realized for the first time how much time I was wasting on indecision and regret. And I decided right then and there that I should never again leave room in my life for either of those thieves.[42]

Dr. Charles Edwards, head of internationally known Scripps Research Foundation, constantly made life and death choices as a neurosurgeon. He said of that experience, "You are always in a situation where you must make a decision that you can't go home and think about. It may be the right or the wrong choice. In this world there's probably more harm done from no decisions than from wrong decisions." He went on to say that we aren't *trained* to be decisive:

> The average American household isn't involved in decision making. Things just happen. You can go through life pretty well without

> making choices, and the older you get, the bigger small decisions seem. I am dumbfounded by the number of people who think they are putting their reputations on the line over decisions that are not quite as big as they think they are . . . I think that one of the attributes of a good leader is that he can make a decision and recognizes it. Even if the choice is wrong, it is better than apathy.

Make a decision and follow through with it. Forrest Shumway, former Vice Chairman of the Allied-Signal Companies, learned that the first day on the job, after graduate school. His first boss told him, "I will tolerate anything but indecision."

One of the reasons many of us have difficulty making decisions is we have not first worked out what is most important to us. As Philip Caldwell, formerly of Ford Motor Company, said in my interview with him for Nightingale/Conant's "This I Believe" audiotape series:

> It's always seemed to me that it is necessary to have some order in the thought process, and I tend to think in terms of trying to define, at the outset, what the object of the game is. It's awfully important to do that before we spend a lot of time saying, "Well, how many players will there be, and are we going to play at a square table or a round table?"

Reflecting on his military years, he said:

> In other words, it is better to find out why it is important to take Hill 875 than spend all of our time talking about how to take it. Then, when we find that we have taken it, well, why are we here? It doesn't really achieve anything. [43]

Just doing something to be active is not necessarily the most intelligent approach. Don't forget that sometimes an option is deliberately not doing anything at all.

Barriers to Decision Making

Probably the number one enemy of decision-making is procrastination. Some of us make decisions by default, putting them off until we no longer have a choice. Why do we procrastinate? Usually it's from fear. Fear of failure, fear of rejection, fear of not having the skills or the time or the talent to follow through, or even a subconscious fear of our own success.

Sometimes we are frightened because something demands a *change* that we don't believe we can carry off. Change can be painfully slow and hard, but since the pattern took many years to develop, it is understandable that it may take time and effort to change. *Not* dealing with a situation or a person only postpones the confrontation while you continue to spend your time in non-productive worry.

Procrastination can be our way of avoiding responsibility. This behavior often starts between the ages of five to nine, when children want to exert their influence more. For example, procrastination was an effective way to handle the situation when we were small children who did not want to go to bed. Procrastinating and prolonging play when we were told to stop gave us the feeling we had some power over the authority figures in our lives.

If you are an adult and still rebelling against "authority," you might ask yourself who is really in charge of your life. Are your rebellious choices really your choices? If you work at building inner strength, you will more easily manage your external environment. It means committing yourself wholeheartedly to the direction of your life.

Well adjusted adults continue their internal growth process throughout life. Individuals can do this by educating themselves on the subject through reading books, attending lectures, keeping a diary of dreams, charting life experiences, or listening to tapes. The Native American Indian has a ritual of going off by himself on a Vision Quest to discover for himself his next step in life. Some people do not continue to grow emotionally or make choices because of low self-esteem, lack of adequate role models, or just plain fear. Who can fault them? But what we see in the lives of the successful indicates that a person works through these obstacles if he wants to go to the next stage.

Alan Garner, author of two best sellers, *Conversationally Speaking* and *It's OK to Say No to Drugs*, says it is important to differentiate between those tasks that are important and those that are just interesting.

So what can you do to become more decisive and disciplined?

- *Weigh the pros and cons. Analyze the results. Ask yourself what is the worst thing that could happen. If you know the outer limits, you will be less likely to fear a decision. We often create "dragons" that disappear when we examine them closely.*
- *Consider your options. In most cases we become blocked in an area when we can see only one option. We usually see a situation in terms of black or white when more likely there are many variations of grays that give us a wider range of choices.*

- *Write it out. Sometimes a simple step like sitting down and listing the options helps clear up our scattered thinking, whereas, if we keep it in our head, it can seem more complex than it really is. Putting it in writing enables us to be more specific and concrete in our focus.*
- *Don't spend a lot of time on decisions that aren't important. Focus on areas that are worthy of your full attention. Don't "sweat the small stuff." Is the subject really worthy enough of your emotional investment to get upset or angry about it? If you care and feel challenged by a decision that needs to be made, your investment in the outcome will bring out your best abilities. It will also maximize your chances for success.*
- *Are you procrastinating? If so, examine the reasons: Can you identify an underlying fear that keeps you from facing the decision head-on? Go for it!*
- *Finally, evaluate your decision. Are you on target for the decision you made? Can you chart a definite improvement in the way you now handle a situation compared to the way you would have handled it six months or a year ago? Would you make the same decision if you had to do it over? What have you learned—is this an event your family and close friends might learn from? If so, can you share it with them?*

Identify Specific Goals

Once you've decided what is important, then the process of setting goals follows.

The successful are *strategists*. They have specific goals and plans for obtaining them and the discipline to see them through. If the first plan does not succeed, they have alternative strategies. Their game plans could be compared to those of a football quarterback's sequence. If the first "straight-up-the-middle" play does not bring the desired yardage gain, the second-down play might be an end run (option play) or attempt at a lateral pass. Having one plan "blocked" does not stop the successful from pursuing their goal. Possessing, as we have seen, the trait of persistence, they do not take "no" as an ultimate verdict.

In an interview with Philip Caldwell, when he was Chief Executive Officer of the Ford Motor Company, I asked him how much of strategy thinking is intuitive and how much is learned. He explained:

> The best strategic planning is based on a careful collection of facts in an organized way that can be arranged to serve your interest—narrow the gap of guess.
>
> In complex, competitive situations, with many persons' lives involved, you must try to be *orderly* about this process and have *strategic* plans . . . intuition, however, may play a part in *timing* . . .

My observations are that successful people often use strategies which are unconventional and, thus, they are often viewed by the more conservative as "mavericks." As they forge new frontiers, their objectives may seem far-fetched and unattainable. Their self-confidence, however, combined with determination and courage, proves them to be creative realists, rather than impractical idealists.

One of the methods some successful people use is visualization. This technique enables the individual to picture in his mind what the end result will actually look and feel like. He is able to get the feeling of what his life will be like when he achieves his goal, whether it be graduating from college, becoming office manager, being married, or even treating his children more lovingly.

This technique has long been used by some athletes who, in addition to practicing long and hard, also do the mental work of seeing themselves kicking a field goal or sinking a golf ball in the hole. Billy Jean King visualized her entire tennis match with Bobby Riggs before her resounding victory over him several years ago.

Neil Bergt, Chairman of Alaskan International Industries, has used this technique since childhood. In fact, he says, "Everything that I have ever done in my life I had an image of myself doing first."

He incorporated his own visualization techniques into those taught by Lou Tice at a seminar he attended.

> I can put an image in my mind of what I want to accomplish and I can hardly think of anything else but that . . . that's all I can see until that image comes true. I find that whatever I'm doing, somehow it's working toward making that image come true.

The theory is that we hold in our subconscious a picture of what or who we are, what we can and can't do. That image may or may not be in alignment with reality. "Our subconscious perceives truth as we see it," explains Bergt. "It may not be reality, but it is the truth as we perceive it. You can program truth as you perceive it if you can put the proper affirmations of images in your subconscious. Your creative subconscious will make you live up to those images."

This process sometimes requires changing an underlying belief we hold about ourselves. Simply visualizing oneself in a loving relationship, for instance, will be ineffective if the individual doesn't feel worthy of love. And visualizing is only part of the goal-attaining process. There still remains the most important part: doing the footwork through hard work and discipline.

- *Decide on the goal and commit yourself to it!*
- *Write the goal down and post it in prominent places, where you can look at it frequently throughout the day, so that it is constantly in your mind. Describe it carefully and specifically. Put it on your desk, your mirror, your refrigerator, your dashboard.*
- *Break the goal down into practical, workable steps.*
- *Set realistic time limits for accomplishing each phase.*
- *Outline a strategy for accomplishing each task, with an alternative plan in case the first approach doesn't work.*
- *Visualize yourself as if you have actually attained the goal. How does it feel? What are people saying to you? What do you look like in your new setting?*
- *Identify individuals and other resources that can help you reach your goal.*
- *Tell a supportive friend who might give you encouragement. Sometimes we're more likely to keep a commitment if others are expecting it. And if you get stuck or discouraged, that person can help. Admitting sometimes you need help may be a sign of strength and a healthy first step toward resolving a problem.*
- *Reward yourself for the little successes as you go along, and plan a big reward—a party, a trip, a present to yourself—when you reach your final objective.*

Discipline

Once you've committed yourself to the goal, it takes discipline to achieve it. Be realistic about how much time and energy you're willing to invest in the effort.

Golfer Lee Trevino believes we all have God-given talents, and the reasons some succeed where others fail are *discipline* and *sacrifice*:

> Every time I meet a superstar or a very successful individual in any field, I know he's not only done it on his own, but he did a tremendous amount of sacrificing to get there . . . The main reason he was more successful than the other is because he was willing to sacrifice.

Self-discipline requires that you keep working at your goals and shutting out distractions. Ted Geisel, creator of the *Dr. Seuss* books, said, "There is no simple way, and the discipline is essential. I never leave the room during my work day, even if all I do is sit there." [44] It is important to set aside a certain period of time each day to work toward your goals. Reward yourself only when that day's objectives are accomplished. The reward might be an activity that you enjoy, a hobby, a sport, or other form of recreation or entertainment.

Philip Caldwell advises us to focus on the job at hand:

> Whatever you are assigned to do, do it very well. Don't spend all your time on the [present] job trying to get to the next job . . . I think people hurt themselves, and they're not effective when they're doing that.
>
> You should do the job at hand better than anybody else. That is the biggest key I know to open the next door.

It often helps to make a daily chart, hour by hour, of all of our activities. In my seminar groups, students do this, and, after two weeks of such notations, they are often surprised at the number of non-goal-oriented tasks in which they had been involved, which had detracted from their major goals.

U.S. Navy Captain Lloyd N. Bucher, captain of the *U.S.S. Pueblo,* learned discipline at an early age in Boys Town, where he was raised. He later adapted those disciplinary methods to the prisoner-of-war situation he encountered when his ship was held hostage by the North Koreans. For him, discipline is a sign of caring. He believes this was one reason he and his men were able to stay together as a cohesive military unit and withstand the privations and pain to which they were subjected. He believes too many of today's children are products of overly permissive parents and advocates discipline and establishing limits as sound ways of showing love and caring, as Father Flanagan did for him in Boys Town:

> Those around me could have kissed me and cuddled me, but what I really needed to learn was a sense of my own limits; and being bounced on the bottom firmly but without excessive force was an excellent instructional method. We never went without meals or a place to sleep; but Father Flanagan never abdicated his authority.

WAYS TO DEVELOP SELF-DISCIPLINE:

- *Make a daily chart, hour-by-hour, of the way you spend your time. Evaluate it to see if it is the most productive schedule to accomplish your goal.*
- *Focus on the task at hand. Don't allow yourself to be sidetracked by distractions.*
- *Give mental affirmations for maintaining your schedule.*
- *Reward yourself at the end. Have that big party. Take that trip. You deserve it.*

5. DO YOUR ACTIONS REFLECT YOUR INTEGRITY AND DO YOU ENCOURAGE OTHERS TO WIN?

Treating people fairly is not just a matter of morals. It also makes good business sense, and no one knows that better than the successful. Integrity is imperative to success, particularly in the business world. You go back to the same customers time and again. If you have not treated them fairly, there will be no second time.

I think the remarks of Jess Hay, Chairman and Chief Executive Officer of Lomas and Nettleton Financial Corporation, capture particularly well the essence of integrity:

> I value integrity. I believe that honesty and integrity are the hallmarks of character and essential components of long term functioning in this or any other society. Integrity involves more than just not lying. It involves being true to yourself and being truly yourself in dealings with others. It involves "being you" but not in the Hedonistic sense of "doing your own thing" without regard to the needs of others. "Being you" is to be true to your own values, your own convictions, your own

> potential, your own responsibilities without inordinate or overriding concern for reward, pleasure, or penalty in any given moment. The antithesis of integrity and of character is the tendency to do, in response to every situation, that which is easiest and least demanding of you as a person.

The individual with integrity, Jess said, is able to keep his head, his purpose and direction, his sense of right and wrong, even when others are pushing him in other directions. Jess includes in his definition the qualities of being slow to judge and quick to forgive, as well as to accept forgiveness when it is offered. "A person of integrity is, in every sense of the word," he said, "a man or a woman endowed by God's creative hand with the determination to be a fully functioning responsible human being, a contributor, a participant, a risk taker, a doer, a lover."

Mahatma Gandhi was such a man. One of the greatest men of his time, he left an indelible impression on the world. Albert Einstein said of him when he was assassinated at age 78 in 1948 that "Gandhi . . . demonstrated that a powerful human following can be assembled not only through the cunning game of the usual political maneuvers and trickeries, but through the cogent example of a morally superior conduct of life." [45]

Bill Daniels, as owner of Prime Ticket sports cable TV network, partial owner of L.A. Lakers basketball team, and a business magnate, is highly thought of in the business world. He said he has earned that reputation by making "Integrity" the watchword of his company:

> You never lie. You tell people the facts. You avoid conflict of interest; if you have one, you tell somebody. You do what you say you're going to do. All that's combined into the word "integrity," and that's the motto of our firm.

He went on to say he would rather lose a deal than sacrifice integrity:

> I've walked away from a lot of deals when I've sensed something going on that wasn't right, or we were involved in a situation where our integrity was on the line. I've done it many, many times. So you lose a couple of hundred thousand dollars. Hell, that's short term.

The true entrepreneur has a top-notch product in which he believes strongly. Quality is essential if he is to stay on top. He is totally dedicated to his "baby" and transfers that enthusiasm to those around him. He chooses quality employees and expects—in fact demands—high performance. If an employee does not meet the required professional standards, the successful move quickly to correct the situation.

They also realize the importance of keeping their top-level staff happy and compensate them well. In addition to financial rewards, they make it a point to treat them with respect and fairness. Keeping all parties in a relationship happy, whether employees, customers, family, or friends, is of prime importance.

Robert Dedman, who has 15,000 employees working at 225 clubs around the nation, said:

> The only thing you should do in any relationship is to try to be the most giving partner. As a rule you'll prosper in direct proportion to how the relationship prospers . . . I think success in life is primarily a result of the ability to set up win-win relationships personally and professionally.

He has certainly met that criterion. He has been married for 35 years, has close relationships with his two children, and has many employees who have worked for him for 28 to 30 years.

Bob Magness, Chief Executive Officer of Tele-Communications, said:

> If you don't have a deal that is good for both parties when you start, then you're dealing with the wrong people. I make lots of deals, and I make them so they come out good for both sides. That's the only kind of deal I make.

Asked to sum up his life's philosophy, Ace Greenberg, Chief Executive of a financial investment firm, said, "I hope that everybody I have come in contact with feels that they received more than they gave from our relationship—that they never had the feeling of being taken advantage of."

- *Choose a boss who has integrity.*
- *Follow your gut-level instincts on the trustworthiness of an individual.*

How supportive are you in your business and personal relationships? Ask yourself the following questions:

- *Are you authoritarian in your relationships, or are you supportive?*
- *Do you act out of a desire for mutual serving and sharing?*

- *Do you let people be themselves? Do you respect their decisions and allow them to make their own mistakes and have their own victories?*
- *Are you realistic in what you expect of others, given their present capabilities?*
- *Do you make it a point to look at a situation from the other person's point of view and find a solution that is mutually rewarding?*

6. BE PERSISTENT!

"You have to bang on doors and bang on doors and never stop!"
— Ray Kroc

If someone tells you something you don't want to believe, don't believe it! One well-known author told me she submitted an article, in which she had a great deal of faith, *seventy-seven* times to different publishers. It was accepted on the *seventy-eighth* try. Another author mentioned submitting an article fifty times before acceptance. Many of the successful say their work is tough, but that does not deter them from continuing to work on a project they love.

Karen O'Connor, in *Sally Ride and the New Astronauts,* writes:

> Persistence—hanging in there—is important. More than half of the astronauts selected in 1980 had been turned down in 1978. Anna Fisher's husband, Bill, was one. And Mike Collins, who flew on the historic Apollo II moon mission, was rejected twice before he became an astronaut.
>
> Before applying a second time, Bill Fisher went back to school and earned another degree. In addition to his M.D., he got a master's degree in engineering. [46]

Ironically, Norman Vincent Peale, who is well-known for his book, *The Power of Positive Thinking,* was nearly talked out of writing it. In his magazine, *Guideposts,* he described the persistence which eventually enabled him to continue the project.

> I had an idea for a book that I thought might help people, but a well-known expert in the field told me my approach was all wrong. I listened to him for a while, but finally I sat down with a pad and pencil and began to outline a series of chapters. With the help of my wife, Ruth,

> I tried to push the fears and hesitations out of my mind and complete the book. Together we did it. Today, they tell me that the book, *The Power of Positive Thinking*, has sold over 15 million copies since it first appeared in 1952. [47]

It took perseverance for Florence Chadwick to complete 16 channel swims, often requiring her to be in very cold water for as long as 17 hours! "My coach used to say swim till you're tired," Chadwick said, "Then swim till you're exhausted. Then swim another two lengths. If you want something bad enough, you'll get it. It must be in your capability—it would be foolish of me to say I want to be an opera singer." She applied the same principle to business, "If you want to do better, you just work harder, longer hours." [48]

In addition to working harder and longer, Don Koll adds another element to his formula for being able to persist until his goal is met—Keep it simple:

> If you come up with an idea that is sound and that you think will work, odds are you can find somebody to put up the money. The key is the idea. There's plenty of money around. I think it's really simple. I don't think the world is that tough. I don't even want to know how complicated it is.

Remember that people respond to requests and ideas differently—some by analytical persuasion, some by needing to hear the request repeatedly; but some don't respond until you become assertive enough to get their attention. Persistence, coupled with polite self-assertiveness, I find, is extremely effective. However, if after a while this strategy does not work, just raising your voice and stating clearly what you want may make the difference.

Persistence enables you to return to a problem over and over, seeing it in a new light, looking for new options. The successful learn how to tap into creative new ideas by looking at familiar ones in a new way. My own fresh ideas often come by talking with people knowledgeable on a subject. Many times, when my creative flow is blocked, I wander along the beach. Getting involved in conversation with open, relaxed beach people often gives me a new perspective.

For many, the creative process is renewed after three steps:

- *Thinking about the problem.*
- *Analyzing it.*
- *Letting the idea go, while still being aware of the problem.*

The last step, releasing the problem from your conscious mind, can be quite effective. The solution suddenly becomes clear, often after sleep, when a dream has offered a suggestion, or simply after the subconscious has had a chance to work on it.

Research also shows that some people can be persuaded through verbalization and others through visualization. The Sears study (Weiss-McGrath Report, McGraw-Hill) confirms these findings:

Life Expectancy of Information:

By Telling (only)	3 hours later	70%
	72 hours later	10%
By Showing (only)	3 hours later	72%
	72 hours later	20%
By Telling and Showing Concurrently	3 hours later	85%
	72 hours later	65% [49]

As you can see, "show and tell" is more than just for school children. It provides the longest memory retention for most people.

The successful recognize that "no" does not necessarily mean "no." Sometimes a person is just testing the waters to see what you will do next. From the successful, I learned that "no" often means that the acceptable time or option has not been discovered yet. Remember Ray Kroc's eight trips to the bank before he got his loan for McDonald's.

Of course, in most cases, only projects with merit will succeed. According to Ely Calloway, founder of Calloway vineyards, and known as a marketing genius, to be successful an idea must be:

- *New*
- *Different*
- *Better*

If these three ingredients are not present, a product or idea probably won't succeed.

If, however, your deep gut feeling tells you it will be a winner, despite what others say . . . PERSIST! Successful people keep trying! Sometimes you may need a break from your work. Take it. It may enable you to return to your pursuit with more enthusiasm.

7. TAKE MORE RISKS

> "Don't be afraid of a few risks. Other people have already taken most of the really big ones for you."

Lee Iacocca, Chairman of the Board for Chrysler Corporation, was referring to the 17 million immigrants who took the ultimate risk in leaving their homelands to come to America. Speaking at the Duke University graduation, he talked about America's tribute to those risk-takers during the 1986 relighting of the Statue of Liberty, which he headed:

> The Statue of Liberty stands for the ideals of America, but Ellis Island symbolizes the reality. Once those people got off the boat, they were herded like cattle through chutes, interrogated in a language most of them didn't even understand, and put through humiliating medical exams. If they were lucky, somebody stamped a piece of paper that said they were Americans. Then they had to go to work and build something called America that was true to the ideals that drew them here. [50]

What have you got to lose? That's more than a rhetorical question for the successful. They are avid risk takers, and their ability to judge when to take risks comes from studying the situation, considering their options, and weighing the possible losses, not just wildly jumping in.

The risks the successful take vary according to their careers. Some interviewees, Mary Kay Ash, Venita Van Caspel, and Forrest Shumway, take financial risks. Others such as Ronald Reagan, Abigail McCarthy, Clare Booth Luce, and Judge Sandra O'Connor are known for political risks.

The successful artists, Charlton Heston, Norman Lear, Francoise Gilot, Maria Martinez, and Ann Ruth, face the risk of public rejection and criticism in order to publicly share their noteworthy talents.

Those in athletics, Lee Trevino, Steve Garvey, and Florence Chadwick, know the tensions of a contest where there is only one winner out of many competitors. Their skills and determination frequently bring them the joys of being that laureled victor.

It takes courage to develop a new skill. Learning a new sport, for instance, may entail risking physical strain or injury. If you are a natural in some sports but not in your most recently chosen one, you may experience awkwardness and humiliation, as well. Some people do not want to weather the beginning frustrations of mastering a new skill. The successful, on the other hand, meet new challenges with gusto.

Successful people are definitely "doers." They take on a new hobby or sport with the same enthusiasm and determination they put into their careers. They see new connections between what is, what has been done, and what might be. They seem to acquire new skills to renew themselves.

In addition to the risks he takes in business, Malcolm Forbes provides us many examples of risk taking—from international motorcycling to skin diving. Intrigued with hot air balloons, he read all the information he could find on the subject and integrated the facts before starting on his daring trip to become the first to cross America in a hot air balloon. Although his was a risky venture, he lessened his chances for failure by thorough preparation.

Ann Ruth, paralyzed from the neck down since age five, continues to "spice up her life" with new challenges. Her most recent adventure was sky-diving, which required faith and trust that her instructor would reach the ground before she did and catch her.

Philip Caldwell, formerly of Ford Motor Company, recommended that people "not be afraid to be torn up a bit. Get out in the world. Have a lot of experiences." He went on to say, "Accept assignments when you can't fill in all the blanks . . . If I had studied any offer too much, I probably would have said no. And if I had said no to any of those jobs, there probably wouldn't have been the next one."

As a counselor, I see people who are stunted and unwilling to expand their horizons in one or more areas. Recognizing an area of resistance is the first step to growing beyond it. Life seems to continually present us with opportunities to grow. We can refuse to move beyond our chosen limitations, but I can say with a great deal of certainty, today's lesson will present itself to us tomorrow if we procrastinate receiving its message.

Lawyer, businessman, and philanthropist, William E. Murray believes in protecting his risks by building in a factor he calls "Planning for Failure":

> If the project does not go as planned, or if a relationship becomes unsatisfactory there must always be a provision in the agreements where you can get out with modest losses.

It is important to temper our "Yes!" to new challenges with wisdom and balanced living. To take on too many novel experiences at once is to invite possible failure and setback. Timing is critical in learning new skills. At one extremely busy stage in my life, I attempted one new skill too many and stopped just short of my goal.

I was a single parent raising a young family, working at two part-time jobs, and moderating and producing my first 16-part television series.

Producing was a new field in television work for me, and it required much of my time and energy. A friend had given me scuba diving lessons as a gift. The class was fun, but I was a long-distance swimmer, and it was difficult to let go, sink into the depths of the ocean, and relax in the strange environment. I had completed the classes, passed the written test, and was prepared for my final ocean dive, some 40 to 60 feet deep. I started through the shore break and, in spite of a very patient instructor whom I had told about my apprehension, I panicked. I kept getting thrown into the waves and could not get beyond their breaking zone. I chose not to complete the training at that time, deciding I was already learning too many new skills to take on one more. It was as if my system was verging on "overload."

Maybe, like me, there are times when you don't want to take on any more challenges and just want to tread water or lie in the sun and rest. Completing the dive for me would have required talking my way through a big risk that I was not ready to take at that time. The ability to say "no" or "not yet" to a challenge when wisdom cautions against it can also be a strength. The appropriate time is usually when our internal gut feeling says it is time.

If you haven't been a risk taker up until now, give it a try. It may not be as comfortable as staying stuck in a less desirable, more comfortable situation, but it can certainly be more rewarding.

- *Start by making a list of things you've been wanting to do but, perhaps because of fear, have avoided. They can range in magnitude from asking someone to lunch to going on a vacation by yourself.*
- *Next to each item, list your fears about what might happen if you acted on it. Is it fear of rejection? Fear of looking foolish? Fear of losing what you already have? You may find that the possible consequence is miniscule compared to the probable reward. Ask yourself: What is the worst thing that could happen? Once you've identified it, analyze whether there is a way of preventing that outcome or dealing with it if it does occur.*

I had a woman in therapy who, like many women of her generation, had been protected and told not to take risks. One day she walked into the office, and it was obvious that a great change had taken place in her personality. She was more assertive, more in control, held her head with a sense of dignity, and even began the therapy session by directing the conversation.

Finally she talked about her breakthrough. She had been in her kitchen working when she suddenly whirled around and caught a glimpse of a big, ugly, larger-than-life rat. This woman, like many of us, knew what she was most frightened of and on the top of her list came R-A-T-S. She was so scared that she almost couldn't say the word.

But, being a conscientious mother of three young children, she was more concerned about a rat running around her house and possibly harming her youngsters. She grabbed a bamboo pole and, baring her teeth to the ferocious animal, began the attack. She shouted to her kids to get up on the couch where they would be safe. She said she might scream during the encounter but she would get the critter! Twenty minutes later, an exhausted mother put down the bamboo stick and scooped up one large, now very mutilated, rat!

That day she identified 20 other fears which she dropped.

- She was assertive to the receptionist and got the appointment she wanted.
- She spoke up to her husband and stopped taking criticism that he hadn't expressed at his job because there he wanted to be the "nice guy."
- She even said no, politely, to her mother-in-law's usual barrage of complaints.

Because she had killed a rat, which had been on the top of her "Most Feared" list, she no longer needed to be controlled by the smaller fears.

Philip Caldwell was a firm believer in this process, which worked well for him at Ford. He made a practice of entering into negotiations thoroughly prepared. Confident that he had done the most detailed planning possible, he could turn the problem off and relax in the knowledge that he had done all he could to influence the outcome.

- *Decide which, on your list, is the easiest, least threatening risk and go for it! Once you can bask in the glory of having conquered one fearsome task, your next risk will be easier.*
- *What if you fail? Do what the successful do: Learn from your mistakes. Take time to get very clear on what went wrong. Was it the timing? Did you trust someone who was not responsible? Did you not listen to your instincts? Were you undiplomatic? If there is a way to correct the situation or to give it another try, do it. If not, chalk it up to experience and know that you're better prepared for the next time. We can't expect to succeed all the time. As Ray Kroc said, "When I make a mistake, I throw it off by saying, 'That's*

why they put mats under cuspidors.' " More importantly, learn from the mistakes of others through reading or observation. Then make a practice, as Dedman said, of learning from what you do well. What new creative ideas can you make out of this?

8. *HONE UP YOUR COMMUNICATION AND PROBLEM-SOLVING SKILLS*

Written and oral communication are two of the characteristics that set us apart from other species. Being able to come up with creative ideas is an important talent, but even the best idea is useless unless it can be effectively conveyed to others. A major talent of the successful is this ability to effectively verbalize ideas to employees so their ideas can be carried to fruition. How clearly and efficiently you can express your ideas to customers and to persuade, motivate, and work out a deal can be a key factor in your success.

One of our biggest fears is speaking in front of an audience. But this is something successful people are often called upon to do—either to inform or motivate others by sharing their stories as guest speakers or to give reports and direction to staff and board members. Some have a natural gift for it or develop it early in life. Others have made an effort to gain experience, often by jumping in and doing it, even though it did not feel comfortable. However they procured them, the successful realize what a powerful tool good communication skills are.

The successful have also learned the ability to build "esprit de corps" among their staff. They set up situations for employees which make them feel like active team members. The Chief Executive Officers serve not only as coaches but as cheerleaders as well, inspiring and motivating their teams on the new heights.

They remember to give accolades. Some chief executives send around memos in a personal form. Each morning, Robert Dedman sends what he calls "warm fuzzies," thanking staff members for special efforts. Ken Blanchard and Spencer Johnson, in *The One-Minute Manager*, suggest managers walk around to see if they can "catch" someone doing something right so they can praise him, rather than catching someone doing something wrong. [51]

Being good communicators, the successful are able not only to motivate, but to handle the negative aspects of a situation, as well. Knowing how to address a problem in a constructive way is essential. Somehow these people usually know how to attack the problem rather than the person, thus leaving the individual with his dignity intact. However, they don't skirt the issue. They get to the heart of the matter quickly, often without mincing words.

Just as important as being *able* to communicate effectively is being *willing* to take the time to communicate and listen to others. The management style of seeking input from employees is a fairly new one in large corporations, but many at the top now realize its importance—not just for fresh input from a different perspective, but also for the sake of employee morale, so they believe their ideas are valued.

Ed McNeely, formerly chief executive officer of Wickes Corporation, had a practice of allowing each of the 180 employees in his corporate offices to come in to talk to him once a year for five minutes—and only five minutes. Even though the time allocated was short, he made the effort to establish a personal contact with his employees.

Philip Caldwell, as head of Ford Motor Company, developed an "EI" or "Employee Involvement" philosophy of production. More than 18 months before production began on the Ranger compact pickup, be brought the employees of the Louisville plant into the planning of the assembly line process. The workers offered 376 suggestions, most of which were implemented.

Norm Brinker, Chief Executive Officer of Chili's restaurant chain, believes the most important form of communication is what the employee tells the boss:

> Most people think communication is from the top down. Actually it's the opposite. That's 180 degrees off. It's from the bottom up. It doesn't make any difference what I say to the employee. It's what he says to me that really means anything.
>
> The only thing that works is what he perceives I've said and, more importantly, what he commits back to me to do. So communication really should be up: "I will do thus and so." And then I either accept it or I don't. I've really been able to get people to commit up. I listen very, very carefully and ask them for a commitment. I don't give answers. I'll give some hints, but I will not, absolutely will not, give the answer. They commit to do something and then it's up to them—it's not up to me—for them to do it.

He also stressed the importance of "wrapping it all up with a sense of humor." Laughing, he said, not only relieves tense situations but also makes work more fun.

Ted Geisel has long been admired for his ability to communicate imaginatively with children through his *Dr. Seuss* books. In fact, I suspect many parents use their children as an excuse to enjoy his books themselves. I asked Ted what he thought gave his books their timeless, wide-ranging appeal, and he said, "I think they're kept alive primarily by the fact they're

in rhyme and are amusing. Whether they say anything or not is another matter. But I think people go for them because they are easy reading and fun and make people laugh."

Anyone who has read Art Buchwald's syndicated column, is familiar with his wit and satire. He described the role that laughter plays in his life:

> It's very therapeutic for me. I have to laugh at things or I'll go crazy. And I decided that everybody else would go crazy if they didn't laugh, too. Norman Cousins did a book explaining that laughter really is a therapeutic thing for people who are sick, and I believe it, because when you laugh, you feel better; and if you can make people feel better, they like you. And I want to be liked by a lot of people, so it really pays off for me.

Outside the company, chief executive officers are skilled negotiators who are able to work out a deal, and most enjoy the challenge of it. This calls for intuition, persuasion, and diplomacy. It involves careful research, sizing up and finding out what the other side wants, and deciding the minimum acceptable offer, while still being fair to the other party.

When asked if he had a regular plan to negotiating, Wall Street investment CEO Ace Greenberg said:

> No I don't. I'm usually very direct. I certainly don't want to waste their time, so I usually get right to the point and see if there's a possibility of doing something. I like to be fair to everybody, including me.

We all have a voice that is constantly chattering away in our heads. Unfortunately, for many, this self-talk is more often negative than positive. We often chide ourselves for past experiences, without even being fully conscious that we're doing it: "Why did I say that?" "I should have . . ." "When am I going to stop . . .?" Becoming aware of this is, of course, the first step to breaking the habit. And equally important is remembering to give ourselves positive acknowledgment when we've done something well. Many people have a subconscious fear of success or don't feel worthy of it. By consciously recognizing each small achievement, we can set the wheels in motion for greater, more frequent successes.

Positive self-talk is especially important when there is no one else around to give us accolades. This is particularly true in the single parent family in America today. Formerly, parents teamed together to teach children respect and to verbalize affirmations. We can teach our children to affirm others, while giving ourselves a pat on the back, by saying out loud, "That was a good dinner," or "I did a good job of fixing that bike." In the office, a manager who has had tough decisions on the job may not receive praise from his boss or his employees but can still remember to give himself applause.

Another form of self-talk is the dialogue we carry on with ourselves for problem solving. Jim Fowler, host of Mutual of Omaha's long-running TV show, "Wild Kingdom" and a new show, "Spirit of Adventure," considers problem solving one of his most valued traits. In his line of work, he confronts some unusual challenges that call for creative thinking. For example, he said, "If you want to get a rhinoceros into a cage when it has never been in a cage before, you have to be innovative and try to reason like you think the rhinoceros might."

He talks about his experience when he was just out of college and went to the Amazon to study the harpy eagle. This eagle is so big that monkeys are its favorite meal. Jim had to use several problem-solving techniques in his study. First he had to figure out how to find a harpy eagle, second how to trap one, and third he had to study it. There was little information available at that time about such a procedure so Jim had to come up with some new ideas. Looking back on the experience, he said it enabled him to do more complicated things later in his research, and it was a great challenge. The successful love a challenge!

But what was the message that Jim got from his parents and from his college experience? "My parents and Earlham College didn't tell me what I couldn't do. They left me free to find out for myself," Jim said. They never limited him. Today Jim doesn't limit himself and continues to find new, innovative ways of doing things.

- *How are you making it possible for your co-workers, children, and yourself to be open to new ideas and options?*
- *Are you encouraging the best in your children, friends, and co-workers by acknowledging their achievements? Take Dedman's advice and, every day, write a memo acknowledging an employee's quality work.*
- *Improve your verbalization skills. Take a speech class. Join Toastmasters. Start "risking" by speaking up in groups. If you start small, you'll gain the sense of accomplishment that will fuel your self-esteem and confidence, making it easier for you to take on more challenging audiences.*
- *Practice expressing your feelings by sharing them with people you know will respect you for doing so. As you get used to doing this,*

expand the circle of people you share with. Don't look for praise for being open. You will quickly discover that openness is its own reward. Try to encourage people around you to do the same and try to be supportive when they do.

- *Be aware of your inner voice and of what it is saying to you. Let go of the past experiences that didn't turn out the way you wanted. Congratulate yourself for little triumphs, even though the outside world doesn't. Let your inner voice say to yourself, "Good for you" when a job is well done.*
- *Keep pads and pencils in handy places around the house and in the car so you can record those "inspirations" that pop into your head before they slip away.*
- *Keep a pad or recorder by your bed to capture those messages your subconscious sends you at night in the form of dreams or on awakening. Get a pen with a light on it so you don't have to turn on the light.*
- *Don't be afraid of big, noisy, aggressive, or powerful people. Inside they are probably feeling vulnerable. In fact, it is often true that the more aggressive a person appears, the more frightened that person probably is. Such people are following the strategy that the best defense is a good offense—and so they become truly offensive.*

9. *SURROUND YOURSELF WITH COMPETENT, RESPONSIBLE, SUPPORTIVE PEOPLE*

An old proverb states, "He who lies down with dogs gets up with fleas."

All of the successful realize the importance of associating with competent, reliable individuals. Whether they started out as team players or as dictatorial heads of their companies, they know that they cannot grow, develop, and flourish without the help of others. And perhaps more important, they know how to pick and retain responsible, loyal, supportive people.

General Jimmy Doolittle believes the increasing technology and sophistication of the world today makes it even more necessary to solicit the help of others:

> Today the entire world has become so complex that, in order to come up with a new and outstanding technical advance, it requires, of course, a concept from some individual. But the individual can't sell and carry

> that to fruition single-handedly as he could in the past. Now he needs a team. A team of scientists, a team of experts, each one of whom is outstanding in his own discipline.

Norman Brinker, who was on the winning polo team of the U.S. Open in 1966, used the principles he acquired in sports to run the Bennigan's and Steak and Ale restaurant chains and now puts them into practice as Chief Executive Officer of Chili's restaurants:

> I view business like an athletic contest. I feel it's just like a team. You've got to have it balanced. So many companies are all out of balance. A salesman-type person who starts a company tends to hire all salesmen. If I'm an engineer, I hire all engineers. You must keep the whole thing in balance and not hire people just like you but people who keep it in balance. I know what I'm good at and I know what I'm not good at. So I try very hard to get people with me who are good at other things.

In an interview with *Transportation News*, Robert Dedman talked about his policy of motivating employees, both as CEO of his Club Corporation of America and as Texas Highway Commission Chairman. In each of those roles he is responsible for approximately 15,000 people! His style is to be supportive of the staff who are on the scene and give them as much responsibility as possible. He believes this encouragement inspires them to improve their skills and confidence, to the benefit of all involved:

> Quite frankly, the more my employees have done through the years, and the less I've done, the better we've done . . . I think when people realize the respect I have for them, it causes them to go ahead and solve the problems, not just try to push them up the ladder or push them down the ladder.

In the article, which the employees read, he verbalized his appreciation for them, further motivating them to their highest potential:

> They're a very highly educated group of people, well-trained, well-motivated, very high-integrity people. They're really one of the major assets that this state [Texas] has. [52]

At age 25, Jane Evans was Vice President of Genesco. Later, as Vice President of General Mills' fashion group, she was responsible for 7,000 employees. Asked what traits enabled her to handle those positions, she replied:

> I really am a manager and a leader who works through people. You know, there is absolutely no way I could run this business by myself. I really enjoy the stimulation of working with other people and seeing that people are motivated, so that they know what is required of them, so they can do a good job, and then rewarding them as they do a good job. [53]

Trusting one's employees frees those at the top to put their attention where they choose. Forrest Shumway's motto, when he was Vice Chairman of Allied/Signal Companies, was "Pick a good man for the job. Then leave him alone." Bob Magness agrees, saying this is the single most important factor in his business success:

> I think the big difference is I can delegate. We've got good people and I let them develop. I don't mess around saying, "Let's change it," unless it's a deal I'm personally working on.

But a warning comes to us from a branch of the justice system. San Diego's Chief of Police William Barnet Kolender believes America's greatest weakness is in not developing responsible people. He says our country suffers because "we do not hold people accountable for what they do, whether that be in employment, in the home, in education, especially, or in the criminal justice system . . . When you can graduate people who can't read, that tells you something is wrong."

Many successful men and women I talked with recognize the business value and the personal reward of helping people grow. Peter Coors took young adults who were basically unemployable out of Denver's inner city, trained them, took them on Outward Bound trips to develop self-esteem and teamwork, and then put them to work. He said:

> We really had pretty good success with that program. The ones who didn't stay at Coors, primarily because of the difficulty in shift work, went to work for other companies. We contributed to getting them actively back into productive employment.

Another leader used the Outward Bound program to develop his team of already-established middle and upper executives. Colorado Governor Roy

Romer, at age 58, and his staff of 28 state executives traded their business suits for crash helmets for a weekend of climbing and rappelling several hundred feet of sheer, vertical rock cliffs. Sometimes blindfolded, the primarily middle-aged cabinet members learned to rely on a rope, their own instincts, and their colleagues. They were counseled to "set yourself up to win" before beginning. If they felt they were in trouble, that they couldn't make it, they were reminded to take time to picture themselves succeeding.

Romer made the climb three times, choosing a more difficult route each time. He believes the process encouraged his top staff members to take greater risks in their jobs. "Competition is not the issue," he said. "The question is, 'Can we help the most timid of us along?' That's what success is . . . if you can, as a team, bring along someone who might be reluctant to try new things, create new ideas." [54]

It is important not just to pick competent subordinates but to associate with able colleagues and choose role models, as well. Businesswoman Mary Cunningham lists the fact that she has always had a mentor as the most important factor in her many careers. At every step along the way she has had someone to coach her, not just in the management principles she learned at Harvard Business School, but in more subtle tips, such as "whose desk to put the memo on, whose name to put on a copy list, what time to set the meeting because John Smith doesn't like morning meetings or Jane Doe is not good after lunch."

Another person who is not always as visible but who plays a major role in the lives of the successful is the spouse or confidante. Certainly Ronald Reagan would agree! And so does Sol Price, founder and Chairman of the Board of Fed Mart and now of the highly successful Price Club. He described the characteristics of this special person as someone who has both feet firmly planted on the ground and can see the executive as a human being with his strengths as well as his weaknesses without being overly enamored with his power. This person can be called upon night or day to give honest, intuitive input with an objectivity that the CEO doesn't necessarily get from those who work for him.

WHY NOT HANG OUT WITH THE BEST!

- *Choose a boss you respect.*
- *Remember that success breeds success.*
- *Identify someone you respect, study his traits, ask for his advice, and extract what is helpful to you.*
- *Choose only people you can count on to get the job done.*

- *Become a motivator of your employees.*
- *Treat your employees as a select group of people, and they will respond as special people. This advice is supported by the research of the Pygmalion Research Studies.*
- *Learn who the givers and the takers are.*
- *Recognize that there are some people you may want to help but with whom you do not necessarily choose to work.*

10. *SCHEDULE TIME FOR EXERCISE AND RECREATION! STAY HEALTHY!*

Given the demanding schedules of these people, it is remarkable that they find the time to exercise and schedule recreational activities. But the majority told me they do just that. In fact, they place a high emphasis on exercising, saying it is essential to maintaining the high energy level required for their long hours of work.

President Ronald Reagan is one who schedules recreation time regularly. He said in our interview, "I still retain my love of the outdoors and get a feeling of claustrophobia from cities." He continued:

> Every once in a while I just have to get out (to the hills) . . . We have a ranch . . . we renamed it Rancho del Cielo, which means Ranch in the Sky. It's up at the top of a pass in the mountains. You can sit on horseback and see the Channel Islands and the other way you can see the San Inez Valley . . . Some of it is rock formations, and then there are meadows and deep oak forests . . . It's a total getaway from the world!

Justice Sandra Day O'Connor incorporates a morning exercise into her schedule. An active participant in golf, tennis, horseback riding, and skiing, she is considered one of the most athletic members of the court. In his 50s, Ace Greenberg says he is only three pounds heavier than when he was playing high school football. Caroline Hunt spends an hour nearly every morning exercising and doing aerobics at the Crescent Club. She said, "I don't expect to become a female jock, but I find it makes me feel energetic." Her only regret is that she didn't start exercising regularly earlier in life.

Realizing the importance of having healthy employees, many companies now integrate fitness into their employee benefit programs. Some have comprehensive programs including fully equipped gyms, running tracks, saunas, stress management counseling, aerobics classes, and company sporting teams. To encourage participation, some companies are even offering such incentives as lower insurance deductibles and cash bonuses for those who participate regularly.

The last time I saw Peter Coors, he was on his lunch hour but was not planning to spend it in the cafeteria or in a fancy restaurant over a calorie-laden meal. Instead, duffel bag in hand, he was headed for the company exercise room.

Rent on New York's Fifth Avenue does not come cheap, but Malcolm Forbes thinks fitness is worth the price. He has installed a 3,500-square foot gymnasium in the penthouse of the Forbes' building—space that would go for nearly $100,000 a year. [55]

Norm Brinker, now CEO of Chili's restaurants, formerly founder of Steak and Ale, has long incorporated athletics into his life. A member of the United States Equestrian Team, he has competed in rodeo competitions as well as polo. The diversity of his athletic ability is demonstrated by his competition in the Modern Pentathlon in the Olympics. He regularly runs, bicycles, skis, or works out in his mini-gym at home. He encourages his employees to exercise and says a large number of them are regular runners. He believes athletics, and particularly competitive sports, rejuvenate us:

> There is something about vitality that you can't put your finger on. Some people are vital and some people aren't. To me, being a competitor helps in that regard. Not just going out and doing some exercise, but being a competitor seems to keep your adrenalin going and keeps you up.

Definitely one of the successful who work hard and play hard, Norm commented:

> I was blessed with a very high energy level and tremendous stamina. I've worked many, many 20-hour days—not just a few. And there was a period of about three years when I worked every single day.

High energy is a common trait among those who have made it to the top. They have a zest for life and are enthusiastic about whatever they are doing. Many of them report requiring less sleep than average and, thus, they give themselves more waking hours to be active.

Neil Bergt, Chairman of Alaska International Industries, lists rising early high on the list of successful traits, "I don't know anybody who is successful in the business world that sleeps late in the morning. Maybe you could find a few in the arts world or movie industry but not in business."

He says he requires little sleep and is often up in the middle of the night wrestling with problems. He rises early to make phone calls, a habit which worked well for him when he lived in Alaska. "There was a five-hour time zone change from the east coast, so I could be up at 3 a.m. and calling people at 8 in New York." His early morning calls are not so well received, however, now that he lives in California, only three hours behind the east coast. "Now my friends on the east coast are getting calls about 6 in the morning from me. My attorneys and everybody. I know they probably wish I'd move a couple of time zones farther away," he said with a laugh.

Knowing and honoring your "body clock" is important, too. TV and business executive Bill Daniels says that he functions best in the early hours. Bill rises early, reads three newspapers at home, and then goes to work and reads the *Wall Street Journal*, "My best times are from 7 in the morning to 1 p.m. So I try to do the work I've got to really concentrate on in the morning and then, in the afternoon, I do my administrative work, dictation, reading, and so forth."

Shared exuberance for life was a factor uncovered in a Gallup poll of 450 men and women over 95 years of age, "All these remarkable individuals had one thing in common. They all wanted to live a long time. They were full of curiosity, they were alert, and they did not worry excessively. A zest for living seemed to be one key factor in their longevity." [56]

Allied Signal, Inc.'s retired Vice Chairman, Forrest Shumway, believes it is unnecessary for even a top executive to work excessively. Seldom did he bring work home with him at night, nor was he away from home more than four or five weekends during his last ten years of work. Does he bring his problems home from the office? "No," he told me:

> Somehow I am able to turn it off and really be home when I am there. After dinner, I watch TV with my family or go to some of the athletic events. Whatever I do, I turn off work and relax. The next day I am ready to get involved in work again.

Unlike many harried executives, he always took his vacation, and at Christmas-time the whole family goes skiing. He manages to find time for hunting and fishing in the summer, believing that relaxation is important.

Helping Americans maintain their health through nutritious food was Bill Galt's goal when he founded his chain of "The Good Earth" restaurants:

> It's quality of life . . . real optimum performance that I'm looking for . . . You are what you eat, and I think the American diet is what is killing us off. It's been destroying that ol' vim and vigor which made this country so great in the early days.

He admitted, though, that he was not always so health-conscious:

> I was a junk food junkie. I drank a lot of coffee, ate sweets, and all the fatty foods . . . at the time I was 40. Most of my friends in the restaurant business were dropping dead . . . and I took a long look."

I was surprised to hear Bill say it was his experience working with Colonel Sanders that set him on the health food path:

> I helped Colonel Sanders set up his new businesses. He was 85 at the time and a high-energy type, so I watched what he ate. He basically lived on fresh fruits and vegetables and foods containing no chemicals or preservatives. He worked 16 to 18 hours a day and died at 93 or 94. His example was what inspired me to develop a new type of food establishment.

Galt has sold the restaurant chain and now heads Galt International, a diversified business firm. He plans to pursue his concerns about health into entirely new areas:

> My next step is to build holistic health clinics throughout the country. They will be places that don't use the traditional methods of medicine . . . where the doctor tells the person what to do, but basically they will be clinics where people are taught to take responsibility for their own health, with good nutrition and supplements. I'm not knocking the medical fraternity, but it's just a new phase of medical health . . . our medical system is not working today. It's almost bankrupting the nation.

Debra Szekeley, founder and owner of The Golden Door, one of America's most prestigious health spas, obviously places a high value on fitness. She sees the results of people abusing their bodies when they come to her spa for repair. In her busy schedule, she says that, although she really doesn't have time for exercise, she nevertheless schedules at least an hour a day. She knows she needs to move or do exercise to get rid of stress as well as to keep fit. She insists that her guests at "The Door" take a walk after their evening meals. She believes everyone should schedule at least one hour of some kind of movement every day.

Seventy-eight year old Aida Grey, author of *How to Grow Older and Look Younger,* is an innovative international authority on beauty. Her Institut de Beaute in Beverly Hills is a mecca for famous actors and actresses and the successful. After more than 45 years in the cosmetology business, she now has more than 100 Aida Grey Salons throughout the U.S., Europe, and Africa.

Aida, who had acne as a teen-ager, but now has flawless skin, believes "There are no ugly women—only lazy ones." She says beauty is based on three factors: your attitude toward life, proper skin care, and what you eat. Water is vital and she drinks 15 glasses a day—three of them before she even brushes her teeth.

Ms. Grey, as she is called, never had to be concerned about money. Although she is almost 80, every day she goes to her salon in Beverly Hills or visits one of the other locations.

There can be a fringe benefit to taking time to relax, which is what one of the men I interviewed found out. Don Koll, President of Koll Construction Company in California, was perplexed by a business problem. He went to Mexico for ten days to "let go" of the issue while he ate, swam, relaxed, and drank beer. Finally, a new tactic for dealing with a company came to him without his consciously focusing on it. He returned and the company did indeed buy his idea, even though he had consistently been told it would not work. Today, Don Koll is one of the most successful developers in Southern California.

Many of the successful, however, consider their work the best form of play. Play, for these people, is doing exactly what they are doing. Mary Kay Ash admitted, "I've never learned how to play."

Athletes, of course, have the benefit of exercise built into their lives. Some, such as golfer Lee Trevino, have had to learn to take time away from their sport for other activities. The key is not allowing yourself to become obsessed with one activity to the exclusion of all other areas of life. Finding a balance prevents you from "burning out."

No matter how successful or well balanced your life is, there are inevitably going to be times of stress. How do these individuals handle it? Mary Cunningham said:

> The important thing to do is get a good night's sleep, look at the situation fresh the next day, and don't extrapolate from your low moment. Give yourself another 24 hours—maybe even another 48 hours—look at the problem fresh, and really identify what it is that is so awesome about this task . . . The chances are it won't look quite so awesome after a good night's sleep and with a fresh perspective brought to bear on it.

Conky Johnston, as president of her own consulting company, Conky

Johnston's Sales & Marketing, encounters stress from time to time. I asked her how she handles it. She told me she had developed a system some years ago while working on a sales presentation for her former company, Johnston's Food. Upon pitching it to an Alpha Beta grocery store, the manager told her it was "the best presentation he had ever heard," but he turned her idea down.

Totally discouraged and disappointed, she continued to mull over the incident as she was driving. Then she realized that she was going to give her whole day to Alpha Beta if she wasn't careful. She decided to allow herself to fully indulge in the negative thoughts for a *limited period of time* and then totally release them. Since she was driving, she "clocked" this time period with stop lights, allowing her negativity to last through three stop lights. At the end of that time, she was feeling so much better that she decided to call the manager who had turned her down and re-introduce the idea in a slightly different way. This time he bought the idea. As it turned out, she ended up giving Alpha Beta the rest of her day—but in a productive, positive way. Now, when a negative or stressful experience occurs, she consciously asks herself: "Is this a one, two, or three stop light stress?"

PROCESS FOR RENEWING YOURSELF

> *First, do not dwell on the past or anticipate the future. Experience each hour of the day where you are.*

A slogan that succinctly expresses this thought is: "May you live *all* the days of your life!"

Since many of us have difficulty dropping the events of the day, the members of a Canadian Indian tribe suggest a procedure. They believe that "Each night, when you go to sleep, you die. A new you is born the next day." How wonderful to look at each day as a totally new beginning.

Ceremonies are one means by which people renew themselves. Although there are many rituals we could consider, one of the most abused is the vacation. Instead of using vacations as intermissions from our hectic lives, many people take work with them so they won't be bored or even lonely. In planning ahead, they worry about how they will spend all the unstructured time. Instead, vacations would be more relaxing if they were truly used for recreating and renewing your life. During such periods, you can shift gears, if necessary.

How do you spend your vacations?

In addition to long, planned vacations, give yourself permission to have a "collapse day" now and then. How do you take care of the need for renewal? I sense the need for such a day when a strong voice deep inside says, "You need a rest." When this happens on a day that I have an important commitment, I have learned to make a pact with myself to accept a "collapse day" just as soon as the commitment is fulfilled. I believe that, because of this pact, my body has somehow carried me through what might otherwise be difficult times and collapses at a later time.

Anne Morrow Lindbergh speaks to the need for our continued renewal in her book, *A Gift From the Sea.* She talks about the "oyster bed" stage of life. This period involves a dispersed family, with children going away to college, marriage, and careers.

When this happened to her, she saw that her oyster bed was left high and dry. Following this family transition, she experienced a most uncomfortable level she called "the abandoned shell." She believes this period requires a lot of solitude. Panic can set in about how to fill the empty space. In her case, filling the space was not the problem because she was very busy. But when a mother is left the lone hub of a wheel, with no other lives revolving about her, she faces a total reorientation. It takes time to discover her "center of gravity." Again, after her husband's death, Ann faced a woman's recurring lesson: "A woman must come of age by herself—she must find her true center alone. The lessons seem to need relearning about every 20 years." [57]

The last time you experienced this sense of loss or purposelessness, what finally helped you "rediscover" yourself?

To aid in our renewal, we must recognize that some people nourish us and other people drain us. Nourishing people leave us feeling refreshed and invigorated.

Do you surround yourself as much as possible with supportive, nurturing people?

How else can we renew ourselves? Three ways that seem helpful to people are laughter, hugging, and verbal communication. A friend of mine told me his relationship with his girlfriend is especially valuable to him because "she generates verbal communication. I never laughed so much until I was around her. It seems to be contagious. I end up feeling so renewed." Laughter relieves body tension, and research has confirmed that it releases healing endorphins into the body. Tense muscles become noticeably looser after a good laugh.

Hugging has the same effect: recent research indicates that a man who hugs his wife each morning before they go their individual ways, lives an average of *five years longer* than men who do not hug their wives.

In addition to laughing and hugging, people need to be able to talk about themselves with a sympathetic person. Often the best listener is someone who sits quietly but really pays attention to the conversation. Many people have difficulty listening because they feel they must try to "fix" the other person's situation or the listener may feel the need to tell his own story. Truly listening to someone is a gift.

Develop a close relationship in which you each take turns talking. Learn to laugh together. It could be one of the most invigorating and renewing experiences in your life.

Many people in therapy mentioned how suffocated they felt by too much responsibility. This was true, particularly, of people who have been made to believe that they are responsible for everyone's happiness. I devised a process whereby they could construct a time and place where they could go to feel the freedom from this "burden" for brief periods. I called it "Wild Abandonment." It became the topic of a speech and questionnaire that I gave to groups. They liked the idea of finding other options to what seemed to be an unpleasant "given" in life.

WHAT WOULD WILD ABANDONMENT BE LIKE FOR YOU?

Whatever your idea of wild abandonment, I suggest that you find ways to bring at least a little of it into your life. With some creative imagination, you can still plan vacations in lush places. You may not be able to go to Tahiti but you can take yourself out for a sumptuous dinner in an exotic restaurant near home, transporting your thoughts to that location. Take mini-vacations, if only on a day off from work. Plan a theme party, watch a travel movie, have your lunch in different surroundings, get away from people, go without shaving, drive a trail bike through the dirt, or feel wild abandonment while skiing down a mountainside. It is important for our mental health to break out of old ruts at times and do something "outrageous" or unstructured.

11. KEEP THE FAITH!

What do you do when problems seem insurmountable? When you just can't figure out what to do next? When you know a change or a risk is called for, but you just can't master the courage?

Many of the successful, whether or not they attend church, say they call on their religious faith during such difficult times. And this is not surprising. From the earliest times, man has sought help from a power greater than himself. From the most primitive tribes to the most sophisticated societies, man has realized he alone was not responsible for his destiny.

This religious or spiritual belief shows up in a variety of forms. Church and synagogue attendance, prayer, meditation, ceremonies, and rituals all testify to man's recognition of this faith. Some individuals may not participate actively in an organized religion but, nevertheless, believe in this power and call upon it when they need help or guidance. Some choose to call it an "inner voice" that speaks to them and gives them direction when a systematically formulated, intellectual decision isn't enough.

Cable television communications magnate and ranch-owner Robert Magness says that, although he doesn't attend church regularly today, he is a strong believer in God. "When I get in trouble, I'm not too proud to call for help . . . I think church is important, but I believe God is more important."

Golf champion Lee Trevino attributes his religious conviction to several close brushes with death, the most dramatic of which was surviving a lightning strike.

Actress Shirley MacLaine, who has written books and starred in a TV series about her spiritual experiences, said she believes, "That the higher self knows everything if we just trust it. And trust the guidance even when you may not understand where it came from." [58]

Dr. Francis MacNutt, a former priest, described his belief: "The law is the thing that tells you the way you are supposed to be. But grace is God helping us become what we can't possibly become because we're trying to live up to that law." He went on to describe how his deep religious convictions had helped him overcome a weakness in his personal life:

> One of my basic problems has always been fear and shyness and timidity. I thought it was part of my character. Over the last ten years, Jesus has freed me of that excessive shyness that pulled me back from really entering into relations with other people.

Connie Engel claims that she achieved the confidence through religion that enabled her to become the first female U.S. Air Force flight instructor. "It was the fact that I found the Lord that made the difference. Before then, although I had been secure outwardly, I was insecure inwardly in a lot of situations. The Lord gave me that inner peace."

Senator Edward Kennedy, when asked what was the most important characteristic he had received from his mother, Rose Kennedy, responded, without hesitation, "Clearly the overwhelming one has been the enormous devotion and faith and belief in God and in religion."

Gregory Peck's faith led him to do audio tapes of the complete New Testament, which might be considered unusual for a Hollywood actor, but it has had an impact on people in all walks of life. A truck driver pulled along-side Peck in his convertible and shouted, "Hey, Greg, I've been listening to your New Testament reading all across the country, and it's great! Thanks." Later, on an "Hour of Power" television program, Gregory said this man's enthusiastic comment was one of the best reviews he ever had.

As a cancer specialist, Dr. Anita Figueredo's work in treating patients earned her the honor of Pro Ecclesia from Pope Paul XII and the San Diego Woman of the Year award. She maintained that a belief in a personal God is of great help for patients during the struggle with cancer. She said that she sees many people who have a deep faith, and that their religious convictions keeps them from experiencing as much fear of this life threatening disease.

Peter Coors lists religious faith first in his ingredients of success: "When my life is completed, success, for me, would be standing in front of God and feeling that, although I've made some mistakes, I've always had Him at the center of my life."

Conky Johnston, President of Conky Johnston's Sales & Marketing Consulting Co., says her religious belief helps her get through her busy day in a more relaxed way. "I want to talk to God in the morning but often get in a hurry," she said, "so I talk to Him on the way to work."

Dr. Norman Vincent Peale believes that God has a plan for us in this world but has structured it so that we must take an active part in the creative process. In his inspirational magazine *Guideposts*, written for people of all faiths, he makes a declaration for the new year. He says that this will be a great year but qualifies it with the word "if." He suggests that your resolution consist of two short words with only two letters each, but which are filled with power that can generate energy, can "sweep away discouragement and failure." They can help a person accomplish any worthwhile goal. What are those two words? "DO IT!" He elaborates:

> Have you got a promising idea? Do it! Do you have a cherished dream? Do it! Do you have a hidden ambition? Do it! Have you some great impulse, some burning desire? Do it!

He also suggests you "take a few moments every morning and look closely at your life . . . Don't just contemplate it. *Do it!*"

> If there are areas in your life where you put off needed action, these unfulfilled tasks can become a fatigue factor. They are like tiny leaks in your reservoirs of energy. [59]

Barron Hilton, Chairman of the Board of the Hilton Hotel chain, puts a copy of *Guideposts* for his guests in his hotel rooms, with the following message:

> We are pleased to place the publication, *Guideposts*, in your room with the thought that it will bring refreshment at the end of a busy day or inspiration at the beginning of a new one. [60]

Some call it "being blessed." Others call it luck. TV and Business Executive Bill Daniels falls into the latter category. He says he isn't particularly religious, but feels he is simply a lucky guy: "Make no mistake about it: you can work hard, but there's a lot of luck involved. Luck or fate."

It was luck, Bill said, that led him out of the oil business and into cable TV.

> If I hadn't gone to Casper, Wyoming from Hobbs, New Mexico, I wouldn't be in the cable TV business today. And when I decided to move, I just looked at the map, made some phone calls, talked to some people, and asked how big is the oil business in Casper; and bang, I said "That's where I'm going." Now if I had said I'm going to Dallas, I would never have been in the cable business. That's fate and it's a form of luck.

Whether or not you believe in an organized religion, most of us acknowledge that certain events or circumstances occur in our lives over which we have no control and, thus, recognize the influence of a higher power. The miracle of birth provides us with a number of givens: intellectual ability, physical stature, predisposition to medical conditions. We are born into a situation with a given set of parents who determine our early lives.

They provide us with a set of basic values that comes from their own belief systems. Although we have the freedom to change those values later, we are nonetheless influenced by our heritage. It is up to us later in life to discover, or rediscover, the guiding philosophy that gives us direction and inner peace.

The following suggestions may be helpful to you when you're experiencing difficult times:

- *When you're overwhelmed by a situation or a decision that you can't "figure out," ask for answers from a source other than your analytical mind. This may mean going to a church or synagogue. It may mean meditating in a quiet room. It may mean sitting in the woods or walking on the beach to attain peace of mind and communion with nature. Use whatever method works to allow you to "hear" the answer that your wonderfully busy, and yet often fearful, rational mind sometimes just won't acknowledge.*
- *When you feel wounded, bruised or shaken up by events from the outside world, how do you become renewed?*
- *Ask yourself how much in life you totally control.*
- *Does the concept of being co-creator with a higher power fit your experience?*
- *Do you create something on your own and then let the higher power/God/Universe contribute another dimension?*
- *What are the most rewarding parts or times in your life? Were you solely responsible for setting those experiences in motion?*

12. ARE YOU MAKING A CONTRIBUTION TO WHATEVER IS MOST MEANINGFUL TO YOU?

Former World War II three star General Jimmy Doolittle said:

> We were put on this earth for one purpose and that's to make it a better place. We should, therefore, be contributing members of society. And if the earth, as a result of our having been on it, is a better place than it was before we came, then we have achieved our destiny.

Many of the successful share this feeling of having a life purpose. Pittsburgh, Pennsylvania opera director Tito Copobianco said, "I feel we each have a destiny, but we can't sit and wait; we must participate in our destiny." Once these people have reached a certain level of success, they usually want to make a contribution to society.

They are frequent volunteers, giving support with their status, talent, time, and money. Sometimes this stems from a sense of obligation—a desire to repay the system which has so richly rewarded them. Other times it comes from a desire to change an unjust system now that they are in positions of influence. And sometimes it emanates from their realizing that the wealth and prestige they have amassed simply do not bring them the true sense of fulfillment they seek.

Volunteerism is so prevalent in America that we assume it to be worldwide, but that is not the case. At international conferences, Americans are often lauded for our willingness to help one another. The pioneer spirit is a part of our heritage. In the early days of our nation, families relied on other families to assist in building houses and raising barns—tasks which would have been nearly impossible for a family alone. Modern technology has eliminated much of those needs, but human needs continue. The American volunteer continues this tradition in a variety of forms: Boy and Girl Scouts, Salvation Army, drug-abuse programs, American Red Cross, Cancer Society, battered-women's shelters, AIDS benefits, muscular dystrophy telethons, and many more.

Many successful women have known from an early age what special causes they wanted to pursue. All her life, Lady Bird Johnson had a strong desire to help beautify the nation and preserve America's wildflowers. She created several beautification programs earlier in life and finally, at age 70, founded the National Wildflower Research Center, donating money, land, and time to it. The reason she gave for undertaking such a major conservation project was "to pay my rent for the space I've taken up on the planet."

Men have traditionally held the role of bread-winners. For that reason, they often wait until their middle thirties or forties to think about their fellow man, after their careers are well established.

Many of the men I interviewed are very generous with their contributions. One such person is Ace Greenberg. He not only plans to donate his entire annual salary to charity, but has instituted a company policy at Bear, Stearns that each of the managing directors must give away four percent of his income. He also is an active fundraiser for a number of charitable organizations. He is not interested in attending meetings, but makes key calls to potential donors to solicit.

Robert Dedman, CEO of Club Corporations of America, has donated more than $45 million to educational institutions. His viewpoint is, "I'm very proud of having made a lot of money, but I'm a lot more proud of knowing what to do with it—and plowing it back into the system." In his position as Chairman of the Texas Highway and Public Transportation Commission, he incorporated a wildflower program to beautify Texas highways.

Sometimes a personal accident causes a person to re-evaluate his philosophy of life. Charles Woods spoke of his brush with death in the fiery crash of his military plane. "It gave me a much more serious outlook on life and a feeling of wanting to help my fellow man."

The most exciting thing about Bill Daniels' world today, in addition to owning the sports TV channel, Prime Ticket, and being part owner of the Los Angeles Lakers, is the unique new bank he set up for children. The first such institution in the world, Young Americans' Bank is dedicated to teaching children aged 10 to 22 about managing their finances. The $1.8 million which Bill donated to establish the bank was put into a trust fund. Children not only learn about mortgages and repaying loans, they get hands-on experience at being shareholders.

The success of "The Kids' Bank," as it is popularly known, is demonstrated by the fact that in its first five months of operation, over 3,200 accounts were opened—nearly five times the average for a bank during that period of time. Although the average account balance is hot high, Bill's main mission, teaching financial responsibility at a young age, is being accomplished. "Women declared their independence some years ago," Bill said, "and in a similar manner, young people have wanted to have their independence. This is one step in that direction."

Golf champion Chi Chi Rodriguez also has an interest in helping children. He has sponsored several foundations for young people; one helps abused youths, and another provides surgery for any child who needs it. He credits his charitable nature to his heritage. From an early age he watched his father give to and help others. "You see," Chi Chi said, "most Puerto Rican people by birth are philanthropists. They have a good and generous heart."

Dr. Jonas Salk has dedicated his life to helping others. Most of us know him for discovering the Salk vaccine, which brought an abrupt halt to the devastating polio epidemic of the 1950s. He is now so busy working on an AIDS vaccine that he hasn't had much time to write or speak about it. I had the honor of presenting him with the San Diego Chapter 100's Man-of-the-Year award, but he was so busy working on research that he wasn't able to be present for the actual ceremony so I had to tape his comments at an earlier date. When I asked if I could interview him for another project he said, "Right now I'm into vaccine—not words."

Many celebrities are now giving their time, actively working to help overcome AIDS. Elizabeth Taylor headed a national campaign on behalf of that project. Singer Dionne Warwick's efforts to help fight the spread of the disease prompted the Department of Health & Human Services to name her Ambassador of Health. The song she released in 1986, "That's What Friends Are For," raised more than $1 million for AIDS research by February of 1988. [61]

Another medical concern for which many of the successful raise money is cancer research. The Cattle Baron's Ball has been an annual event in Dallas for 17 years. It is the largest fund-raiser in the country to benefit cancer research. The volunteers raise approximately $800,000 each year. Local socialites don their boots and cowboy hats, procure a huge ranch, and work for one solid year to put on the two-day event. Celebrities such as Larry Hagman ("J.R."), Linda Gray, Jane Russell, "Iron Eyes" Cotty, and others add their celebrity status and color to the event.

Nancy Brinker (Mrs. Norman Brinker) heads another Dallas foundation which helps cancer research. It is named for her sister, Susan G. Komen, who died of the disease. The foundation, which honors people such as Betty Ford, Happy Rockefeller, Barbara Bel Geddes, and Jill Ireland, raises over $1 million for cancer each year.

Outstanding volunteer Billie Leigh Rippey chaired the first Rita Hayworth Gala in the Southwest, which benefited Alzheimer's research, the disease from which Rita died. The event cleared nearly $200,000 which was turned over to the University of Texas Medical Center at Dallas and the National A.D.R.D.A. center for further research on Alzheimer's disease.

A familiar face at benefits and charitable events where there is a cause to espouse is Bob Hope's. For years he has given up his holidays—and put his life at some risk—to entertain troops in the war zones. For those efforts and others, he has received awards and medals from Presidents Kennedy, Johnson, and Eisenhower as well as from all branches of the armed forces.

Bob's latest crusade focuses on the drug problem facing America's youth. With his unique style combining humor, enthusiasm, and his strong sense of purpose, he solicits the active involvement of friends and cronies as well as young people. At a kick-off event for the "Hope for a Drug-Free America," introduced during the 1988 Super Bowl weekend in San Diego, I realized what a master plan he and his committee had devised to focus national interest on this important cause by choosing a time when much of America was attending or watching the Super Bowl.

He highlighted the new project in a one-hour special which USA Cable Network televised. The program included personal comments by such prominent individuals concerned with the drug problem as Walter Cronkite, Jimmy Stewart, and Charlton Heston. Referring to his role in *The Ten Commandments*, Heston emphasized the magnitude of the situation by saying,

"I didn't really part the Red Sea. That was just an illusion. This is the real challenge—a tough one. No special effects."

Also featured were pro-football coaches such as Tom Landry and Don Shula, who presented awards to NFL players and gave them the opportunity to present to the television audience their feelings about the drug-free program.

Many astronauts were present, and Alan Shepard spoke for all of them when he said, "We're proud to be a part of this program. It is seemingly impossible, but we've accepted that challenge before. It is one that we can meet, and we're pledged to support." [62]

Other prominent names involved with this project include the following members of its Board of Directors: U.S. Congressman Jack Kemp, Kentucky Governor Martha Layne Collins, Los Angeles Mayor Tom Bradley, Lamar Hunt, Lee A. Iacocca, Grant Tinker, Pete Rozelle, Peter Ueberroth, and others.

To get students directly involved, Bob arranged for some of the young leaders in the area to be bussed to the Convention Center the following day for a pep rally. He encouraged their cooperation by calling on their self-esteem through his comments:

> All you youngsters are picked as ambassadors of this project to go out and help other youngsters get connected. Can you imagine if we had all the young people in this country connected as members of this unit in the drug-free America? Do you know what that would do? I know you do, because you've got those young, bright minds. And I'll tell you, it would just mean a lot of health and happiness to a lot of people in this country.

But this was just the kick-off event. "Hope for a Drug Free America" continues as an active organization.

Another man who has devoted many of his later years to making a contribution is highly successful businessman Ross Perot. He is well known for freeing his own employees from an Iran prison. The account is described in detail in the book *On Wings of Eagles* by Ken Follett. Later he accepted the chairmanship of "Texans War on Drugs Committee" which has been a model used by other states in their drive against drugs.

Successful people are often involved in the arts, as well as other related activities. Former actress and television hostess Marylou Whitney is founder of the National Museum for Dance in Saratoga Springs, New York. She and her husband Sonny, who founded Pan American Airlines, contribute their time, status, and finances to worthy causes in the towns where their numerous homes are located. She is the hostess par excellence who brings together many political, international, and business figures as well as socialites for various causes. Her activities range from serving on the National Committee of the Whitney Museum of American Art, to working for the U.S.O. of New York City, which in 1987 honored her as "Woman of the Year" at their annual luncheon.

Another woman who uses her wealth for assisting others is Joan Kroc, widow of Ray Kroc who founded McDonald's. She established the Joan B. Kroc Foundation, which had programs on alcohol and drug abuse. Later she supported programs on nuclear disarmament and education. Today, the foundation is building a hospice facility in San Diego.

Many of the successful are concerned about the future of our wildlife, too. Chairman of the Board and Founder of worldwide Determined Productions, Connie Boucher is known mostly for the stuffed Snoopy dogs and other Peanuts characters she designs, produces, and markets. Having experienced business success, she is now directing her attention to making contributions to the outside world. She has a line of "endangered species" stuffed animals, from which she donates a percentage of her profits to the World Wildlife Federation.

Tom Mantzel, a businessman who is also concerned with wildlife preservation said, "I think that we're all just passing through. We're here for a blink of an eyelash. I think we need to take care of what we have here and provide for the future so others can enjoy it." And he has done just that. He used the fortunes he made in the oil and gas industries to purchase the Fossil Rim Wildlife Ranch. He acquired and raised endangered species from Africa, providing an opportunity for guests—particularly school children—to see the animals and learn about conservation and erosion. "I think we have an obligation to future generations," he said, "to maintain not only the land, but wildlife, so they can enjoy it just as we've enjoyed it."

Now is a good time to take stock of the projects you are most concerned about and how you are investing in them.

- You may have more time than money at certain points of your life. At other times the reverse is true. Regardless, give yourself the opportunity to experience the rewards of giving. Sometimes this means making a financial contribution, or sometimes it's just a matter of giving praise or support to a friend—or a stranger, for that matter.
- Pick an area of special interest. Find a way to volunteer. It may be Boy Scouts, a medical cause, a religious group, feeding the hungry, or teaching English as a second language.
- Many discover that the act of giving is its own reward.

CONCLUSION

You have read about the traits of the successful. You have specific examples as to how they organize their lives to move in a focused direction toward their goals. You have also read suggestions on using these very traits in your own life. In the chapter called "Stumbling Blocks," you had the chance to assess what traps you might consciously or unconsciously fall into.

Now comes the BIG CHALLENGE: actually putting these traits into use. This book, as helpful as it may be, will only stay on a shelf in your mind if you don't move it to the next step—which is ACTION!

One of the great contributions of the successful is the wisdom that their achievement was not just a one-time event, but an ongoing process. In addition, it was not just the money which motivated them, although of course that does create more options. I call the special qualities these people have "MEGATRAITS," as you recall, which I define as an explosive force that continues to ignite itself and progressively spreads to new areas.

Choosing a forward movement will entail success not just now or with your next project, but will continue to build. One success will lead to another and yet another.

A race horse that was born to race, will not be happy just eating grass in a pasture. His excitement will be in training and actually running the race. So it is with you. If you find or have found your special niche/talent, it will set you free to be all you can be. Success will surely follow.

Each of us has his own destiny. Norman Lear describes it as "the special tapestry of our lives . . . the way we dip our paintbrush into the paint. The color is unique, the design is unique, and each of us is unique." At times we must pay a price for being unique, for going "against the flow." However, conforming to the status quo is much more costly if, in doing so, we neglect our own destinies.

You can run away from your true and special talents, but life, I guarantee you, has a way of pulling you back and confronting you with two questions, "Who are you?" and "Why were you born?" We continue to find out more and more about life and ourselves as we peel down the covering layers to reach closer to the core.

I wish you well on your *journey*. **May you be all you were intended to be!**

INDEX

FOOTNOTES

No.		Page
1.	Earl Nightingale, *"The Strangest Secret,"* Nightingale Conant audio tape.	2
2.	"Portraits of Durants," *Los Angeles Times,* July 5, 1987, p. 4	2
3.	"Visibility Doesn't Equate with Success," *Stanford Observer,* June 1986	4
4.	*Parade,* August 3, 1986, p. 1	4
5.	Michele Willens, "Cosmo Talks to Malcolm Forbes: Businessman-Editor," *Cosmopolitan,* April 20, 1987, p. 214	9
6.	Mary Cunningham, Nightingale/Conant audio tape album "This I Believe" series.	9
7.	Erik Erikson, *Childhood and Society* (New York: Norton, 1964), p. 37.	14
8.	George E. Vaillant, "How the Best and the Brightest Came of Age," *Psychology Today,* Sept. 1977, pp. 34, 37-41, 107-110.	19
9.	Robert Seidenberg, *Corporate Wives, Corporate Casualties,* New York: Amacon, 1980.	10
10.	Warren Farrell, *The Liberated Man* (New York: Random House 1974)	20
11.	Sandra Lipsitz Bern, *Stanford Observer*	22
12.	Cleiaia Halas and Roberta Matteson, *Why Do I Feel So Bad?* (New York: MacMillan, 1978)	25
13.	Margaret Hennig and Anne Jardim, *The Managerial Woman* (New York: Simon & Schuster, 1977), p. 30-54.	25
14.	Mary Cunningham, Op. Cit.	25
15.	Mark Fastead, "The High Price of Male Macho," *Psychology Today,* September 1975	27
16.	Betty Friedan, *The Feminine Mystique*. 2nd Ed (New York: Norton, 1964)	29
17.	Hennig and Jardim, Op. Cit., p. 85-117.	32

18. Ruth Mehrtans Galvin, "Goal Consciousness: You Have to Have a Strategy," *New West.* 32

19. "Women Narrowing Salary Gap with Men," Reprinted by permission of Associated Press. 35

20. "O'Connor: Equality Gaps Remain," Permission granted by *USA Today,* Article: Feb. 12, 1988, p. 3-A. 35

21. This material is from Dr. McCoy's interview for Nightingale/Conant's "This I Believe" audio-cassette album series. 47

22. Mary Cunningham, Op. Cit. 76

23. *Forbes* Magazine, October 26, 1987, p. 160. 96

24. Michele Willens, Op. Cit., p. 212 96

25. This material is from Dr. McCoy's interview for Nightingale/Conant's "This I Believe" audio-cassette album series. 97

26. President Gerald Ford's speech at Congress of the Laity, Los Angeles, Feb. 17, 1978. 100

27. "Former President Ford in Good Health," *San Diego Union,* June 20, 1982, p. A-3. 101

28. Barbara Haskel, Introduction to Francoise Gilot's book, *Francoise Gilot: An Artist's Journey,* (New York, Atlantic Monthly Press, 1987.) 107

29. Mrs. Lyndon Baines Johnson, Preface to *A White House Diary,* (New York: Holt, Reinehart, Winston, 1970). 126

30. "Jewell J. McCabe, 41: The National Coalition of 100 Black Women," *Fortune* magazine, Aug. 17, 1987. 153

31. Pamela Noel, "New Battler for Black Women," *Ebony* magazine, Feb. 1984. 155

32. "King of Ketchup," *Forbes* magazine, March 21, pp. 58, 59, 62, 65. 167

33. "The New Economy Suits Heinz's Stingy C.E.O., *Fortune* magazine, June 23, 1986, p.22. 170

34. "H.J. Heinz: Power in the Pantry," *Dun's Business Monthly,* Dec. 1986, pp. 30-31. 171

35. *Cosmopolitan,* April 20, 1987, p. 212. 225

36. Tom Stacey, "Success is Matter of hard work to Sam Huff," *La Jolla Light*, Dec. 1985, p. B 13-14. 228

37. W. Timothy Gallwey, *Inner Tennis: Playing the Game* (New York: Random House, 1976) 231

38. Eric Sherman, "What's Hot (Stars Who Care)," *Ladies Home Journal*, Sept. 1987. 237

39. Robert L. Veninga, "A Gift of Hope: How We Survive Our Tragedies," *Ladies Home Journal*, Nov. 1985. 239

40. Elisabeth-Kubler Ross, *On Death and Dying* (New York: MacMillan, 1969) 240

41. Dr. Francis MacNutt, *The Power to Heal*, (Indiana: Ave Maria Press, 1977) p. 117, 151. 240

42. "You and Your Vital Long Life," *Prime Time*, a publication of Scripps Memorial Hospital, 1987, pg. 1 242

43. Phillip Caldwell, in an interview with Dr. McCoy for Nightingale/Conant audio tape album, "Lessons in Success and Leadership" from the *This I Believe* series. 243

44. Dr. Seuss' traveling art exhibit, 1986 244

45. Walter Scott, *Parade*, 1977 250

46. Karen O'Connor, *Sally Ride and the New Astronauts* Franklin Watts: New York, 1983 252

47. Norman Vincent Peale, "Things Will be Great in 88!," *Guideposts*, Jan. 1988, pp. 2-4. 253

48. "Chadwick is Back in the Swim," *San Diego Union*, May 24, 1987, pg. D-2. 253

49. Sears Study, Weiss-McGrath Report, McGraw-Hill. 254

50. Lee Iacocca, Chairman of the Board, Chrysler Corporation at graduation, Duke University, Durham, N.C., 1986 255

51. Dr. Kenneth Blanchard and Dr. Spencer Johnson, *The One-Minute Manager* (Berkley: Berkley Publishing Co., Sept. 1987). 259

52. *Transportation News*, Jan 1988. 264

53. "The Changing Woman" Television Series 265

54. Kris Newcomer, "Outing Puts Officials to the Test," *Rocky Mountain News*, July 12, 1987 266

55. A. Donald Anderson, "In the Office: See How They Run," *The New York Times*, Jan. 3, 1988, pg. F13. 268

56. "You Have to Want to Stay Alive," *Prime Time*, 1987, pg. 1. 269

57. Anne Morrow Lindbergh, *A Gift from the Sea* (New York: Random House, March 1978) 273

58. Shirley MacLaine in Dr. McCoy's interview for "The Changing Woman" television series. 275

59. Norman Vincent Peale, "Things Will Be Great in 88!," *Guideposts*, Jan. 1988, pp. 2-4. 277

60. Barron Hilton, Ibid. 277

61. "Let's Open Our Hearts to Victims, Families," Permission granted by *USA Today*, Article: Feb. 12, 1988. 281

62. "USA Cable Network TV Superbowl Special, Feb. 11, 1988. 282

BUSINESS AND PROFESSIONAL BOOKS

MegaTraits $17.95
Dr. Doris Lee McCoy 1-55622-056-1

Dr. McCoy traveled extensively to interview over 1,000 "successful" people. Interviews with such people as Charlton Heston, Malcolm Forbes, and Ronald Reagan led Dr. McCoy to discover 12 traits of success. She sought consistencies and success patterns from which you can benefit. Are there specific points to help all of us become more successful? The answer is a resounding YES! There are traits consistently found in the lives of successful people. Read *MegaTraits* to discover how you too can develop and utilize these unique attributes.

Business Emotions $14.95
Richard Contino 1-55622-058-8

Revolutionize your thinking, conditioning, and approach. Learn why emotions are a controlling factor in every success and failure situation. This practical book will guide you through the maze of hidden psychological issues in a simple and straightforward manner. Achieve predictable, positive, and immediate results.

Innovation, Inc. $12.95
Stephen Grossman, Bruce Rodgers, 1-55622-054-5
Beverly Moore

Unlock your hidden potential to reach a new plane of creative thinking. Seek out new avenues of problem-solving by elevating your ability to conceive ideas. Techniques and exercises in this book expand your creativity. The authors take you on a journey designed to spark confidence by reorganizing your thinking processes and patterns. Learn to use innovative thinking to inspire fresh ideas and formulate imaginative concepts.

Investor Beware $14.95
Henry Rothenberg 1-55622-055-3

Create your own luck with this book detailing the essentials for safe investments. Avoid shady, risky, and unsuccessful investments. Learn how to anticipate and interpret various investment climates and analyze a business from financial statements. The average investor will find what he needs to know about economics, financing, taxes, operating entities, and types of investments. Discover the ramifications of diversified investments such as real estate, franchises, oil and gas, gold, tax shelters, and syndications.

Steps to Strategic Management $13.95
Rick Molz 1-55622-050-2

This book is the story of one individual. . .YOU. Put yourself in the shoes of Joe Clancy, the imaginary entrepreneur in this book. By following the clear, ongoing example of Joe, you will discover how strategic management works. A series of nine steps will help you develop a systematic approach to strategic management. With honesty and hard work, you can use this book to help shape your future.

Call Wordware Publishing, Inc. for names of the bookstores in your area.
(214) 423-0090